I0213678

RELATIONSHIPS IN THE MESSIANIC TIME

Relationships in the Messianic Time

A Commentary on Philemon

David McClister

Relationships in the Messianic Time: A Commentary on Philemon

P.O. Box 290696, Tampa, FL 33687
www.deward.com

Cover design by Barry Wallace.

Unless otherwise noted, all Biblical quotations are the author's translation.

Printed in the United States of America.

ISBN: 978-1-947929-25-8

To My Children:

Melissa, Matthew, Meghan, and Michelle

CONTENTS

PREFACE

Stanley E. Porter has legitimately complained that "Commentaries for some time have become (rarely otherwise) little more than compendia of other people's knowledge." [1] The implication is that this need not be the case, and I would agree. Of course, no author wants to write in isolation from others. That would be foolish. But the other extreme is the idea (which Porter complains about) that a commentary needs to note, and engage with, everyone else's views in order to be a successful commentary. I have tried to take his point seriously. The present commentary on Paul's little letter to Philemon tries to steer something of a middle course. I will say up front that I have not read everything ever published on this letter, not even all the contemporary publications. There are insights into this letter that I have missed because of that, and in many cases this book is undoubtedly poorer because of it. But this book is not meant to be a critical interaction with everything that others have said before me. This book aims to argue for a particular way of reading this ancient letter.

Since there are already several good commentaries on Philemon available, perhaps a word is necessary about why I have written another one. Through my personal study, I came to realize that my own understanding of this letter was flawed. The more I studied it, the more I came to realize that the view that this is a letter about a runaway slave is only a surface reading (and maybe an incorrect one as well). As I thought about the ancient world in which Paul, Philemon, and Onesimus lived, and the dynamics that shaped their lives, I began to see that this little letter was about something far more significant, and far more practical. This book is my attempt to relate what I have learned in the hopes that it will aid the understanding of others as well.

Bartchy has noted that the epistle's story "is grounded in profound theological convictions,"[2] and Wright has made the important point that

[1] https://domainthirtythree.com/2016/09/05/the-shocking-news-of-peter-obrien-and-plagiarism-august-is-the-cruellest-month/. 27 Jul 2022.

[2] S. Scott Bartchy, "Philemon, Epistle to," *ABD* 5:305–10.

Philemon must be read from the perspective of the worldview from which it was written, and that the letter demands a theological explication.[3] The present commentary takes its cue from these notices and is an attempt to situate the letter in its Biblical-theological context, as well as to account for the human context. I have benefitted from many of the more recent studies on Philemon, so this commentary aligns with several of them in important ways. What is different about this commentary is that I propose a more specific theological explanation for this letter, namely, that Paul's apocalyptic eschatology is what drives it. Philemon is not primarily about a runaway slave, or even about slavery itself. That (or something like it) is the stage scenery, that is the background, but it is not the letter's core concern. The letter is about allowing the newness of the situation that Christ has created to transform the relationship between Philemon and Onesimus, in light of the fact that Onesimus had become a Christian.

Many thanks go out to many people. Librarians, editors, proofreaders, friends, and my family (and especially Lisa, my wife). All had a share, directly or indirectly (and sometimes both), in the writing of this book. I am especially grateful to David Thomley and Dr. Evan Blackmore. Both men read the draft of this book and offered many helpful observations. Whatever errors or flaws remain in this book are mine. I hope that this little volume will be of some help to someone who wants to understand Paul's letter to Philemon better.

David McClister
October 2022

---

[3] N. T. Wright, *Paul and the Faithfulness of God,* vol. 4 of *Christian Origins and the Question of God* (Minneapolis: Fortress, 2013), 6.

ABBREVIATIONS

AB	Anchor Yale Bible
ABD	*Anchor Bible Dictionary*, David Noel Freedman, ed., 6 vols.
AD	*anno Domini* (year of our Lord)
ANRW	*Aufstieg und Niedergang der römischen Welt*
BC	before Christ
BDAG	Bauer-Danker-Arndt-Gingrich, *A Greek-English Lexicon of the New Testament and other Early Christian Literature*, 3rd ed.
BDF	Blass-Debrunner-Funk, *A Greek Grammar of the New Testament and Other Early Christian Literature*
BECNT	Baker Exegetical Commentary on the New Testament
Ben.	Seneca, *De Beneficiis (On Benefits)*
BTB	*Biblical Theology Bulletin*
BZNW	*Beihefte zur Zeitschrift für die neutestamentliche Wissenschaft*
CBQ	*Catholic Biblical Quarterly*
CurBR	*Currents in Biblical Research*
cent.	century
cf.	*confer* (compare)
De Senectute	Cicero, *De Senectute (On Old Age)*
Digest	Justinian, *Digesta (Digest of Roman Law)*
ECC	Eerdmans Critical Commentary
ed.	editor, edition
e.g.	*exempli gratia* (for example)
Ep. Mor.	Seneca, *Ad Lucilium Epistulae Morales (Moral Letters to Lucilius)*
esp.	especially
ESV	English Standard Version
etc.	*et cetera* (and so forth, and so on)
ExpTim	Expository Times

ff	following verses or following pages
fn	footnote
Ibid.	at the same place (previously cited)
idem	the same person (as previously cited)
i.e.	*id est* (that is)
HCSB	Holman Christian Standard Bible
HTR	*Harvard Theological Review*
HUCA	*Hebrew Union College Annual*
ICC	International Critical Commentary
ISBE	*International Standard Bible Encyclopedia* (rev.)
JBL	*Journal of Biblical Literature*
JETS	*Journal of the Evangelical Theological Society*
JGRChJ	*Journal of Greco-Roman Christianity and Judaism*
JRS	*Journal of Roman Studies*
JSNT	*Journal for the Study of the New Testament*
JSNTS	Journal for the Study of the New Testament Supplement Series
JTS	*Journal of Theological Studies*
LCL	Loeb Classical Library (Harvard University Press)
LSJ	Liddell-Scott-Jones, *A Greek-English Lexicon*, 9th ed. with supplement
MM	Moulton and Milligan, *Vocabulary of the Greek New Testament*
NAC	New American Commentary
NASB	New American Standard Bible
NCB	New Century Bible
NewDocs	*New Documents Illustrating Early Christianity*, 10 vols.
NICNT	New International Commentary on the New Testament
NIGTC	New International Greek Testament Commentary
NIV	New International Version
NKJV	New King James Version
NT	New Testament
NTS	*New Testament Studies*
NovT	*Novum Testamentum*
NRSV	New Revised Standard Version
OT	Old Testament

P.Oxy.	Oxyrhynchus (Egypt) Papyri
Phlm	Paul's letter to Philemon
PRSt	*Perspectives in Religious Studies*
rev.	revised
RSV	Revised Standard Version
SBL	Society of Biblical Literature
SBLSPS	Society of Biblical Literature Seminar Papers Series
TDNT	*Theological Dictionary of the New Testament* (Kittel, 10 vols.)
TThZ	*Trierer Theologische Zeitschrift*
v	verse
vv	verses
vol.	volume
WBC	Word Biblical Commentary
ZECNT	Zondervan Exegetical Commentary on the New Testament
ZNW	*Zeitschrift für die neutestamentliche Wissenschaft und die Kunde der älteren Kirche*

Abbreviations of Biblical Books

Gen	Genesis
Lev	Leviticus
Deut	Deuteronomy
Psa	Psalm
Prov	Proverbs
Zech	Zechariah
Matt	Matthew
Rom	Romans
1 Cor	1 Corinthians
2 Cor	2 Corinthians
Gal	Galatians
Eph	Ephesians
Phil	Philippians
Col	Colossians
1 Thes	1 Thessalonians
2 Thes	2 Thessalonians
1 Tim	1 Timothy
2 Tim	2 Timothy

Phlm	Philemon
Heb	Hebrews
Jam	James
1 Pet	1 Peter
2 Pet	2 Peter
Rev	Revelation

Note: In both the Introduction and the Commentary, "Phlm" refers to the letter Paul wrote, and "Philemon" refers to the person.

INTRODUCTION

Part 1: The Letter and Its Problems

Ancient Letter-Writing. We begin with some basics which are not always discussed. First, people in ancient times wrote letters for some simple reasons, chiefly because they could not communicate in person at the moment. Generally, communication by letter could be simply a way of keeping in touch, but a letter could also convey requests or provide information about things that had arisen that were of mutual concern to the parties involved. Paul's letters certainly fall into these broad categories. That is, Paul's letters were always personal. There is a good amount of the "keeping in touch" business in them, but also much of the business of communicating important information. For Paul, this information also had a decidedly theological value. Another way to say this is that Paul did not write letters simply for the sake of producing doctrinal theological essays. Paul was not an academic who wrote theology in the abstract for the general, interested reader. His letters were occasional in the sense that they always arose in response to specific occasions and the questions and issues that were part of them, but they were also, at the same time, personal.

Letter-writing, however, also engages a more specific set of conditions. Petersen proposed the following five elements as implicitly operative, at least on the social level, in the act of sending a letter: 1) there is an implied previous relationship between the sender and recipient, 2) the letter comprises a new "moment" or event in that relationship, 3) the letter implies at least one future stage in the relationship, namely the recipient's response, 4) the parties involved in the correspondence are related to each other in a complex web of roles, positions, and statuses which are in play, and 5) the way the letter is crafted (including its argumentation, tone, *etc.*) corresponds to the sender's understanding of his relationship to the recipient.[1] All of this is relevant to Phlm.

[1] Norman R. Petersen, *Rediscovering Paul: Philemon and the Sociology of Paul's Narrative World* (Philadelphia: Fortress, 1985), 63–65.

In the modern world of global telephone service, emails, and text messages, the practice of writing a letter on paper and sending it far away by courier has greatly diminished in our culture. We can have instant, "face-to-face" conversations easily. In Paul's day, however, where none of these conveniences existed, letters were vitally important, and they served multiple purposes. Stowers has identified at least a dozen different functions that letters served in the Greco-Roman world.[2] Many students of Phlm believe this letter fits best into the category of "a letter of recommendation." In such a letter, three parties are basically operative: the letter's author, the recipient of the letter, and a third person whom the author is recommending to the recipient (and who, often, was delivering the letter). A letter of recommendation vouched for the character and integrity of the third party. As Klauck notes, such a letter would typically address the personal integrity of the person being recommended, explain the relationship between the author and the person being recommended, mention the relationship between the author and the letter's recipient, and request a warm welcome for the person being recommended.[3] Phlm fits this model closely. However, none of Paul's letters fit neatly into any one category, as they regularly include features from familiar (*i.e.*, non-official) and familial letters as well. It appears that Paul used elements of different kinds of letters in order to achieve his own purposes.[4]

Papyrus was a common writing material in in Greco-Roman times. Letters written on papyrus were usually written on one side only, with individual sheets glued together as needed to accommodate the length of the letter. The finished papyrus document was then folded and, if necessary, sealed. The name and location of the addressee of the letter was written on the outside of the folded document. A courier, or multiple couriers at successive points, would then deliver the letter. The official postal system in Paul's day was for official government correspondence

[2] Stanley K. Stowers, *Letter Writing in Greco-Roman Antiquity,* Library of Early Christianity 5 (Philadelphia: Westminster, 1986).

[3] Hans-Josef Klauck, *Ancient Letters and the New Testament: A Guide to Context and Exegesis,* trans. and ed. Daniel P. Bailey (Waco, TX: Baylor University Press, 2006), 73–75. *Cf.* 2 Cor 3.1; Acts 18.27.

[4] "Literary genres and their form-functional components are not monolithic or invariant verbal structures." Authors can manipulate them for their purposes. Ernst Wendland, "'You Will Do More than I Say': On the Rhetorical Function of Stylistic Form in the Letter to Philemon," in *Philemon in Perspective: Interpreting A Pauline Letter,* ed. Francois Tolmie. BZNW 169 (Berlin: de Gruyter, 2010), 79–111, at 84.

only, so Paul could not simply drop a letter into a mailbox. Letters were routinely delivered by private persons. That is, the person who wished to send a letter had to find someone going in the direction of the letter's recipient and ask them to carry the letter there. The letter carrier could be an acquaintance, but often not. Slave owners could use trusted slaves to deliver letters. For others, letters were given to ship captains, merchants, or other people who were travelling. Remarkably, this informal system seemed to work quite well.[5] Paul, however, probably always had his letters delivered by trusted fellow workers in the gospel. It is likely that Onesimus delivered Paul's letter to Philemon.[6]

There was a form that most letters generally followed. It began with the sender's name(s), then the name of the recipient(s), followed by a greeting (usually the Greek word *chairein,* meaning "Greeting"). Then followed the body of the letter, with a closing at the end. The amount of detail in the letter varied, because the courier could communicate some information in person. So Paul said in Colossians 4, "As to all my affairs, Tychicus, our beloved brother and faithful servant and fellow bond-servant in the Lord, will bring you information. For I have sent him to you for this very purpose, that you may know about our circumstances and that he may encourage your hearts; and with him Onesimus, our faithful and beloved brother, who is one of your number. They will inform you about the whole situation here" (vv 7–9, NASB).

Ancient letters often used "stock" expressions. In addition to *chairein* ("greeting"), letters often closed with the word *errōso* ("farewell"). Other common phrases (determined by the purpose and contents of the letter) were "I rejoiced greatly" (at the hearing of some news), "I am amazed" (likewise at the hearing of news), "I want you to know," "I received your letter in which you said …," "Just as I wrote," "I ask you therefore …," "do not neglect to …" or "take care that …."[7] Students of the New Testament documents will quickly recognize versions of these phrases in Paul's letters.

---

[5] See Eldon Jay Epp, "New Testament Papyrus Manuscripts and Letter Carrying in Greco-Roman Times," in *The Future of Early Christianity,* ed. Birger A. Pearson (Minneapolis: Fortress, 1991), 35–56.

[6] Peter M. Head, "Onesimus the Letter Carrier and the Initial Reception of Paul's Letter to Philemon," *JTS* 71.2 (2020): 628–56.

[7] See John L. White, "Epistolary Formulas and Cliches in Greek Papyrus Letters," *Society of Biblical Literature 1978 Seminar Papers, Vol. II,* SBLSPS 14 (Missoula, MT: Scholars Press, 1978), 289–319.

Interestingly, Paul put his own, unique "stamp" on the Greco-Roman letter form.[8] Although it was usual to say *chairein* ("greeting") at the beginning of a letter, Paul never used this word in the introductions to his extant letters. Instead, he used the similar-sounding phrase *charis humin*, "grace to you," or the longer "grace to you and peace." Similarly, he never used the usual *errōso* ("farewell") in the closing section of his letters, but instead substituted a more Christian closing, such as "the grace of the Lord Jesus be with you." He also often qualified himself, the sender, with descriptions such as "an apostle of Christ Jesus" or "a slave of Christ Jesus." These descriptions were closely matched to the circumstances of each letter. Furthermore, Paul adapted the Greco-Roman letter to become a form of instruction and exhortation for churches (although this was not completely unprecedented).[9]

Like many documents in the ancient world, Paul's letters were intended to be read out loud. In the case of Paul's letters, they were to be read to the whole church (Col 4.16; 1 Thes 5.27; *cf.* Rev 1.3).[10]

Although Paul himself could both read and write, his letters reveal that he sometimes (often?) used a secretary to compose his letters (*cf.* Rom 16.22). This practice was not uncommon in Paul's day. Given the general uniformity of style in Paul's letters, it seems clear that Paul gave his scribes very little latitude in the composition process of his epistles. To ensure the authenticity of the final product, Paul would write the last few lines of his letters in his own handwriting.[11] This, too, was a common practice in Paul's time.

The Problems of Paul's Letter to Philemon. Phlm holds several distinctions within the New Testament. It is the shortest "book" or document written by Paul in the collection of his letters,[12] it is the only

[8] See John L. White, "New Testament Epistolary Literature in the Framework of Ancient Epistolography," *ANRW* 25.2:1730–56.

[9] Therefore, as White notes (John L. White, "The Structural Analysis of Philemon: A Point of Departure in the Formal Analysis of the Pauline Letter," *Society of Biblical Literature 1971 Seminar Papers* (Society of Biblical Literature, 1971), 8), Paul's letters were often a cross between, or combination of, personal letters, sermons, literary letters, and official letters.

[10] Literacy rates in the ancient world were low compared to today. Someone in the church who could read would have read an apostolic letter out loud to the assembled congregation. See Paul J. Achtemeier, "Omne Verbum Sonat: The New Testament and the Oral Environment of Late Western Antiquity," *JBL* 109.1 (1990): 3–27.

[11] We have explicit notices of this in 1 Cor 16.21; Gal 6.11; Col 4.18; 2 Thes 3.17 (and note 2 Thes 2.2); and Phlm 19.

[12] Phlm has only 335 words in the original Greek text. By comparison, 2 John has 245 words and 3 John has 219 words. The text of Phlm, either in part or in whole, is known

one of Paul's letters that is directed primarily to an individual Christian (although the church is listening in), and it is possibly the most-neglected epistle in our Bibles. What could such a short letter, about a mostly individual matter, have to teach us today? Plenty, as it turns out.

The New Testament documents are like historical photographs of moments in the history of the early church. In these documents we see Christians struggling with the implications of the new faith, dealing with resistance from without and sometimes within, and learning how to put their beliefs into practice—all at the same time. We cannot always make out every feature of the "photographs," especially in the backgrounds. There are things there in the background, but some of them are not fully in focus, some of them appear only partially, and the things in the distance are hard to discern. In the foreground, however, we see a few Christians caught in a moment of time, thinking about their faith and learning how to translate it into their lives. Such is what we get in Phlm.

The brevity of the document is partly what accounts for its attractiveness to scholars and historians. It captures a fascinating moment in early Christianity, but its lack of detail leaves us with many questions. Since the 1980s there has been a resurgence of interest in this letter because scholars have become fascinated with trying to answer those questions, using what we know about the ancient world, and to reconstruct the letter's background—that part of the "photograph" that is not very clear to us. But the foreground image of Christians working out their faith in a difficult situation is clear enough. It is the intersection of those two parts of the picture that creates the challenge. We know they are related, but exactly how is hard to see in some places.

Of course, anyone who reads the New Testament *as a Christian* does not read it simply as if it were an old photograph, as if it were just an interesting scene from someone else's life in another time and place. We read these documents because we believe they speak across the centuries and through the cultures to address issues that transcend their original contextual confines. We read them because we believe they speak to us today. The "photographs" are templates for our behavior today. Phlm is not just about a problem between a couple of Christians. It is about fellowship, love,

from at least 572 manuscripts (S. Matthew Solomon, "The Textual History of Philemon" (PhD diss., New Orleans Baptist Theological Seminary, 2014). In this commentary I have used the 28th edition of Nestle's Greek text for this letter. The English translation offered in the commentary is my own, based on the Nestle-Aland 28th edition.

peace, humility, sacrifice, acting in accord with truth, serving the interests of the gospel, and imitating Jesus. It is a sample of an approach that finds applications every time Christians must work together. And it is more.

An Intriguing Text. This little letter is fascinating first because of the mystery that surrounds its context and circumstances. What was going on? What was the situation behind the letter, and what prompted Paul to write it? We realize that when we read the epistles of the New Testament, we are reading someone else's mail. The problem with this is that we often do not get the whole conversation. Sometimes we can infer what the other party had said, but even this is tricky.[13] The difficulty, of course, is that some things in the half of the conversation that we can "hear" could be much clearer, and would make much better sense, if we only knew what the other party had said. Statements communicate in contexts. We cannot simply pick up one of these documents and act as if they were written in the abstract or, as a parallel exercise, simply mine them for theological instruction without regard for the situations in which these words were originally written. Those contexts give meaning and precision to the statements. As difficult as it might be, we must try to see the historical context because that will be our first way into understanding what we are reading.

So what was going on? This simple question is much harder to answer than one might think.[14] We can say with confidence that Paul was in prison (vv 1, 9, 10, 13) but that he hoped to be able to travel, and to see Philemon, soon (v 22). Timothy was with him (v 1). We also know that Paul was writing to address a situation in which he had become, somehow, a participant. There was a slave named Onesimus (v 10) who had come to know Paul, who had left the household of Philemon to be with Paul (v 15), and who had obeyed the gospel under Paul's guidance (vv 10, 19). Paul found this newly converted slave to be useful to him (or potentially useful to him) in his work in the gospel (vv 11, 13), but as a slave Onesimus was not free to help Paul either as he wished or as Paul wished. Onesimus' master and owner needed to be part of the conversation, and any decision about whether, or how, Onesimus could help Paul in the future had to come from the slave's owner. So Paul wrote this letter, asking Onesimus's owner to "do the right thing" (v 8). In

---

[13] See John M. G. Barclay, "Mirror-Reading A Polemical Letter: Galatians as a Test Case," *JSNT* 31 (1987): 73–93.

[14] A history of the approaches to, and use of, this letter can be found in Larry J. Keitzer, *Philemon*, Readings: A New Biblical Commentary (Sheffield: Sheffield Phoenix, 2008).

addition, there was apparently some kind of personal problem between Onesimus and Philemon (vv 15, 18–19). Onesimus himself was now returning to his owner (v 12), presumably bearing this letter, as a show of good faith on both his part and Paul's.

Those are the things we know with confidence. Everything else is unclear. This calls for two observations: 1) The facts noted above comprise what Petersen has called the letter's "story," or its "narrative world."[15] Whatever this letter meant, or means, it must be located within that story. Imposing an external framework on the letter will only result in a misreading of the letter. 2) The relative lack of clarity created by the sparse details mentioned in the letter itself is what creates our difficulty with reading and interpreting Phlm today.

Who was Apphia (v 2) and what does she have to do with the situation? Was she a notable woman in one of the churches (comparable to Phoebe, who is mentioned and commended in Rom 16.1)? Or was she the wife of Philemon? Or both? And what role did she play in this situation, either in its creation or its solution?

Where was Paul imprisoned? Was he in Rome, in Caesarea, or somewhere else? This would seem to have a bearing on his plans to visit Philemon soon (v 22). What was the nature of Paul's custody, and what were the conditions? Was he in a prison cell, or was he under a more liberal house arrest, as Acts 28.30–31 describes?

How had Paul and Onesimus met in the context of the letter's situation, especially since Paul was in custody? That is, how is it that a slave had come to be with a prisoner? Was it a chance meeting, or did Onesimus seek Paul out? Where was Philemon, and why was Onesimus not at home with his master where we would normally expect a slave to be? The fact that Onesimus was not with his master/owner does not, by itself, raise suspicions. Masters could send trusted slaves on all kinds of errands away from home. But exactly what was the reason Onesimus was not at home? Did he go at his master's bidding and with his master's blessing, or had he run away? Or had he left at his master's bidding but failed to return, basically turning an errand into an escape? It is clear from the letter itself that something was wrong in the relationship between Onesimus and his master Philemon. Paul was interceding. But what was the problem? Had Onesimus felt threatened? Was Philemon a

[15] See his own construction of the known events, *Rediscovering Paul*, 65–70.

harsh master and Onesimus feared for his well-being or his life?[16] Had Onesimus stolen something? Paul's cryptic promise to pay whatever was owed, if anything (v 18), raises such a possibility. Some runaway slaves were known to leave with some of the master's property to finance their travel.[17] Or had Onesimus stolen or mismanaged something to the loss of Philemon, and Onesimus left before Philemon had found out (knowing that he would be punished when Philemon learned about it)? Or had Onesimus not stolen any property, but his prolonged and unexplained absence from Philemon was now costing Philemon in terms of labor and productivity? Or was it Paul's fault that Onesimus had not returned to Philemon yet, because Paul had kept him busy in some kind of service for the gospel? How long had Onesimus been a slave? How long had he served Philemon? What was the nature of his service? Was he a field hand, a household manager, or what? What had prompted Philemon to think of him as "useless" (v 11)? What was their prior relationship like?

And when did Paul find out that Onesimus was not a free man? Did he know Onesimus from a previous meeting in a place where Paul had preached, or had Paul only recently come to know him? Did Paul know about Onesimus' slave status from the beginning of the situation of this letter, or was it something he was not told until later, after Onesimus had already been helping him? Slaves on the run would often conceal their identity. Had Onesimus done that? How long had Onesimus been away from Philemon? Had he come to be with Paul only recently? Had he decided to go back home before his conversion, or was returning to Philemon the result of his conversion and encouragement from Paul? What did Paul want Onesimus to do for him (that is, for Paul)? Did Paul want Onesimus to become one of his regular fellow workers in the gospel, thus effectively calling on Philemon for a kind of transfer of ownership to Paul, or a prolonged use of his slave? Did Paul want Onesimus to become an apprentice of sorts?[18] What was "the right thing" (v 8) Onesimus' master

---

[16] *NewDocs* 8:36–40 lists the following reasons that were typically causes for slaves to flee: recent enslavement, sale and transport away from home, fear of a new master and a new residence, opportunities arising during transfer, opportunities arising from civil disturbances, avoidance of giving evidence in a legal dispute, cruel treatment by a master, and fear of punishment.

[17] *NewDocs* 8:13.

[18] This is the theory of J. Albert Harrill, *Slaves in the New Testament: Literary, Social, and Moral Dimensions* (Minneapolis: Fortress, 2006), 14–16; also Peter Arzt-Grabner, who notes that in Phlm Paul used terms that were often used in apprentice contracts in his

was expected to do? Set Onesimus free? Or simply allow him to stay with Paul (and possibly forgive any debt this new situation had created)? Was there actually some kind of offence Onesimus had committed against his master, or was there only the perception (on Paul's part) of an offence, or was it that Paul simply wanted to avoid an offence being committed? *We know the answers to none of these questions.*

Where was Paul? Where was Paul? He was in prison (vv 1, 9, 10, 13), but what was the location of this imprisonment? Three possibilities have been offered by scholars: Rome, Caesarea, and Ephesus.

Paul was kept in custody in Caesarea Maritima under the tenure of the Roman governor Felix (Acts 23–24). This lasted for two years (Acts 24.27), from 55–57 AD.[19] However, the idea that Paul's prison epistles were written during his time in custody at Caesarea Maritima has gained little scholarly support.[20] Acts also reports that Paul was imprisoned (actually under house arrest) in Rome at the end of that narrative. The dates would have been 58–60 AD ("two whole years," Acts 28.30).[21] The distance from Rome to Colossae is around 1,300 miles, and the distance from Caesarea to Colossae[22] was well over 900 miles, both as measured mostly by sea.[23] In

day. *Philemon*, Papryologische Kommentare zum Neuen Testament 1 (Göttingen: Vandenhoeck & Ruprecht, 2003), 66–70.

[19] Dates are from Jack Finegan, *Handbook of Biblical Chronology*, rev. ed. (Peabody, MA: Hendrickson, 1998), 397, 402.

[20] See the remarks by Harold W. Hoehner, *Ephesians: An Exegetical Commentary* (Grand Rapids: Baker Academic, 2002), 93. Among modern scholars who support a Caesarean origin of Paul's prison epistles are: Gerald F. Hawthorne, *Philippians*, WBC 43 (Dallas: Word, 2004); Lewis Johnson, "The Pauline Letters from Caesarea," *ExpTim* 68 (October 1956): 24–26; Bo Reicke, "Caesarea, Rome, and the Captivity Epistles," in *Apostolic History and the Gospel. Biblical and Historical Essays Presented to F. F. Bruce on His 60th Birthday*, ed. W. Ward Gasque and Ralph P. Martin (Grand Rapids: Eerdmans, 1970), 277–86; and E. Earle Ellis, *The Making of the New Testament Documents* (Leiden: Brill, 1999), 266–75.

[21] Based mostly on the evidence of Eusebius (Books 2 and 3 of his *Church History*), most New Testament scholars believe that Paul was released and eventually imprisoned again, and that this later and final imprisonment is the context for *2 Timothy* and *Titus* (and possibly *1 Timothy* as well). Most also believe that the so-called "prison epistles of Paul" (that is, letters in which he says that he was in prison at the time he wrote them: Ephesians, Colossians, Philippians, and Philemon) were written during an imprisonment *before* his final imprisonment at the end of his life.

[22] On the usual assumption that Paul's letter was going to Colossae, the home of Philemon. Yet see below.

[23] The distances involved are often cited as support for the theory that Paul must have been imprisoned in Ephesus, where it would have been easier to send letters to Philippi and Colossae. See Eugene Boring, "Philippians and Philemon: Date and Provenance," *CBQ* 81 (2019): 470–94, at 486–88 on some of the distances and times involved. Philippians

either scenario it would have taken most of two months to deliver a letter one way.[24] Between these two options (Caesarea or Rome), what could tip the scales in favor of the Roman confinement is that Luke specifically says Paul could receive all the visitors who came to him there, which would fit the list of several co-workers listed in Phlm. The problem, however, is the distance, especially when Paul implies that he would be visiting Philemon soon enough that he could go ahead and get a room ready for him (v 22).

There is no direct evidence for an Ephesian imprisonment, but it has been proposed on the basis of deductions from statements in the New Testament. In 2 Corinthians 11.23 Paul spoke of having been imprisoned several times. However, if we compare Paul's letters with Acts, by the time we come to the point in Acts where Paul wrote 2 Corinthians (Acts 20.2), Luke has recorded a total of only one imprisonment for Paul, the night he spent in prison at Philippi (Acts 16). Clearly Paul was imprisoned much more than Luke has told us in Acts. Also, since Paul spent almost three years in Ephesus (Acts 20.31), there may have been enough time for him to have been incarcerated there for a while. Paul said in 2 Corinthians 1.8–10 that he came close to getting killed in Ephesus. Exactly what this refers to, we do not know. It could refer to the riot recorded in Acts 19, but it could also be a trial and imprisonment.[25] It is clear from Acts 19 that Paul faced serious opposition there, not unlike the opposition he encountered in Philippi—which led to his imprisonment. Clearly, an Ephesian imprisonment for Paul is not impossible. The problem is that we have no direct evidence for it. The theory, however, offers a ready explanation for Phlm 22. Ephesus was less than 100 miles from Colossae, and this would make good sense of Paul's request for lodging (v 22) because the request would seem to imply that Paul did not have far to go.[26]

---

in particular seems to imply several communications between Paul and the church there. However, long-distance travel in the ancient world was more common than is sometimes supposed. *Cf.* the tomb inscription in Hierapolis of a merchant named Flavius Zeuxis, who made the round-trip voyage from Hierapolis (near Laodicea) to Rome 36 times in his lifetime (text in *Corpus Inscriptionum Graecarum,* no. 3920). See also the analysis of these problems by Moisés Silva, *Philippians,* 2nd ed., BECNT (Grand Rapids: Baker Academic, 2005), 7.

[24] Boring, "Philippians and Philemon," 487 notes that land travel and sea travel happened at nearly the same rates, on average 20 miles per day (depending on conditions).

[25] Prisons were, for prisoners with high social status, the usual place of execution. Brian Rapske, *The Book of Acts and Paul in Roman Custody,* vol. 3 of *The Book of Acts in Its First Century Setting,* ed. Bruce W. Winter (Grand Rapids; Eerdmans, 1994), 13–14.

[26] *E.g.,* N. T. Wright, *Paul and the Faithfulness of God,* vol. 4 of *Christian Origins and the Question of God* (Minneapolis: Fortress, 2013), 7–8.

New Testament scholars are divided over a Pauline Ephesian imprisonment.[27] The evidence is inferential. If Paul was imprisoned in Ephesus when he wrote Phlm, then Philemon could have been at Colossae. But if Paul wrote Phlm while imprisoned in Rome (Acts 28), then Philemon could have been somewhere in Italy (see below), or perhaps in Colossae. Phlm does not contain enough information to speak with confidence about Paul's location or Philemon's.

The Relationship Between Philemon and Colossians. It has often been pointed out that Colossians and Phlm appear to be closely related to each other and that this is a way into the context. The first question we must answer in this approach is whether or not Paul actually wrote Colossians. Some scholars do not believe that Paul wrote all the letters that bear his name in the New Testament. The consensus among such scholars is that 1 Thessalonians, 1 and 2 Corinthians, Philippians, Philemon, Galatians, and Romans are genuine epistles of Paul, and that 2 Thessalonians, Colossians, Ephesians, 1 and 2 Timothy, and Titus were written by others who were imitating Paul or simply signing Paul's name to their work to give it credibility (a practice known as pseudepigraphy). This stance, however, is problematic at least for Colossians, since these same scholars believe that Phlm is a genuine Pauline epistle. There are nine names that both Colossians and Phlm have in common: Paul, Timothy, Epaphras, Mark, Aristarchus, Onesimus, Demas, Luke, and Archippus. No other letters of Paul demonstrate such close overlap, and it is hard to escape the conclusion that these two letters must be related in some way. One could argue that an imitator would include these names to give his work the appearance of having been written by Paul, but upon closer inspection the idea does not hold up. First, why would an imitator choose to create a fictitious letter to the church in Colossae? Colossae was not a prominent city in Paul's day; it was in decline by Paul's time.[28] A larger city and church would have been the better strategy for a forger. Also, if a forger wrote Colossians and used

---

[27] A good overview of the positions against and for the theory of an Ephesian imprisonment respectively are: Ben Witherington, III, "The Case of the Imprisonment That Did Not Happen: Paul at Ephesus," *JETS* 60.3 (2017): 525–32, and Joel White, "The Imprisonment That Could Have Happened (and The Letters Paul Could Have Written There): A Response to Ben Witherington," *JETS* 61.3 (2018): 549–58. See also Peter Head, "Onesimus the Letter Carrier," 636 fn 19.

[28] See Markus Barth, Helmut Blanke, and Astrid B. Beck, *Colossians: A New Translation with Introduction and Commentary*, AB 34B (New Haven: Yale University Press, 2008), 8–9;

Phlm as a guide for which names to use, why did the forger not include Philemon and Apphia in the salutations of Colossians? There would be no good reason to omit them, especially since the supposed forger used several other names available from Phlm. Most importantly, however, the theory that Paul did not write Colossians is, in the end, only a literary theory. It is not based on any historical evidence. We will proceed on the assumption that Paul wrote Colossians[29] and that the easiest way to account for the similarities in names in both letters is that the same author wrote them both.

A second question in the relationship between Colossians and Phlm concerns how we are to interpret the similarities. A common approach goes like this:

- Both Philemon (v 1) and Archippus (v 2) are listed as recipients of Phlm. So where one of these men is, the other is also.
- Archippus is mentioned in Colossians (4.17), suggesting that he is in Colossae.
- Therefore Philemon was also in Colossae.

Another form of the argument is:

- In Phlm, Paul says he is sending Onesimus back to Philemon (v 12).
- In Colossians, Onesimus is going to accompany Tychicus to Colossae, and Paul reminds the Colossians that Onesimus is "one of your number" (v 9).
- Therefore Onesimus is going back to Colossae, where his master/owner Philemon must be.

With these arguments, it seems clear that Philemon was at Colossae, and Onesimus was going back there. Scholars have further argued that the close correspondence of these statements, along with the nine names in common between the two letters, leads us to conclude that both letters were written at the same time, and delivered to the same place: Colossae. Colossians was for the church, and Phlm was for an individual.

But things are not as clear as they seem. Just because Archippus was in the same place as Philemon when Paul wrote Phlm does not mean that these two men must have also been in the same place when Paul

Joseph A. Fitzmyer, *The Letter to Philemon: A New Translation with Introduction and Commentary*, AB 34C (New Haven: Yale University Press, 2008), 8–10.

[29] For further arguments on the genuineness of Colossians, see Michael F. Bird, *Colossians and Philemon*, New Covenant Commentary Series (Eugene, OR: Cascade Books, 2009).

wrote Colossians. The only way to get the logic to work is to *assume* that Paul wrote both letters *at the same time*.[30] But there is no proof for this. The fact is that Philemon and Apphia are *not* listed among the recipients of Colossians. This could indicate that the two letters were not written to the same place. Similarly, there is a problem in the alternate way of framing the argument. Paul refers to Onesimus as "one of your number." Literally, he says that Onesimus is "from you" (*ex humōn*). Nothing says that this can only mean that Onesimus was currently considered a resident of Colossae (and thus his master/owner lived there too). It could just as easily mean that Onesimus was originally from Colossae without implying anything about where his current home was. It is a jump in logic to assume that just because Onesimus was "from there" that his master/owner must have lived there too.[31] Furthermore, designating Onesimus to the Colossians as "from you" would be strange if Onesimus had regularly lived there and if Colossae was commonly known to be his home (*i.e.*, the home of his master/owner Philemon). They would have already known that Onesimus was from there. The designation makes more sense, however, if Onesimus had originally been born there but had not, in fact, lived there (at least for a long time). Telling the Colossians that Onesimus is "from you" (*i.e.*, from Colossae) is therefore new information designed to encourage them to welcome Onesimus who was now basically a stranger to them (as was Tychicus).[32]

Balabanski has argued that if we look at how Archippus and Onesimus are described in these letters, a very different scenario suggests itself. That is, rather than concentrating solely on the similarities between the letters, we should also account for the differences. The key difference is how Aristarchus is described. In Phlm he is called one of Paul's fellow workers. This term regularly denotes those men whom Paul sent to various places to preach and check on the churches. The implication of calling Aristarchus a fellow worker is that he was free—when Paul wrote Phlm—to go where Paul sent him. But in Colossians, Aristarchus is called Paul's fellow prisoner (4.10). He was not able to go anywhere.

---

[30] Vicky Balabanski, "Where is Philemon? The Case for a Logical Fallacy in the Correlation of the Data in Philemon and Colossians 1.1–2; 4.7–18," *JSNT* 38.2 (2015): 131–50, at 137; see also Eduard Lohse, *Colossians and Philemon*, trans. William R. Poehlmann and Robert J. Karris, Hermeneia (Philadelphia: Fortress, 1971), 186.

[31] Balabanski, "Where is Philemon?," 139.

[32] *Ibid.*, 139.

This strongly suggests that Phlm and Colossians were *not* written at the same time.[33] Aristarchus was a free man when the former was written, but imprisoned when the latter was written.

But how should we account for the nine names in common between Phlm and Colossians? Surely, it could be argued, that such an extensive duplication of names means that Paul was in the same situation when he wrote both letters, basically surrounded by and concerned with the same people in both of them. This is undoubtedly correct, but it does not necessarily mean that Paul wrote both letters at the same time. All it must mean is that the same basic group of people served Paul as fellow workers while he was imprisoned (which likely lasted for around two years), and that group changed as the larger ministerial situation changed. With this perspective, the similarities in names does not have to mean that Paul wrote both letters at the same time. It could mean that he only wrote both letters under the same basic conditions, namely, his imprisonment during which he relied on the same basic group of fellow workers until he was released. The composition and sending of the letters could actually have been separated by many months.

This also means that Philemon and Archippus were not necessarily both in Colossae when Paul wrote Phlm. All we can say for sure is that Archippus was either in Colossae or nearby when Paul wrote Colossians (Col 4.17). If we do not assume that Phlm was written and sent at the same time as Colossians, then we do not know where Philemon was when Paul wrote this short letter.

Balabanski and others suggest that Paul wrote Phlm earlier in his Roman imprisonment, and he wrote Colossians later during that same imprisonment. This would account for the differences between the letters, specifically in the ways Archippus and Aristarchus are described in each letter. Also, there is a problem concerning Onesimus that needs to be fixed in Phlm, but there is no indication of any problem concerning him in Colossians. This could mean that the problem with Onesimus had been resolved by the time Paul wrote Colossians and Onesimus was now one of Paul's fellow workers and was traveling with Tychicus.

If Paul did not write Colossians and Phlm at the same time, and if therefore Philemon and Archippus were not necessarily in the same place (Colossae) when Paul wrote Phlm, then it is possible that Philemon lived

---

[33] *Ibid.*,139–41; also Bird, *Colossians and Philemon*, 10.

somewhere closer to Paul, perhaps somewhere in Italy (even in Rome; that is, if Paul's imprisonment was in Rome) or perhaps on the western coast of Greece (*cf.* the mention of Nicopolis in Titus 3.12). Paul's request to have a room prepared for his visit could be taken to mean that Paul did not have a long trip to make.

What, then, is the conclusion? The answer is that we simply do not know for certain where Philemon or Archippus were when Paul wrote this letter. The traditional view that both men were in Colossae *could* be correct, but nothing says it *must* be. It works when we *assume* that Paul wrote Colossians and Phlm at the same time, but if we do not make that assumption, then nothing says that Philemon or Archippus had to be in Colossae.

Onesimus. A natural question related to Phlm is the issue of what was going on with Onesimus, namely, how Onesimus had come to be with Paul. Or, to ask it another way, just exactly what had Onesimus done that made Paul think he needed to intercede and offer to bear the burden himself? The short answer, and of which we must constantly remind ourselves, is that we do not know.

There are at least six ways to imagine what had happened prior to Paul's writing this letter:

1. Onesimus' master (and possibly the church as well) intentionally sent Onesimus to Paul;
2. Onesimus ran away from his master, was captured and ended up being imprisoned along with Paul;
3. Onesimus ran away from his master, was found or met by one of Paul's friends, and this friend brought Onesimus to Paul;
4. Onesimus ran away and could not survive on the run, so he went to Paul;
5. Onesimus was seeking asylum from Philemon, and had run to Paul for this protection;
6. On his own, Onesimus had come to Paul, whom he hoped would help him to be reunited with his master, from whom he was estranged.[34]

The text of Phlm itself explicitly mentions none of these scenarios. That is, every one of them is a guess, an attempt to fill in the blanks so that we might have a more precise sense of what Paul wrote in this letter. As

[34] B. M. Rapske, "The Prisoner Paul in the Eyes of Onesimus," *NTS* 37 (1991): 187–203.

Pearson has shown, however, students of Phlm often see these scenarios as active not because the text of Phlm tells us such, but because we bring them with us to the text and read the text in light of the theories.[35]

The question of Onesimus' status has generated much discussion, and it is appropriate to examine three of the main positions here.[36] The most common approach to this letter has been that Onesimus had run away,[37] that he was what Roman law called a *fugitivus*. The available evidence suggests that runaway slaves were a common feature of the ancient world, and one who knew of the whereabouts of a runaway slave was required by law to bring him to the authorities. Harboring a runaway slave was illegal and punishable by a fine.[38] Some of the papyrus documents from ancient Egypt in the Roman period are public notices describing runaway slaves and appealing to the public to help find them. One such document reads: "If someone found a slave named Philip, about fourteen years old, pale-skinned, speaks poorly, wide nose, wears a thick wool tunic and a worn belt, take him to one of the military posts …." [39] Another notice describes a slave who "… does not speak Greek, tall, smooth-shaven, scar on left side of head, honey-complexioned, pale, thin beard (in fact, his beard does not really have any hair), smooth-skinned, narrow in the mouth, long-nosed, a skilled weaver, walks around pretentiously, talking in a shrill voice, about thirty-two years old …." [40] In a letter from the middle of the fourth century a government official in Egypt said "I order and entrust you to arrest my slave called Magnus who has run away and is staying at Hermopolis, and has taken certain articles belonging to me, and to bring him bound, together with the man who is over [the village

---

[35] Brook W. R. Pearson, "Assumptions in the Criticism and Translation of Philemon," in *Translating the Bible: Problems and Prospects*, ed. Stanley E. Porter and Richard S. Hess, JSNTS 173. (Sheffield: Sheffield Academic, 1999), 255, 278. He notes that some translations give the impression that more is known about the situation than is actually the case.

[36] For a fuller survey of views, see D. Francois Tolmie, "Tendencies in the Research on the Letter to Philemon Since 1980," in *Philemon in Perspective: Interpreting a Pauline Letter*, ed. D. Francois Tolmie, BZNW 169 (Berlin: de Gruyter, 2010), 1–27.

[37] This interpretation precedes Chrysostom. See Margaret M. Mitchell, "John Chrysostom on Philemon: A Second Look," *HTR* 88 (1995): 135–48.

[38] *Digest* 11.4.

[39] P.Oxy. 3616, dated to the third century AD; in *NewDocs* 8:9.

[40] P.Oxy. 3617, third century; in *NewDocs* 8:9–10. The document is damaged (like many ancient papyri) and the surviving part does not specifically have the word "slave" in it, but the type of document and the description seems to fit that of a runaway slave notice.

of] Sesphtha."[41] A late-third century document shows a man authorizing a friend to find a runaway slave: "I appoint you by this my instruction as my representative to journey to the most illustrious Alexandria and search for my slave called ..., aged about thirty-five years, with whom you too are acquainted ...; and when you find him you are to deliver him up, having the same powers as I should have myself, if present, to ..., imprison him, chastise him, and to make an accusation before the proper authorities against those who harbored him, and demand satisfaction."[42]

If Onesimus had run away from Philemon, it could be easy to imagine that once he had been converted by Paul he understood that he needed to return home and fulfill his obligations (*cf.* Col 4.22–25; Eph 6.5–8). If we adopt this scenario as the background to Phlm, it could make sense of Paul's appeal to Philemon to take him back (Phlm 17). The situation would go something like this: Onesimus had run away, costing his master a loss of labor at home (or worse, he had stolen something; *cf.* Phlm 18). Now that he was a Christian, he understood that he could not continue in this delinquent situation, and with Paul's encouragement he wanted to return home. However, he feared that he would not be treated well when he returned, so Paul penned this letter to help reconcile the situation. Some scholars go even farther and suggest that Paul was asking for Philemon to give Onesimus his freedom because Paul wanted Onesimus to work with him in the gospel (v 13).

As logical as all of this might seem, there are a few problems with it. The biggest problem is imagining a credible scenario in which a runaway slave came to make the acquaintance of a man who was in Roman custody. It is reasonable to assume that runaway slaves would naturally avoid places where civil authorities could spot them. In a similar vein, it would not be obvious why a runaway slave would seek out known friends of his master, when those friends could potentially cause him to be arrested and punished.[43] It is hard to imagine, then, how or why a runaway like Onesimus would venture to come to a place which, by its

---

[41] P.Oxy. 1423; in *NewDocs* 8:33–34. Apparently the governor of Sesphtha was complicit the in slave's escape.

[42] P.Oxy. 1643; translation from Bernard P. Grenfell and Arthur S. Hunt, eds. *The Oxyrhynchus Papyri,* Vol. XIV (London; New York; Boston: The Offices of the Egypt Exploration Society, 1920), 70–72. Several other such notices can be found in *NewDocs* 8:1–46.

[43] Peter Arzt-Grabner, "The Case of Onesimos: An Interpretation of Paul's Letter to Philemon Based on Documentary Papyri and Ostraca," *Annali di Storia dell'Esegesi* 18.2 (2001): 589–614, at 605.

nature, was staffed with people who could either turn him in or arrest him on the spot. All kinds of secondary theories have been proposed to avoid this difficulty. Some suggest that Onesimus knew Paul from an earlier experience, and that when Onesimus found out that Paul was in Rome he went to him there (hoping he would not be found out in the process), or he had a mutual friend bring him to Paul. A major problem with this approach is that it puts Paul in the position of illegally aiding a runaway slave under the noses of the Roman authorities. Paul would not have engaged in such behavior. Other scholars have suggested that Onesimus had been caught and imprisoned in the same prison as Paul, and this would explain how the two were now together.[44] The obvious problem here, however, is that if Onesimus was a fellow prisoner, then certainly Paul had no authority to send him back to Philemon! Also, if Paul's Roman imprisonment at the end of Acts 28 is the proper context for his writing Phlm, it would be highly doubtful that a runaway slave would have been thrown in with a man who was under light house arrest, as we know Paul was.[45] The whole exercise quickly becomes a situation in which one conjecture is now necessary to support another one.

Another common theory to explain how Onesimus had come to be with Paul is that Onesimus had not run away, but that Philemon had actually sent Onesimus to aid Paul in his imprisonment as a kind of servant on loan.[46] From what we know of the Roman penal system, the prisons and jails did not supply blankets or even a regular supply of food.[47] Prisoners probably relied mostly on family and friends to bring them provisions while they were incarcerated (*cf.* 2 Tim 4.13). In this scenario, then, Onesimus had been sent as a kindness to Paul, so that Paul would have someone who could regularly bring him food and other such necessities (such as paper and ink to write letters), and to deliver Paul's letters and messages to Christians on the outside. But, as the theory usually goes, Paul had kept Onesimus longer than expected. Philemon might have been thinking that Onesimus had become a slave that Roman law would call *erro*—a slave who was sent on a legitimate errand but had now gone missing (with

---

[44] For example, R. P. Martin, *Colossians and Philemon*, NCB 48 (London: Oliphants, 1974), 147.

[45] Rapske, "The Prisoner Paul," 191.

[46] For example, Sara B. C. Winter, "Paul's Letter to Philemon," *NTS* 33 (1987): 1–15.

[47] A good description of life in Roman custody is Rapske, *Book of Acts and Paul in Roman Custody*.

the presumption that he had escaped).[48] Therefore Paul wrote this letter to assure Philemon that all was well, to apologize for keeping Onesimus so long and for inconveniencing Philemon in the process (v 18), and even asked Philemon if Onesimus could return and help him some more.

An obvious problem with this theory is that it leaves us wondering why Philemon would send a slave who was at first an unbeliever to help Paul whose need was for helpers in carrying on his work in connection with the gospel. But it also seems to run against Phlm 17. If Onesimus had been sent to Paul because Onesimus was known to be a trusted slave, then the request of v 17 is puzzling. "... it does not seem logical, that he should have pleaded for a slave who had been trustworthy enough to be sent to him and bring him a letter or some food or something else."[49] Furthermore, Phlm 13 seems to rule out this theory. In that verse, Paul said he was sending Onesimus back even though he wanted to keep him so that "he might minister to me on your behalf." If Philemon had indeed sent Onesimus to minister to Paul as a gift from Philemon, then "a letter full of such trepidation and pleading would have been unnecessary."[50]

A variant on this theory, and one that is increasingly popular among New Testament scholars, is that Philemon did not send Onesimus to Paul, but that it was Onesimus' idea to come to Paul. This approach says that there was some kind of serious problem between Onesimus and his master Philemon (some even suggest that Philemon had been harsh on Onesimus), and Onesimus came to Paul in a sort of bid for asylum and intercession as an *amicus domini*, a friend of the master.[51] On this reading, Onesimus knew that Paul and Philemon were friends, and so he sought out Paul and asked the apostle to intervene for him for better treatment and for a safe reception back with Philemon.

---

[48] Some scholars have called into question the idea that there was an actual difference between a *fugitivus* and an *erro* in practice. See Harrill, *Slaves in the New Testament*, 6–14; *idem*, "Using the Roman Jurists to Interpret Philemon," *ZNW* 90 (1999): 135–38. For response, see Peter Lampe, "Affects and Emotions in the Rhetoric of Paul's Letter to Philemon: A Rhetorical-Psychological Interpretation," in *Philemon in Perspective: Interpreting a Pauline Letter*, ed. D. Francois Tolmie, BZNW 169 (Berlin: de Gruyter, 2010), 61–77, at 64; also Peter Arzt-Grabner, "How to Deal with Onesimus? Paul's Solution within the Frame of Ancient Legal and Documentary Sources," in *Philemon in Perspective: Interpreting a Pauline Letter*, ed. D. Francois Tolmie, BZNW 169 (Berlin: de Gruyter, 2010), 113–42, at 124–33.

[49] Arzt-Grabner, "The Case of Onesimos," 605.

[50] James D. G. Dunn, *The Epistles to the Colossians and to Philemon: A Commentary on the Greek Text*, NIGTC (Grand Rapids: Eerdmans, 1996), 331.

[51] So Rapske, "The Prisoner Paul."

There is an interesting ancient letter that some scholars think supports this understanding of the background of Phlm. In this letter Pliny, the Roman governor of Bithynia in the first part of the second century AD, wrote to a man named Sabinianus, urging him to accept a freedman who had failed to perform his obligations to Sabinianus and who had then come to Pliny asking the governor to intercede for him. The letter reads:

> Your freedman, with whom you said you were angry, came to me, prostrated himself at my feet, and held on to them as if he were at yours. With many tears and with much begging, and even without words, he convinced me that he was truly sorry. I believe he has amended his ways because he is cognizant of his transgression against you. You are angry, I know, and you are rightly angry, I also know; but now gentleness is especially to be praised when the reason for anger is most legitimate. You loved this man, and, I hope, you will love him yet. You (will) have the right to be angry again, if he deserves it, because, being moved by entreaty, you will be willing to excuse him for all fault. Make allowance for his youth, his tears, and your own gentleness. Do not torture him, nor torture yourself either; for indeed it is torture for you who are so gentle to be so angry. I am afraid it will appear that I am not asking but compelling, if I join my entreaties to his, yet I will join them fully and freely, as much as I have rebuked him sharply and severely, threatening severely that I will never ask this again. This I said to him, for whom it was necessary to be frightened, but I do not say this you; for it is possible that I will ask again, and I will obtain your cooperation again, that it might be in such a way proper for me to ask and for you to perform. Farewell.[52]

Some scholars believe it is possible to read Phlm as this same kind of letter, in which a friend of the master appealed to the master on behalf of an erring slave. Pliny asked for the man to be forgiven and taken back, just as Paul asked in Phlm. Pliny even went as far as to say that his relationship with Sabinianus meant that this request should not be taken lightly, and that he was perfectly within what was proper for his status to make not only this request, but future requests as well. In a similar way (it is argued), Paul (more gently) reminded Philemon that he stood in Paul's debt (v 19). Therefore, as the argument goes, Phlm is not about a runaway, but about a slave who had come to the master's friend for intercession. In this scenario,

[52] Letter 9.21 (my own translation). Apparently the request was met with its desired response, as Pliny's letter 9.24 shows.

it was not that Onesimus had run away and now Paul was taking it upon himself to make things right; instead Onesimus wanted to go home, but he was afraid of harsh treatment and asked Paul to appeal for him.

As tempted as some scholars are to use Pliny's letter as a guide for understanding Paul's letter, there are some significant differences between the two documents and some problems with this approach. First, Onesimus was a slave, but the man for whom Pliny appealed was not a slave. He was instead a freedman, a former slave, and as such his social status was different from that of a slave. Second, Pliny noted that the freedman had expressed true repentance over the wrong he had committed, but we hear nothing of the sort about Onesimus in Phlm. Onesimus' voice is never heard in Phlm. Paul never spoke for him or relayed any of his words to his master. There is nothing of "He says he is sorry," *etc.*[53] Third, Pliny only made a pretense of not commanding that Sabinianus comply with his request. While he acted as if he was going to considerable trouble to intercede for the man while the man was in front of him, at the end of the letter he made it perfectly plain that he expected Sabinianus to follow his wishes not only that time, but for any future request as well. Paul, on the other hand, kept well clear of any idea that he was commanding Philemon to do something (vv 8, 14). Fourth, this reconstruction still involves the unlikely scenario of a slave seeking help from a man who was in Roman custody. Whereas Sabinianus had come to a Roman governor, Onesimus (under this theory) had gone to a man who was legally under arrest. It is hard to imagine that Roman officials, if they found out that Onesimus was improperly away from his master, would have allowed him to stay with Paul (a prisoner!) as some kind of asylum.[54] Fifth, and perhaps most importantly, Pliny was asking for a restoration to the former good relationship between Sabinianus and his freedman. Paul, however, was not simply attempting a reconciliation, he was not calling for a return to the status quo. He was asking for something different from, and something much more than, that.[55] The

[53] Head suggests that Onesimus himself would have had opportunity to speak for himself when he delivered the letter. "Onesimus the Letter Carrier," 647–49.

[54] The ancient evidence may suggest that even the practice of a slave seeking asylum in a temple had disappeared, at least in some places, by this time. William L. Westermann, The *Slave Systems of Greek and Roman Antiquity* (Philadelphia: American Philosophical Society, 1955), 105.

[55] Wright, *Paul and the Faithfulness of God*, 18: "radically different."

letters and situations are, then, different enough from each other to call into question whether Pliny's letter is actually a good model for reading and understanding Phlm.[56] This by itself, however, does not necessarily rule out the theory that Onesimus had left Philemon to come to Paul for help with some kind of intercession.

So which is it? Is Phlm about a runaway slave, a *fugitivus*, for whom Paul is asking freedom? Or had Onesimus been sent to Paul and Paul had now kept him too long? Or is it that Onesimus had wronged Philemon in some way and had come to Paul, asking Paul to intercede for him? We must remind ourselves that none of these scenarios can be established from the text of Phlm itself. They are, at the end of the day, theories about the historical developments behind the text, but none of them can be proven. Of course, something actually did happen that brought Paul and Onesimus together. That is, even though there are problems with just about any scenario we can imagine for how the two men came to be together, one of them must have been the actual historical circumstance in spite of the problems we can imagine about it! But the difficulty for us, 2,000 years later, is that we no longer know what that was.

One of the problems this lack of clarity creates for us is that what we believe about the situation of Onesimus will determine what we think Paul was asking to be done for him or with him. But if we do not know what the situation was, how can we be sure we are reading Paul's request correctly? (We cannot.) Asking for a slave to be "on loan" to Paul for an extended period is one thing, asking for the slave's freedom is another thing. The problem is not academic, because it has a bearing on what we think this little letter is saying to us today. The way we read the original content will have a bearing on what we think the message of the text is for us now. That is, we have to know what it *was* saying (when Paul wrote it) in order to know what it *is* saying (to us today). Specifically, if we read Phlm as Paul asking for Onesimus' freedom, then the letter is asking for a much greater sacrifice on Philemon's part than if we read the letter as Paul simply asking for Onesimus to stay with him for a while. So what is the text "saying"? Is it calling on Christians to make tremendous sacrifices for each other, or is it teaching us to temper the demands we make of each other?

---

[56] Similar is Arzt-Grabner's proposal that Onesimus was a roaming slave, not quite a runaway but not being exactly obedient either; "The Case of Onesimos," 606–7; *idem.*, "Onesimus *erro*" *ZNW* 95 (2004): 131–43. For a critique of Arzt-Grabner's view, see John G. Nordling, *Philemon*, Concordia Commentary (Saint Louis: Concordia, 2004), 140–42.

Herein lies what I think is the biggest interpretive problem for Phlm. Actually, it is the same problem that we face for any of the New Testament documents, but it is perhaps especially acute for Phlm. The fact is that all communication occurs within a set of contexts that, together, give the communication meaning and precision. Context provides a control or limit to interpretation; context is what keeps a text from meaning just anything and everything. But if we do not, and cannot, know those original contexts, then we cannot hear the original communication as precisely and clearly as those who knew those contexts and lived in them. And if we cannot hear the communication clearly, it is difficult to know exactly what to make of it.

We must always read the Biblical text with an ear open to the original contexts—including the historical-cultural contexts—in which they were produced. Of this there must be no question. In fact, skipping this step in the interpretive process is unethical, because the contexts are our guide to understanding and interpretation. When we willfully ignore them, we demonstrate a disdain for the truth. But here is the problem: our ability to recover, recapture, or reconstruct the original contexts is limited. We are dealing with communications that were originally made about 2,000 years ago. They were made in a different historical, cultural, linguistic, *etc.* context than what we live in today. Recovering those ancient contexts proves to be difficult because our knowledge of that ancient world is fragmented and limited. To take only the literary piece of the puzzle as an example, it is commonly estimated that only 5–10% of the literature available in the first century has been preserved to our times. Even the Bible itself provides us with preciously few references to specific historical situations. So how can we interpret those texts correctly if we cannot know the contexts in which those documents originally communicated? Without the context, do we not run the risk of misunderstanding what we are reading? The answer is "Yes, of course we do." This is exactly why Biblical scholars spend so much energy on trying to learn those contexts. They have everything to do with reading the text correctly.

There are a few basic solutions to this problem. The first is to reason our way to the best possible historical reconstruction of the original contexts, and then use those reconstructed contexts to interpret the texts. This is the way historical inquiry is generally done, and in many cases our reconstructions, while never complete, are complete enough for us to interpret ancient communications adequately. We will never have absolute "exegetical certainty" in the sense of knowing every facet of the ancient contexts, or knowing them fully, so that we can know with perfect confidence that we are understanding the ancient texts correctly. But absolute certainty rarely exists for anything. We get along just fine with *sufficient* certainty for just about everything we do in life.[57] For many of the New Testament documents, we know enough about the ancient contexts to get the sense that we are reading those documents correctly, even if at the same time we wish we could have more information.

Phlm, however, seems to pose a special problem. As noted above, scholars have suggested several possible contextual situations by which we should read this letter. This either means that Biblical scholars have wild imaginations (which is always a possibility), or it could mean that the evidence we have for reconstructing the original contexts behind Phlm is so fragmentary that even sufficient certainty about them is not possible. Multiple possible reconstructions probably means that we do not have enough evidence to speak with our usual degree of assurance about them. Pearson has stated the matter honestly: "the exact situation addressed in the letter is simply too obfuscated to posit a definite solution."[58]

So what do we do in a case like that of Phlm, where we cannot sufficiently reconstruct the contexts? How can we know if one interpretation of the letter is better than another if we lack sufficient certainty about the contexts which limit and control our understanding? One might be tempted to go to the other end of the interpretive spectrum, minimize (or ignore) the role of historical context in interpretation, and simply allow a theological (or "doctrinal") reading of the text to dominate. One could argue that this is exactly how the Biblical documents have often been read and interpreted for hundreds of years, sometimes with the barest regard for knowledge of the original historical contexts. Yet the church seems to get the message of those texts anyway. One could even argue that this is how the texts themselves want to be read. Communicating the historical contexts was simply not the chief concern of the Biblical

---

[57] See the excellent discussion in Michael R. Licona, *The Resurrection of Jesus: A New Historiographical Approach* (Downers Grove, IL: IVP Academic, 2010), 67–70. James McGrath said "most of us are aware that we hold many beliefs that we cannot prove to be true, but are nonetheless perfectly reasonable to entertain." Alister and Joanna McGrath, *The Dawkins Delusion?: Atheist Fundamentalism and the Denial of the Divine.* (London: SPCK, 2007), 8.

[58] Pearson, "Assumptions," 255.

writers. Sure, they knew that such contexts existed, they mentioned them from time to time, and we may assume that they understood that their readers would know something of those contexts already. But the essence of those documents is the theological message. So in the case of Phlm, it could be argued that the text itself begs to be read this way. The lack of detail in the text itself regarding an historical interpretive context almost "forces" us to adopt a primarily theological reading.

Before we settle on such an approach to Phlm, however, we need to be careful. The difficulty we may have in recovering the letter's contexts (as illustrated by the multiplicity of theories that have been advanced about them) is not a license to ignore them altogether. In fact, we must realize that the theology which we find speaking so loudly in our texts also demands a context in which it can become operative or "live." There is little use on anyone's part for abstract theological doctrines. The theology of the New Testament was meant to be incarnated, as it were, understood and lived out in historical situations. We cannot escape the matter of context even when we are reading primarily with an eye or ear to the text's theology, because we still have to decide what this text is telling us to do. We assume that it is telling us something, something that we can define with some precision. It is not speaking so generally as to mean anything we wish.

Part 2: The Historical-Social Context

A Way Forward, A Way Out. So what are we do to, specifically with Phlm? I have tried to show, in the preceding discussion, that substantial parts of the historical picture behind the letter are not available to us. They happen to be parts that many people think are the crucial parts. This does not, however, mean that we are left with nothing, or that our reading of this letter must forever remain unsettled and vague. There are some facets of the ancient context that are sufficiently clear for us to make good sense out of the letter. In fact, I hope to show that the part that everyone seems to fret about the most—whether Onesimus was a runaway or not—is not even necessary to understanding the letter. The reason I believe this is because the letter itself points us in this direction. If Onesimus' freedom were the actual point of the letter, Paul could have made that clear. Or if giving Onesimus to Paul for a time for use in the ministry was the point of the letter, Paul could likewise have made that clear. But Paul did not specify either outcome. That is, the text itself does not turn on a singular, specific action as the conclusion of the matter. If we read the letter carefully, Paul was actually asking for something else. Be that as it may, there are some things about the historical background of the text that we can establish with a high degree of confidence, and we may use this background knowledge with profit when reading Phlm.

There are three well known features of the ancient world that will help us understand this little letter more accurately: 1) the matter of status (including the issue of slavery), 2) the use of rhetoric, and 3) the matter of patronage and reciprocity. More importantly, these are not three contextual features that we are pulling out of thin air, as it were, to impose upon the text. No, these features are important because they are mentioned specifically in the text of Phlm. In other words, the correct and most fruitful reading of Phlm lies not in the background of the text, but in the text's own foreground, those contextual elements that are mentioned in the text itself.[59] Let us notice them in turn.

Status. For many people in the Hellenistic world, the social status of oneself, and of others, was an important consideration in their deeds, communications, judgments, interactions, and perceptions. The social statuses of the participants could play an important role in meetings, transactions, letters, requests, evaluations, and deliberations. Lines were drawn and behaviors were adjusted according to the status of the people involved.

In the Greco-Roman world of Paul, Philemon, and Onesimus, a person's status among others fell somewhere along a vertical hierarchical scale. At the very bottom of the social-cultural status scale, or near the bottom, were slaves, and at the very top was the Roman emperor. Everyone else was somewhere in the middle, but it was a middle with many gradations and nuances. However, these gradations were not equally spaced from each other from top to bottom. The highest statuses in the Roman world were concentrated at the top of the socio-economic scale, among the elite. Economically, there were basically two groups in the Hellenistic world: the aristocratic elite, and the commoners.[60] However, a person's wealth

---

[59] See Ronald F. Hock, "A Support for His Old Age: Paul's Plea on Behalf of Onesimus," in *The Social World of the First Christians: Essays on Honor of Wayne A. Meeks*, ed. L. Michael White and O. Larry Yarbrough (Minneapolis: Fortress, 1995), 67–81, at 75.

[60] One could argue that a "thin" middle class existed, but most historians think of them more as the lowest level of the upper class.

was not the only (or even primary) indication of their status, not by far. One's birth (parents and circumstances), age, accomplishments, the public offices one held (and how many times), the country of one's origin, one's citizenship, one's ancestors, one's ethnicity, one's ability to speak Greek correctly, and several other factors all contributed to the creation of the perception of one's status in relation to other people. This made for a complicated situation. One would rarely be above, or below, others in every way.[61] Two men might both be Roman senators, but one might have more political power or personal wealth than the other, or belong to an older Roman family, thus giving him an edge in status. Two men might both be commoners, but one might be the president of the local guild to which they both belonged, and so he would slightly outrank the other in status. Given the fact that there were many markers of status, one had to be careful in the ancient world to know which markers mattered the most or which were in play at the moment.

In the world in which Paul lived, one's own status and the status of others could be important factors in conversations and requests, and these things sometimes had to be taken into account. We see this dynamic operative in Phlm, yet this is, perhaps, an aspect of the letter that we often overlook. We tend to read the interaction between Paul and Philemon as if it were simply an interaction in which one Christian was asking another Christian to do something, or as if it were simply an interaction between socially equal friends. But the letter is filled with indications that the status of both Paul and Philemon were powerfully operative in the way the communication worked. In fact, there is a status-loaded triangle of people primarily involved in the letter: Paul, Philemon, and Onesimus. Each of these people had a particular status relative to each other within the world of the text and which the text itself explicitly acknowledges.

One of the things that makes Paul's letter to Philemon so interesting is that each of the main characters had multiple statuses, all of which are played with, and against, each other. Paul was a prisoner (vv 1, 9), a brother (to Philemon), an aged man (v 9), a "father" (to Onesimus, v 10), a partner to Philemon (v 17), a guarantor (v 19a), and a benefactor (v 19b). It is interesting that Paul did *not* play the "apostle card," at least explicitly. Philemon was a beloved brother and fellow worker with Paul

---

[61] See Wayne A. Meeks, *The First Urban Christians: The Social World of the Apostle Paul*, 2nd ed. (New Haven: Yale University Press, 2003), 54–55.

(vv 1, 20), host to a church (v 2), a benefactor (v 5), a slave owner (vv 10f), a brother to Onesimus (v 16), a partner to Paul (v 17), a debtor to Paul (v 19b), and prospective host to Paul (v 22). Onesimus was a slave, he was Paul's "child" (v 10), a "brother" to Philemon (v 16), a minister to Paul's situation (v 13), and possibly a debtor to Philemon (v 18). Every one of these statuses is called into play at some point in the letter, and each one had their own particular nuance and role in the negotiation that was taking place.

Similarly, in v 8 Paul claimed he could order Philemon to do what he said, if he wanted to. Paul had enough status over Philemon in their church relationship that he could demand Philemon's obedience, and Philemon knew this. The fact that Paul mentioned this is powerful, even if in the very next breath Paul said he would not take that route in the present situation. There was a boundary in play here, and even if Paul himself should decide to set it aside in this case, the prerogative was Paul's, not Philemon's. Philemon was bound to honor it, and Paul's statement in v 8 was a subtle reminder of that fact. In v 9, in the middle of the sentence where Paul said he was not going to pull the "boss" card on Philemon, he also reminded Philemon that he (Paul) was an older man, which again carried a message about Paul's status in relation to Philemon.[62] The mention of that fact placed a burden on Philemon. In v 19 Paul reminded Philemon that he was indebted to Paul (a topic we will address below), which is another form that status took. And yet from an economic perspective, Philemon was undoubtedly higher up the socio-economic ladder than Paul. Under any other set of circumstances, Philemon would have been reckoned as the man with the highest status among the three, at least socially. In this letter, however, that is not how things proceeded. Although Paul was kind and respectful in the letter, and he used his apostolic authority in the gentlest way, it is clear that Paul measured the relationship between himself and Philemon by the scale of the perspective of their Christian fellowship, and when that scale was used, the highest status belonged to Paul.[63]

Beyond the relatively "horizontal" social dynamic of status between Paul and Philemon (although it involved a hierarchy), Paul reminded

---

[62] John M. G. Barclay, "There is Neither Old nor Young? Early Christianity and Ancient Ideologies of Age," *NTS* 53 (2007): 225–41.

[63] See David A. deSilva, *An Introduction to the New Testament: Contexts, Methods, and Ministry Formation* (Downers Grove: InterVarsity Press, 2004), 672–73.

Philemon that there was a "vertical" dimension to the situation as well, and that Philemon was also indebted to Christ the Lord. We must remember that when Paul said "Christ," although it has become something of a second name for Jesus to us, to Paul it was primarily a title. The Christ is the Messiah of Israel, the promised king from the line of David who came to establish and reign over God's kingdom. To refer to Jesus as Christ was to inject the matter of his kingship into the discussion. Paul used the word "Christ" seven times in this short letter, a subtle reminder to Philemon of who was really in charge of the situation in the text. Similarly, Paul referred to Jesus as "the Lord" five times in the space of the letter's twenty-five verses. The rhetorical effect of these repetitions would have been significant. Recall, as we noted earlier, that Paul's letters were read out loud to the churches to which they were addressed (and to other churches as well, Col 4.16; *cf.* Rev 2.7). Imagine you were listening to Phlm being read out loud, and every few seconds you heard either "Christ" or "the Lord." It was a verbal reminder of where the importance in the letter's issue was to be found, a reminder of where the ultimate status and authority lay.

Additionally, the horizontal and the vertical are intimately connected for Christians. How God through Christ has related to us now determines how we are to relate to each other. To put that more drastically, to join into fellowship with God through Christ is, at the same time, to join in a fellowship with everyone else who has joined God through Christ, and this dual fellowship brings with it a redefinition of the one who joins. These relationships have an overriding spiritual dimension, but they are worked out in the context of the social world of people.[64] We will return to this below.

All of this indicates that the issue of status is all over the letter to Philemon, and we would miss an important part of the interpretive task to ignore it. It is precisely here that we may begin to see just how sensitive and difficult the issue that was addressed in this short letter really was. It would be one thing for one man to ask another, equal man to do something, or to exhort him about the right course of action in a situation. When the issue of the unequal status of the two men relative to each other is layered onto the scene, the situation takes on a new character and becomes more complex. Then, when a third man is brought into the

---

[64] Marion L. Soards, "Some Neglected Theological Dimensions of Paul's Letter to Philemon," *PRSt* 17.3 (1990): 209–19.

situation, and this third man can be thought of as "belonging" in some sense to both of the other men, the recipe for conflict exists. Paul had a claim on Onesimus, whom he now called "my child" (v 10). This way of referring to Onesimus is important in the letter, because it invoked a counter-status to the way Philemon thought of him. Paul's right over Onesimus as a father, it is subtly suggested, trumped Philemon's right over Onesimus as master. Similarly, the claim of a bond through Christ was presented as greater than Philemon's claim on this man as his legal owner. *This counter-status, or this re-drawing of the lines of status, lies at the heart of the letter to Philemon.* Two different planes or modes of existence intersected here, and Paul claimed that one of them was invested with a higher authority than the other. Although the master had the right (socially and legally) over his slave, the other man (in this case, Paul) argued that he also had a status that gave him authority to tell the slave owner what he must do with the slave, and thereby overriding the legal owner's authority. In the Hellenistic world, one man did not generally tell another man what to do, or not to do, with his slaves. The only person who could probably pull this off would have been the emperor himself.[65] In the situation with Onesimus, therefore, the potential for serious conflict and social embarrassment was high all around. Who was Paul to ask (in strong terms, nonetheless) Philemon about what to do with one of his slaves? How would Philemon ever be able to act like a master to Onesimus if Onesimus was aware that Paul had told Philemon what to do with him? In the eyes of Onesimus, Philemon will have lost a good deal of his authority to Paul. The master's authority would be diminished in the eyes of his own slave. Why would Paul ask for such a potentially embarrassing thing? If Paul felt compelled to engage in this risky request, how should he go about doing it so as to save the maximum amount of face for Philemon in front of his slave?

[65] The story is told in Seneca, *Dialogue* 5: On Anger, 3.40, of a time when Augustus was visiting Vedius Pollio. A slave broke a glass and Vedius ordered him to be killed by being thrown into a pond of lampreys (which he kept for such purposes). The slave ran to Augustus and pleaded for a less painful way of execution. The emperor was shocked at Vedius' cruelty and ordered the slave to be set free (and to break all the glasses in Vedius' house, and the pond of lampreys to be filled in). And yet when a crowd called for the emperor Hadrian to free a slave who had performed well as a charioteer, the emperor refused saying "It does not befit me, nor is it fitting to request of me, that I should free a slave belonging to another person, or compel his owner to do this." In Dio Cassius, *Roman History* 69.16 (Cary, LCL).

Slavery. While we are discussing status, this is a good place to note some things about slavery in the Hellenistic world. In many ways it was different from the slavery with which we are familiar in American history. Slavery in the Hellenistic world was not primarily a racial phenomenon. Many slaves in antiquity served in the country of their birth, and people of all ethnicities could, and did, become slaves. There has been great debate through the centuries over the legal status of slaves in the Roman empire. Westermann is probably correct to note that in the eyes of Roman law, a slave was both a person and a "thing."[66] As a person he had no legal or political standing, but a slave was not merely a "thing" and nothing else. Since slaves lacked legal standing in Roman law, there was technically no crime that a master could commit against one of his slaves. However, there were laws that protected slaves in some ways by limiting what masters could do with them, and more of them appeared as time went on.[67] In addition, slaves were a costly investment, and it was in an owner's interests to treat them well.

Slaves were taken from several segments of the Roman empire.[68] Prisoners of war who were brought to Rome were at one point a subgroup that was largely put into slavery, but as Rome's need for war subsided, this segment of the population diminished.[69] Slavery through kidnapping by pirates also basically ended as the Romans got control of the Mediterranean Sea by 31 BC. In the Greco-Roman world, unwanted children were often taken outside the city and abandoned to die. Some people collected such children and raised them until they were old enough to be sold as slaves. Other people became slaves through kidnapping, or because of unpaid debts (either their own or their parents'; in Roman law, a father had the right to sell his children into slavery), and some as punishment for crimes. Some people were slaves from birth, because they were children of a slave woman. The size of the slave population varied from place to place. In Italy, and especially closest to Rome, the number of slaves was possibly around a third of the total population. In

---

[66] *Slave Systems*, 104.

[67] Westermann cites several examples from Roman Egypt, *Ibid.*, 102–103; see also 114–115. Also Richard R. Melick, *Philippians, Colossians, Philemon*, NAC 32 (Nashville: Broadman & Holman, 1991), 342.

[68] See W. V. Harris, "Demography, Geography and the Sources of Roman Slaves," *JRS* 89 (1999): 62–75.

[69] Westermann, *Slave Systems*, 101, 106.

rural, poorer areas the slave population was likely under ten percent of the total, although the slave population would have been higher on the large-scale farms of the wealthy.[70]

The life of a slave could be hard or relatively easy,[71] depending on the nature of the work he did and the disposition of his master. Some slaves did back-breaking work in the fields, but this was decreasing in New Testament times. Other slaves were tasked with the management of other slaves or of a farm's operations. In the surviving literature, we find slaves serving as field workers, cooks, messengers, tutors and guardians for the master's children, scribes, accountants, nurses, skilled workers, and even musicians. Some slaves even worked for the Roman government and lived, in many cases, better than most free people. Many slaves were paid for their labor, although it was a pittance. Yet it was enough, in some cases, that a slave could save it and eventually pay for his freedom.[72] We hear in the ancient literature of some slave owners who were notoriously hard on their slaves, and there were few considerations to prevent it. Physical abuse certainly existed, although the extant literature mentions it relatively infrequently (possibly suggesting that it was not commonplace), but this does not erase the fact that slaves were undoubtedly, by their nature, people who were exploited in many ways. The picture that comes from the ancient literature is that masters and slaves were often on cordial terms with each other, and some were even close, but cordiality should not be taken to imply that slaves were content with their situation.

In most cities, one would routinely encounter and interact with slaves in the daily course of business. Slaves could have been seen just about anywhere in public, without chains or special clothing to identify them as slaves, if they were doing business or running errands for their masters. In most places slaves were allowed to attend public sacrifices and festivals, games, and the theater. With their owners' permission

---

[70] *Ibid.*, 87, 91.

[71] For a good summary of how scholars have viewed slavery in NT times, see John Byron, "Paul and the Background of Slavery: The *Status Quaestionis* in New Testament Scholarship" *CurBR* 3.1 (2004): 116–39. For the varied condition of slaves, see John T. Fitzgerald, "The Stoics and the Early Christians on the Treatment of Slaves," in *Stoicism in Early Christianity*, ed. Tuomas Rasimus et al (Grand Rapids: Baker Academic, 2010), 141–75.

[72] See G. Francois Wessels, "The Letter to Philemon in the Context of Ancient Slavery in Early Christianity," in *Philemon in Perspective: Interpreting a Pauline Letter*, ed. D. Francois Tolmie, BZNW 169 (Berlin: de Gruyter, 2010), 143–68, at 155–57.

they could join trade guilds and local associations where they could hold office and be accepted as full members without the distinction of being labeled as slaves.[73] Most classicists agree that in Paul's time and afterwards the general attitude toward the treatment of slaves in the Roman empire was improving.[74]

The experience of slavery in the Roman world therefore stretched across a range from the horrible to the comfortable, with most slaves probably living at about the same level of comfort as a poor free person. Even if most slaves were not subjected to torture or abuse at the hands of their masters, their lives were still such that runaway slaves were a major social problem.[75] Many slaves undoubtedly felt trapped by their status as slaves,[76] and many spent their lives in fear of physical abuse.[77] Their lot was unfortunate at best, and there was no reason for a slave to wear himself out with extra labor, nor was there much incentive to be scrupulous or to be a person of integrity, because working harder did not generally improve their life. Upward social mobility through hard work was not usually an option for them. Having integrity did nothing to right the unfairness of their situation, because their situation was sanctioned in law. Many slaves probably felt exploited, and some of them likely had no qualms in exploiting their masters in return. For this reason, slaves were routinely caricatured as a lazy, scheming, mischievous and immoral lot who were not to be trusted.[78] However, we must understand that the greatest part of this characterization should be read as a stereotype built by those further up the social scale, constructed to give themselves a sense of superiority. It is not likely that the stereotype described the true reality of the ancient world. Nevertheless, slaves, even those in relatively good places, were likely to have been dissatisfied with their lives for the most part and harbored the desire to be free.[79] This sentiment was fueled by a growing social trend to recognize the basic equality of all people. For example, Seneca said "What we have to seek for, then, is that which

[73] Westermann, *Slave Systems*, 108.

[74] *Ibid.*, 113–117.

[75] *Ibid.*, 105.

[76] K. R. Bradley, *Slaves and Masters in the Roman Empire: A Study in Social Control* (Oxford: Oxford University Press, 1987), shows the extent to which slaves were completely controlled by their masters.

[77] Fitzgerald, "The Stoics and the Early Christians," 163.

[78] *Ibid.*, 146–47.

[79] Head, "Onesimus the Letter Carrier," 649–56.

does not each day pass more and more under the control of some power which cannot be withstood. And what is this? It is the soul,—but the soul that is upright, good, and great. What else could you call such a soul than a god dwelling as a guest in a human body? A soul like this may descend into a Roman equestrian just as well as into a freedman's son or a slave. For what is a Roman equestrian, or a freedman's son, or a slave? They are mere titles, born of ambition or of wrong."[80]

Many slaves could reasonably expect to be freed before their deaths (although nothing guaranteed this). Roman slave owners routinely provided for the freedom of their slaves upon the master's death with a manumission clause in the master's will. In fact, this happened so often that laws were passed that limited the number of slaves that could be freed in this way.[81] Slaves could sometimes buy their freedom with the help of family and friends, or by a special arrangement known as sacral manumission,[82] and many male slaves were free by their early thirties. Once a slave was freed, he became known as a freedman, or an ex-slave. If the master freed a slave before the master's death, the slave was still considered indebted to serve his former master like a client when called upon to do so.[83] Freedmen could go on to attain better lives, as the well-known example of the Roman procurator Felix reminds us,[84] but it is important to note that the stigma of slavery clung to a person for the rest of their lives.

This brings us to the important point that slavery in the ancient world was more than a physical circumstance of one's life. It was also part of the ancient scale of status. Slaves were considered to be the lowest,

---

[80] *Ep. Mor.* 31.11 (Gummere, LCL). See also Seneca's Epistle 47, against the abuse of slaves (esp. 47.10; and 44.1). On the topic of Stoic attitudes about slavery, see Fitzgerald, "The Stoics and the Early Christians." We should note, as Fitzgerald does, that even as the treatment of slaves was being debated, basically no one in the ancient world was calling for the abolition of slavery (the only exceptions being the Therapeutae and the Essenes; John M. G. Barclay, "Paul, Philemon and the Dilemma of Christian Slave-Ownership," *NTS* 37 (1991): 161–86, at 177).

[81] The basis for the law was to guard against dilution of the "Roman stock" that would occur if too many outsiders were admitted into citizenship and into Roman society in general. Head, "Onesimus the Letter Carrier," 89.

[82] Many scholars believe that Paul uses the imagery of sacral manumission in Rom 6.22.

[83] See R. Zelnick-Abramovitz, *Not Wholly Free: The Concept of Manumission and the Status of Manumitted Slaves in the Ancient Greek World* (Leiden: Brill, 2005).

[84] That Felix was a former slave is reported by Tacitus, *Histories* 5.9; and Suetonius, *Life of Claudius*, 28.

or nearly so, on the social scale. They were often given demeaning, humiliating work to do and, as we noted above, had no rights under the law. When a slave was to be punished, he was punished with forms of punishment that were considered humiliating and demeaning, such as bodily beating (scourging) or crucifixion (Roman citizens were exempt from such degrading forms of punishment).[85] The ancient terminology also spoke to the negative power attached to the social status of slavery. A former slave was not known as a free person; such a description was used only of people who had never been enslaved. Nor was a former slave the equal of free people. He was known as a freedman, a man who once bore the lowest status possible and for whom, in a sense, that status still had some effect. Furthermore, as we noted in Part 1 of this Introduction, owners would post notices of runaway slaves that included physical descriptions. These descriptions obviously had the practical goal of enabling someone to identify the runaway when they saw him, but these descriptions were also caricatures. They were composed so as to create a demeaning impression of the runaway, to portray him as a ridiculous, sub-standard person who obviously, just from the looks of him, could never pass as a respectable free person.[86]

We do not have any information about the quality of Onesimus' life as a slave. We have no idea of how Philemon treated him, what kind of work he did, whether his life was pleasant or not, *etc.* We do not know his age, nor how long he had been a slave. We do not even know his birthplace or ethnicity, since it was common practice for owners to rename slaves with Greek or Latin names.[87] All we can say with certainty is that as a slave he would have held the lowest social status of those who were involved in the case that Paul made to Philemon. This was part of the world in which they lived. It could not be ignored and

---

[85] In the Roman world, one's appearance and outward demeanor was considered to be a reflection of one's character, identity, and status. To be forcibly overpowered by another person, to be arrested or put in chains, and to have one's body abused, was considered shameful, an offence against one's dignity. Crucifixion maximized these indicators of shame with its involuntary nakedness and physical torture. Since slaves lacked social dignity, such treatment was considered appropriate for slaves, but it was considered greatly insulting when it was directed against free people.

[86] Harrill, *Slaves in the New Testament*, 43–44.

[87] Westermann, *Slave Systems*, 92; see also David Lewis, "Notes on Slave Names, Ethnicity, and Identity in Classical and Hellenistic Greece," *Studia Źródłoznawcze. U Schyłku Starożytności* 16 (2017): 169–99.

was a factor in the situation. It is obvious from the letter that this is an important consideration in our understanding of what Paul was asking Philemon to do, and appreciating the social reality of the situation impresses us with how delicate the matter actually was.

Rhetoric. Related to this appeal to status is Paul's use of rhetoric with Philemon. Rhetoric was, formally, the art of persuasive speaking. It was a crucial part of the education of anyone who wanted to participate in public service in the Hellenistic world. Formal rhetoric followed accepted canons. Public speeches for the courtroom (called forensic rhetoric) followed certain conventions, and another set of conventions governed public speeches for or against political positions (called epideictic rhetoric). The elements of these various types of public speeches are not our concern here. Instead, the point is that many people would have encountered formal rhetoric in the public speeches they heard, and the use of public rhetoric was a highly-developed art in New Testament times.

Whether Paul had any formal training in rhetoric is a matter of ongoing debate among scholars. Some have argued that Paul knew the formal features of rhetoric and used them in his speeches and letters. Others claim that Paul's knowledge of rhetoric would have been second-hand, having picked it up through hearing and reading it in the course of everyday life.[88] And then there is Paul's famous statement in 1 Corinthians 2.1, "when I came to you, brethren, I did not come with superiority of speech or of wisdom, as I proclaimed the testimony of God to you." On its face, it sounds as if Paul was saying that even if he did know rhetoric—whether having studied it formally or just having picked it up through exposure—he made sure not to let the gospel sound like it. Paul did not want the gospel to be lumped in with the mass of rhetorical appeals being made for Hellenistic philosophies. Of course, what we have left of Paul's voice are thirteen of his letters in the New Testament. From these letters it is not possible to conclude that Paul consciously used the features of formal Hellenistic rhetoric in them,[89] and we should undoubtedly also

[88] As argued by Ben Witherington, III, " 'Almost Thou Persuadest Me…': The Importance of Greco-Roman Rhetoric for the Understanding of the Text and Context of the NT," *JETS* 58.1 (2015): 63–88.

[89] There is no evidence that elements of rhetoric were taught to be incorporated into letter-writing. See Jeffrey T. Reed, "The Epistle," in *Handbook of Classical Rhetoric in the Hellenistic Period, 330 B.C.-A.D. 400,* ed. Stanley E. Porter (Leiden: Brill, 1997), 171–93; and in the same volume, Stanley E. Porter, "Paul of Tarsus and His Letters," 533–85. Also Michael Bird, "Reassessing a Rhetorical Approach to Paul's Letters," *ExpTim* 119 (2008): 374–79.

take Paul's claim in 1 Corinthians 2.1 seriously, that his oral preaching was not styled after the canons of Hellenistic rhetoric.

This does not mean that persuasion has nothing to do with Paul's letters. It is possible that Paul had picked up a few features of Greco-Roman rhetorical techniques by exposure to them in everyday life. However, a better argument could be made that Paul simply used the kinds of arguments that were common in everyday conversation, as well as those he learned from his training as a rabbi.[90] In any interaction in which two people have different positions on an issue, and there is dialogue between them, each party is going to make appeals and arguments that are persuasive in nature. People who had no training in the more formal aspects of classical rhetoric routinely participated in this ordinary, everyday kind of persuasive speech. Its production was not bound by the structural rules of formal rhetoric, but simply followed patterns of thinking and speaking that were in common use.

It is this less formal and more flexible "everyday" kind of rhetoric[91] that, I believe, permeates Phlm.[92] Even the casual reader of this little letter is impressed with how Paul was constantly recasting a problematic situation as one that was an opportunity to do good. Paul reminded Philemon of the goodness he had shown in the past and of which he was capable in the present situation (vv 4–7). He played on Onesimus' name, which in Greek means "useful" (see v 11, 16).[93] He asked Philemon to refresh his heart (v 20). These were rhetorical touches of the everyday kind that Philemon would have understood well.

Persuasion, or the use of rhetoric, was part of the process of negotiating one's way through the various levels of power and status in the ancient world (as it still is today). From certain perspectives, it might be possible to judge Paul's words as manipulative, as flattering Philemon because

---

[90] Modern scholars generally agree that the methods of argumentation used by the Jewish teachers were influenced by Greco-Roman models. See David Daube, "Rabbinic Methods of Interpretation and Hellenistic Rhetoric," *HUCA* 22 (1949): 239–64.

[91] This was once called "New Rhetoric" in the scholarly literature, but that designation seems to have fallen out of use.

[92] See Stanley E. Porter, "Ancient Literate Culture and Popular Rhetorical Knowledge: Implications for Studying Pauline Rhetoric," in *Paul and Ancient Rhetoric: Theory and Practice in the Hellenistic Context*, ed. Stanley E. Porter and Bryan R. Dyer (Cambridge: Cambridge University Press, 2016), 96–115.

[93] See Wright, *Paul and the Faithfulness of God*, 21: Paul did not do this for its effect as entertainment, but to make a serious point.

Paul wanted something from him, and rationalizing every possible objection so as to leave Philemon with no choice but to do as Paul asked. Such objections may say more about our Western sensibilities and our infatuation with the perception of our independence than they say about Paul's letter.[94] Although it was indeed possible to act and speak in such deceptive ways in Paul's time (see Col 2.4, 8), it is doubtful that Philemon would have judged the rhetoric Paul employed here as exhibiting such underhanded motives. The use of persuasion by itself was not perceived as manipulative or deceitful.[95] The Sophistic overuse of rhetorical flourishes by a writer or speaker was considered objectionable (especially in a letter),[96] but not the use of persuasion itself. Witherington has noted

> What we see in this document is the limits to which Paul was prepared to go rhetorically to achieve an important aim. While of course he was not prepared to resort to dishonesty or trickery, nor would he conjure up feigned emotions, he was prepared to use all the normal rhetorical conventions, pulling out all the stops, including combining references to persuasion and command and playing the emotion card repeatedly, to give a discourse the necessary weight to achieve its goal. If this makes us uncomfortable because it seems manipulative by modern standards, it is because we do not live in the kind of social and rhetorical environment Paul did, where this kind of discourse was not only commonplace but actually relished and applauded, and where power inequities in relationships and social iniquities such as slavery presented the orator with situations requiring very strident and bold rhetoric to accomplish some purposes.[97]

---

[94] *Cf.* Ben Witherington, III, *The Letters to Philemon, the Colossians, and the Ephesians: A Socio-Rhetorical Commentary on the Captivity Epistles* (Grand Rapids: Eerdmans, 2007), 94; and John M. G. Barclay, "*Koinōnia* and the Social Dynamics of the Letter to Philemon," in *La Lettre à Philémon et L'Ecclésiologie Paulinienne / Philemon and Pauline Ecclesiology*, ed. Daniel Marguerat (Leuven: Peters, 2016), 151–69, at 163, 166. Wright put it this way: "Yes, yes, think many readers, this simply reveals Paul as a master of manipulation. The hermeneutic of suspicion casts its usual wet blanket over all possibilities other than the reinscribing of narratives of money, sex and particularly power, and it is power that people often see at work here. Sometimes this proposal is part of the contemporary drive to make Paul simply yet one more hellenistic thinker and writer. He can't, people think, be as different as all that! It *must* 'really' be all about social manipulation ..." *Paul and the Faithfulness of God*, 6.

[95] One should consider 2 Corinthians 8–9 from this same standpoint.

[96] Ben Witherington, III, *Conflict and Community in Corinth: A Socio-Rhetorical Commentary on 1 and 2 Corinthians* (Grand Rapids: Eerdmans, 1995), 42–43, quoting Quintilian; Wilhelm Wuellner, "Arrangement," in *Handbook of Classical Rhetoric in the Hellenistic Period, 330 B.C.-A.D. 400*, ed. Stanley E. Porter (Leiden: Brill, 1997), 74–75.

[97] Witherington, *Philemon, Colossians, Ephesians*, 87.

And,

> Pathos was the stock-in-trade of much communication that was intended to persuade, and people of that rhetoric-saturated culture were not merely used to it, they knew how to read it. They knew when it was deliberate hyperbole and when it was not. They knew when it was genuine and when it was for rhetorical effect, whereas we do not always pick up the rhetorical signals. Indeed, if we have never studied ancient Greco-Roman rhetoric we *often* misread Paul's rhetorical signals.[98]

Paul certainly was trying to persuade Philemon "to do the right thing" (v 8). To this extent, Paul's letter is persuasive. It makes arguments and presents an appeal (v 10). That is, to this extent the little letter is rhetorical. In fact, all of Paul's letters can be called rhetorical in this broader sense. Paul was not in the business simply of conveying information, much less commands. Of course, he taught so that people would know the truth about Jesus and his work, but he also persuaded people to become followers of Jesus and to live after his example. "Knowing the fear of the Lord, we persuade men" (2 Cor 5.11). Ultimately, this is how we should understand Paul's persuasion in Phlm. Paul saw the situation between Philemon and Onesimus as one that involved obligations to the Lord, and it was the fulfillment of their commitment to Christ, that translates into commitments to each other, that Paul had his eye on here. Paul's persuasion was the expression of his passion for the fulfillment of this reality among Christians.

Benefaction and Reciprocity. A third facet of the ancient culture that was at work in Paul's letter was the powerful dynamic of benefaction and reciprocity. This dynamic was woven into the fact noted above, that a person's status was often an important consideration in one's interactions in the ancient world. Many of the things we might do today were done differently in ancient times. If a there is a job opening at the Post Office today, nearly everyone who is interested has the right to apply for it. If one meets the qualifications for the job, he/she has a decent chance of getting it. In the ancient world, getting such a position, or even getting what one needed, was not simply a matter of applying for it nor even of proving that one had the skills necessary to do the job well, but of

---

[98] Ben Witherington III, *Paul's Letter to the Philippians: A Socio-Rhetorical Commentary* (Grand Rapids: Eerdmans, 2011), 179.

knowing the right people and entering into a good relationship with them. Social interactions at all levels were the keys to advancement and opportunity in life. In order to obtain something beyond one's reach, one had to form a relationship with someone who had access to the desired goal. This often meant that one had to appeal to someone with a higher social status than oneself because resources and opportunities were limited and were closely guarded by those who had social power.[99] The ability to control opportunity and resources often gave the wealthy and those with high social status tremendous social leverage. Such a system of advancement through favorable relationships is generally known as benefaction, and these interactions created bonds of obligation. The greater the giver's status, and the greater his gift, the greater were the obligations that went with the gift. Recipients of favors were obligated to the giver in several ways, but the basic expectation was always that an understanding of reciprocity was in place.

The patron-client relationship was a specific form of benefaction in the ancient world. Because people of greater wealth and status were naturally in a position to help others, people of lesser means and status could appeal to them for favors in exchange for future service and the promotion of the giver's name (*i.e.*, of their honor). In such cases the giver was known as the patron, and the recipient of the gift became the client. The patron-client relationship was the key to many things in the ancient world, so much so that we can say without fear of exaggeration that the ancient system of things was built upon it. This, in fact, was what Seneca said about it: "For how else do we live in security if it is not that we help each other by an exchange of good offices? It is only through the interchange of benefits that life becomes in some measure equipped and fortified against sudden disasters."[100] To us, "patronage" is a term associated with unfairness and corruption. To the ancients, however, patronage was a vital part of how their world (including religion[101]) worked. Access to resources was mainly through relationships with the people who had them.

The patron-client relationship was a strictly social arrangement. There was no formal law that said things had to work this way, nor were there any laws that regulated the relationship. The system worked

---

[99] David A. deSilva, *Honor, Patronage, Kinship & Purity: Unlocking New Testament Culture* (Westmont, IL: InterVarsity Press, 2012), 96.

[100] *Ben.* 4.18.1 (Basore, LCL).

[101] John M. G. Barclay, *Paul and the Gift* (Grand Rapids: Eerdmans, 2015), 27–28.

entirely upon social consent, upon the agreement that patrons and clients had obligations to each other. If one party failed to honor their obligations, there was no legal recourse for the other party. There was, however, a significant social recourse available. Ancient Hellenistic culture was an honor culture, in many ways different from the culture of 21st-century America. This is not to say that American culture lacks a moral category of honor (or shame), but that the importance accorded to honor in the ancient world was, generally, much more significant than in our culture today. One author has said that "Honor, whether ascribed or achieved, is the greatest social value in antiquity, valued more highly even than life itself."[102] In an honor culture, all actions are weighed not primarily against the law, but against the social standard of honor. People were expected, by each other, to do the honorable thing in any situation (and their society determined what the honorable thing was). The fear of shame tended to drive many people in the ancient world to a degree that does not generally compare to modern America, except in some American subcultures.[103] A failure to respect the obligations of patronage resulted in shame.

One of the reasons that honor drove the thinking and behavior of many people in the Hellenistic world was that, for many of the cultures within the Roman empire, the group played a more significant role in their thinking than it does in ours. Our modern American culture tends to emphasize, if not praise, individuality and independence, but the ancient world was more a world of groups: family, ethnicity, city, religion, trade guild, *etc.* The groups to which a person belonged identified a person. Many people did not consider individuality, uniqueness, and being different from others to be a good thing. Instead, conformity was generally expected and commended. Within the group, certain expectations adhered to the identity. Those who failed or, even worse, refused to conform to the group's expectations brought shame upon themselves and the group. Acting honorably, then, was important not only for one's own sake, but also for the sake of the group to which one belonged. Acting against the group's values could result in rejection and ostracism by one's group,

---

[102] Stephen C. Barton, "Social Values and Structures" in *Dictionary of New Testament Background: A Compendium of Contemporary Biblical Scholarship*, ed. Stanley E. Porter and Craig A. Evans (Downers Grove, IL: InterVarsity Press, 2000), 1127–34, at 1129.

[103] See Tamler Sommers, *Why Honor Matters* (New York: Basic Books, 2018). Modern examples of honor cultures would be Japanese culture and Middle Eastern cultures.

which was, generally, a more serious thing in the Hellenistic world than it is in ours today. To be rejected by one's group was a kind of "death," it meant that one lost important elements of their identity.

This group-oriented aspect of ancient culture, and its relationship to the control of honor, is part of the fabric of Phlm. The delicate conversation that was taking place between Paul and Philemon was happening in front of others. As the letter arrived at its destination, it was addressed not to Philemon only, but also to Apphia, Archippus, and the church there. The normal practice was that Paul's letters were read to the church (Col 4.16), and so this negotiation, already sensitive because of the conflict of status involved between Paul and Philemon, took on another dimension, that of a kind of public hearing in which Philemon's response would be on display for all to see and evaluate.[104] The church was called upon not simply to listen to Paul's appeal, but to help turn it into a reality by encouraging Philemon to resolve the problem in a way that befitted the behavior of those who make up the church of the Lord.[105]

Benefaction, then, was built on the back of the ancient culture of honor, and the shared importance of honorable behavior before the group is what made the system work. We noted a quotation above from Seneca in which he commented on the value of the patron-client system in his world. He prefaced that remark with these words: "Ingratitude is something to be avoided in itself because there is nothing that so effectually disrupts and destroys the harmony of the human race as this vice."[106] In other words, since the patron-client relationship was one of the foundations of Greco-Roman culture, gratitude was essential. The person who failed, out of ingratitude, to fulfill his part of the relationship threatened the entire fabric of society. Seneca's remark basically wonders "What kind of world would we have if everyone was ungrateful and did not fulfill their obligations?" It was unimaginable to them.

At the core of benefaction in the ancient world, including the patron-client relationship, lay the concept of reciprocity. The basic idea was, "If I do something for you, you are indebted to do something for me." This unspoken "law" operated in nearly every transaction. Failure to reciprocate was shameful. To put it another way, the doing of a favor

---

[104] Harrill, *Slaves in the New Testament*, 13.

[105] Timothy A. Brookins, "'I Rather Appeal to *Auctoritas*': Roman Conceptualizations of Power and Paul's Appeal to Philemon," *CBQ* 77 (2015): 302–21, at 320–21.

[106] *Ben.* 4.18.1 (Basore, LCL).

created the expectation of loyalty to the giver of the favor. The recipient of the favor was honor-bound to reciprocate. How the reciprocation was to be accomplished depended on several factors. Sometimes it meant doing a favor in return. Sometimes it meant doing a service for the giver. If the nature of the gift was such that the recipient could not repay it, then the recipient was expected to publicly praise and honor the giver, to tell others what a great thing the giver had done and thus build up his stock of public honor.[107] Furthermore, the person who failed to honor his obligations shamed himself in the worst possible way. The result would be socially disastrous. Such a person would be known as the person who lacked honor, and few would be eager to do business with, or do a favor for, this person again.

We noted concerning rhetoric that Paul may have avoided the use of formal rhetoric in his preaching and writing, but there was still a more common kind of rhetoric or persuasion at work in his letters. A similar thing holds true concerning Paul's involvement in benefaction. The patronage that characterized the relationships between social elites and non-elites was one thing, but a similar kind of relationship also existed on lower social levels as well.[108] That is, benefaction is not something that existed only between the wealthy and those of lower economic status. Bonds of benefaction could and did exist between people who were otherwise socio-economic equals.[109] Examples would be the relationship between neighbors, the relationship between friends, the relationship between a teacher and a student, the relationship between an employer and an employee or apprentice, or, to use a more familiar example, the relationship between elders and a church. In all of these

---

[107] *Cf.* 1 Pet 2.9: "that you may proclaim the excellencies of him who has called you."

[108] See Richard Saller, "Patronage and Friendship in Early Imperial Rome: Drawing the Distinction," in *Patronage in Ancient Society*, ed. Andrew Wallace-Hadrill (London: Routledge, 1989), 49–62.

[109] Carolyn Osiek, "The Politics of Patronage and the Politics of Kinship: The Meeting of the Ways," *BTB* 39.3 (2009): 143–52, at 146–47; *cf.* J. Brian Tucker, "Paul's Particular Problem—The Continuation of Existing Identities in Philemon," in *T&T Clark Handbook to Social Identity in the New Testament*, ed. J. Brian Tucker and Coleman A. Baker (London: Bloomsbury T&T Clark, 2016), 407–24, at 417. However, Erlend D. MacGillivray ("Re-Evaluating Patronage and Reciprocity in Antiquity and New Testament Studies," *JGRChJ* 6 (2009): 37–81) is undoubtedly correct to insist that "patronage" should only be used for the formal system known in Roman culture, and cites Danker's preference for the more comprehensive term "reciprocity system" (p. 41, fn 18) to describe lesser or other kinds of reciprocal relationships in the ancient world.

examples, everyone might well be on basically the same socio-economic level. None of them might be wealthy, yet there would exist among them gradations of status. "A student is not above his teacher," Jesus said. The social distance between a teacher and student might not be great, and it certainly might not be as great as the distance between people in the classic patron-client relationship (where the patron was definitely one of the social elite), but what could be called a lower form of the patron-client relationship existed between them nonetheless. Because it existed, it was to be respected and brought with it expectations for both parties.

It is precisely here, at what we might call a common (non-elite) level of the patron-client interchange, that we may locate the relationship between Paul and Philemon. This little letter is surprisingly saturated with the language of benefaction. In the text we hear terms such as "fellowship" (v 6), "partner" (v 17), talk of owing and repaying (v 19), and "benefit" (v 20). Paul clearly presented himself to Philemon as a benefactor to whom Philemon owed something—even his own life (v 19). Philemon would have understood, and accepted, these clues. And yet Paul stopped short of demanding action from Philemon (v 8). Instead he demonstrated his awareness of Philemon's status as well. Philemon had benefitted the saints from his own resources (v 7), he prayed for Paul, and would be his (hopefully) future host (v 22). The disposition of Onesimus remained in Philemon's control, as Onesimus' master, as Paul would not force him to do anything (v 14). But I suggest that although the dynamics of benefaction were in play between Paul and Philemon, and Paul put rhetorical pressure on Philemon, Paul used these things only to get at something else, something much more important and more fundamental for people who relate to each other as Christians.

Of course, it is easy for us to assume that since Paul was the apostle among the parties involved in this letter, he would have been the one with the greatest status among them, that he would have been viewed as the benefactor. This is, of course, possible, but some scholars have suggested that a different scenario might have been at work. According to this alternate interpretation, it is Philemon who had presented himself as the benefactor. He was acknowledged to be the host to the church (it met in his house, v 2), he had given gifts to Christians (v 7), and he was the owner of the slave that was helping Paul (v 13). For these reasons, Philemon could have thought of himself as the "patron" in this situation.

This approach also favors the theory that Philemon had deliberately sent Onesimus to Paul, which could be interpreted as another expression of Philemon's generosity. In this reading, Philemon's liberality had placed Paul (either intentionally or not) in the place of being a kind of client (indebted) to Philemon. This scenario, then, placed Philemon in the "driver's seat" of the relationship, as it were. With such an approach, Phlm reads very differently: the letter becomes Paul's tactful resistance to Philemon's attempt to control the situation and the people in it.[110]

The problem with this reading of the situation is that it lacks support from the text of Phlm itself. It is a reading between the lines, as it were, with certain assumptions filling in the gaps. As noted previously, when we read Paul's letters we are reading other people's mail, and we are only getting Paul's side of the conversation. We simply do not have any evidence that Philemon was thinking inappropriately toward Paul or that he had selfish motives. It could be true, but as it stands it is another piece of the background that we simply do not know. It is not part of the narrative world of the text itself, and this indicates that it is not "in play" in the letter. Even more, however, Paul clearly pointed out in vv 9 and 19 that he occupied no such position in relation to Philemon.

The ancient social world was an interlocking web of status, honor, group, benefaction, reciprocity, and rhetoric. All of these things (plus others, of course) worked together to create the social environment in which every person lived and worked, including the Christians. When Paul reminded Philemon that he owed Paul his very self (v 19), Paul was claiming that he stood in the position of a benefactor, spiritually, to Philemon, and this rhetorical claim was a subtle reminder that Philemon was honor-bound to reciprocate by granting his benefactor's request.

This section of our introductory survey raises an important point about the gospel, a point that is powerfully operative in Phlm. The point is this: *our unity in the kingdom of God does not erase the social realities in which we each live.* A fellow Christian may be my boss at work. The fact that he is a fellow Christian does not eliminate his status or authority as my boss. The fact that we are both Christians does not mean that I am unaccountable to him as my boss, or that I do not have to follow his orders, *etc.* As Christians, we are called upon to respect the social structures that

---

[110] See Scott S. Elliot, " 'Thanks But No Thanks': Tact, Persuasion, and the Negotiation of Power in Paul's Letter to Philemon," *NTS* 57.1 (2011): 51–64.

make up our world. After conversion to Christ, the social hierarchies still exist and we must live and work within them. So in passages like Colossians 3.18–4.1 and Ephesians 5.22–6.9 (the well-known "household codes"), Paul did not call for the abolition of roles either within society or within the church, even though before God we are all of equal worth. Parents are still parents and are to be respected as such. Children are still children, husbands are still husbands, wives are still wives, slaves are still slaves, and masters are still masters in this world. In the cases of parents and children, and husbands and wives, those social structures are God-ordained (as is the role of human government, Rom 13.1–7). Each is to fulfill their assigned social roles "as to the Lord." Those roles do not disappear between us when we enter the fellowship of Jesus Christ. Within the local church, elders "rule" over the congregation. The fact that the rest of flock are also Christians does not mean that they need not pay attention to the directions of the overseers (Heb 13.17). More broadly, within the kingdom of God men are still men, women are still women, Jews are still Jews, and Gentiles are still Gentiles. Christian unity is not the result of distinctions between people disappearing, but the result of the gospel overcoming, or transcending, these distinctions in an important way. Christian unity is not a uniformity in which all social distinctions vanish and everyone becomes somehow "the same."

So what does Galatians 3.28 mean, then? The passage says "There is neither Jew nor Greek, there is neither slave nor free man, there is neither male nor female; for you are all one in Christ Jesus" (NASB). Galatians 3.28 is a statement about the overcoming of separations and barriers. In the ancient world, men and women were two distinct social groups, as were free people and slaves, and Jews and Gentiles. The world in which Paul lived (much like ours) was a world in which social separations were important, especially for identity. Distinctions make uniqueness, so identities were constructed around the differences between groups of people. Perhaps even more importantly, one's membership in a group could also mean that one faced inherent barriers to access and privilege. For the Judaizers, access to God was a privilege of the Jews and the Jews only. In a similar way, being female or being a slave meant that access to many things in life was simply impossible. The distinctions were barriers. In the context of Galatians, the Judaizers were arguing that God himself regarded Jewishness as the key distinction, or barrier, for salvation. It is to this incorrect idea that Paul was responding in Galatians 3.28. Paul's assertion is that the determining identity for salvation is "in Christ," and that this new sphere of relationship encompasses, or subsumes, males, females, Jews, Gentiles, *etc.* Or, as Paul put it in Ephesians 2.18, "through Him we both have our access in one Spirit to the Father." That is, God has created a new group in which those classic barriers that were determinative in the world of men are not determinative for salvation. Contrary to the world of men, within God's kingdom one's ethnicity, gender, or social position does not create a barrier to access to God. The division between those who are in relationship with God and those who are not consists of the criterion of faith in Christ Jesus. No other criterion exists, and this is Paul's point in Galatians 3.28. They had all been baptized into Christ, and no other criterion of acceptance with God was operative (especially the criterion of Jewishness, as the Judaizers were insisting). It is in this way that the gospel eliminates "boasting" in worldly, fleshly distinctions (Rom 3.27).

As Martin has put it,

> This unity, however, is not uniformity. In Christian baptism, Jews are baptized as Jews, Greeks as Greeks, slaves as slaves, free persons as free persons, males as males, and females as females. Baptism does not abolish such distinctions but treats them as irrelevant for entrance into the community of faith. Once in this community, of course, the baptized person must still contend with her or his cultural, economic, and gendered status as well as with the differing status of others. Nevertheless, all have full standing in the community in that all are baptized. The diversity produced by these distinctions creates many members in the one body according to 1 Cor 12:12–14. When Gal 3:28 proclaims that in Christ there is neither Jew nor Greek, slave nor free, and that in Christ there is no male and female, the proclamation only pertains to the absence of these distinctions as requirements for baptism in contrast to the requirements in the covenant of circumcision. This verse does not proclaim the absolute abolition of these distinctions but only their irrelevance for participation in Christian baptism and full membership in the Christian community.[111]

Galatians 3.28 strongly implies that there is equality of worth among all who are in Christ, even if that is not its primary point.[112] Problems

---

[111] Troy W. Martin, "The Covenant of Circumcision (Genesis 17:9–14) and the Situational Antitheses in Galatians 3:28," *JBL* 122 (2003): 111–25, at 121–22.

[112] Fung has thus correctly noted about this verse: "If the notion of equality in Christ

are created when we confuse, or conflate, social status (whatever its basis, whether in gender, ethnicity, *etc.*) with personal worth. In Paul's world, ethno-social status and judgments about the perceived value or worth of a person went together.[113] Rich people were considered more valuable than poor people. Aristotle famously asserted that some people were natural slaves because of deficiencies that made them less than fully human.[114] Greeks considered themselves intellectually and culturally superior to barbarians, and some Jews considered themselves of greater worth to God than Gentiles.[115] As deSilva notes of the categories mentioned in Galatians 3.28, "Each of these three pairs [Jew and Greek, slave and free, male and female] reflects the racism and chauvinism that pervaded the ancient world."[116] Paul's assertion was that the categories of status, as well as the perceptions of value that went with them, were of no account when it comes to determining a person's fellowship with God.

Asserting that human categories of identity or status are of no account before God with respect to salvation does not mean that those categories have now ceased to exist once one becomes a Christian, or that they do not exist within the group of God's people, or even that they mean nothing to God. Personal identities and relationships are not erased. Upon baptism, a Gentile is still a Gentile, that is, he/she is still not Jewish. "To be in Christ does not represent a fusion of identities so that Christ-followers are a fusion of Jewish and gentile identities. ... Paul's struggle was for gentile equality in Christ, not to make gentiles and Jews the same in Christ."[117] The same is true concerning distinctions in nationality, or gender, and also concerning social distinctions. The rich are still rich, the poor are still poor, slaves are still slaves, and governors are still governors. Differences

---

is also involved, it is only secondary and has regard to incorporation into this 'one person' and membership in the community." Ronald Y. K. Fung, *The Epistle to the Galatians*, NICNT (Grand Rapids: Eerdmans, 1988), 176.

[113] What we today call racism (the ancients did not have a word for it) was indeed part of the Greco-Roman world. See Benjamin Isaac, *The Invention of Racism in Classical Antiquity* (Princeton: Princeton University Press, 2004).

[114] In his *Politics* 1.5.

[115] See E. P. Sanders, *Paul and Palestinian Judaism: A Comparison of Patterns of Religion* (Philadelphia: Fortress, 1977), 87.

[116] David A. de Silva, *The Letter to the Galatians*, NICNT (Grand Rapids: Eerdmans, 2018), 339.

[117] William S. Campbell, *Paul and the Creation of Christian Identity* (London: T&T Clark, 2008), 158.

in social status have always existed among Christians, but within Christianity social status (membership in a particular social grouping) does not come into play when determining a person's worth or value, nor does it have a role in determining either the possibility or the degree of their standing with God. This further means that all such judgments among Christians about each other that are based on such worldly standards are to be rejected.[118] Unity in Christ is not accomplished by the elimination or destruction of all differences between Christians. We do not become one by every one of us becoming a hybrid. Unity in Christ is the result of a transformation of our minds in which we no longer count the differences between us as barriers or as markers of superiority before God. In Christ a man is still a man, but he is a different sort of man, a man in whom selfish notions of status and difference do not shape his view of the value of other people. In Christ a Jew is still a Jew, but a different kind of Jew who now regards his ethnicity as a call to invite the world to Israel's Messiah. In Christ a slave is still a slave, but in Christ he is a different kind of slave, a slave that uses his servile condition to proclaim Christ-like service; and a master is still a master, but a transformed master whose sees himself first as burdened with the high calling of showing the masterly love of Christ to those who belong to him. The marvel of this unity in Christ is that the very differences that the world uses to separate and judge people remain, but they no longer mean what they meant outside of Christ. Instead, the differences, the social situations, become contexts and vehicles for expressing service to Christ. As one has put it, "By this social dynamics are—in a sense—turned into theology."[119]

The notion of transformation is key here. It would be incorrect to think in terms simply of addition, where a new status is now added to a person's old status. The result of such an approach is the compartmentalizing of the aspects of our lives so that I think of a man as a brother at church, but I think of him as an employee at work (for example), and my attitude toward him is determined by where we are. Thinking of myself, or of other people, in two different ways depending on the situation is not what Paul was calling for. "Onesimus cannot be Philemon's brother on Sunday only and his slave

---

[118] *cf.* 1 Cor 1–4, 12–14, Rom 2, Jam 2.1–13, and other places where status judgments within the churches became an issue.

[119] Reidar Aasgaard, *"My Beloved Brothers and Sisters": Christian Siblingship in Paul* (London: T&T Clark, 2004), 309–10.

the rest of the week."[120] He did not ask Philemon to think of Onesimus now as a slave *and* as a brother. He asked him to think of Onesimus as *more than a slave*. The distinction is crucial. Onesimus' slave status was not erased by his conversion, but it now had a completely different character than it had before. He was a Christian slave, not just a slave.

In Phlm, then, Paul did not attempt to erase the fact that Onesimus was a slave or that Philemon was his master and owner, nor did Paul put himself in the place of the neutral outsider. The social positions of each of these men was part of the situation. Perhaps this is one of the reasons why we never hear Onesimus' voice in the letter. Paul simply recognized that "in a master-slave dispute the master held all the cards,"[121] and Onesimus' conversion did not change that. The fact that they were all Christians did not eliminate their social positions or the status each had in relation to the others. In Phlm, Paul *used* his position in relation to Philemon to encourage Philemon to transform his relationship with Onesimus. Social roles are employed for, or become subservient to, the accomplishment of God's will and the glory of God. As Barclay has stated it,

> What matters about Onesimus, what gives him worth, is his status as a "beloved brother"—which is precisely what matters also about Philemon and what gives him his worth. Whatever else might be said about them—unfree and free, slave and master—is not thereby erased, as if their status in human law was magically altered, but neither is it endorsed or reinforced. It is not ignored, as if their new status operated in a wholly different sphere unrelated to their everyday interactions…, but neither is it merely supplemented by, or encompassed within, the master category "brother." Rather Onesimus' "slave" categorization (and by implication, Philemon's categorization as "master") is made subordinate to the category of "beloved brother" and is relativized in importance.[122]

Here, then, is where we find the "mechanics" of Phlm. The appeal works within the machinery of the social positions of the three main parties, Paul, Philemon, and Onesimus. Paul used his social advantages

---

[120] de Silva, *Introduction*, 675.

[121] James D. G. Dunn, *Beginning from Jerusalem*, vol. 2 of *Christianity in the Making* (Grand Rapids: Eerdmans, 2009), 1032.

[122] John M. G. Barclay, "*Koinōnia* and the Social Dynamics," 160–61. *Cf.* Tucker, "Paul's Particular Problem," 407–24; he says (415) "Paul's construction of a superordinate identity does not seek to eliminate or obliterate existing subgroup identities."

(as an old man and as a benefactor to Philemon) to leverage an appeal for Onesimus, yet without destroying Philemon's position and role in the process. But the appeal itself was neither explicitly nor primarily for a change in Onesimus' social ("worldly") status. Specifically, Paul nowhere asked Philemon to give Onesimus his freedom. That would have been an adjustment to Onesimus' social position, but that was not what Paul was after. Instead, the appeal was for Philemon to adopt a view of Onesimus *in the Lord* in a way in which the different social statuses of the two men are not the primary determiners of their relationship. It results in a change for Onesimus *within* his role as a slave.

In effect, Paul was simply asking Philemon to do with Onesimus what God has already done with us in Christ. God sees our ethno-social positions (in fact, a case can be made that our differences are God-given, and that God even takes our differences into account in judgment), but he does not employ them to determine our acceptability with him (as Gal 3.28 says). Similarly, Paul was not asking Philemon to ignore what Onesimus was (a slave), but to accept Onesimus as a brother on the basis of his inclusion in the group that is "in Christ."[123] Paul was asking Philemon to adopt a way of looking at Onesimus in which Onesimus' social status had nothing to do with the acceptability or valuation of a person within Philemon's circle of fellowship.

What Paul was asking for in Phlm is not all that different from what he demanded in his letters to the Galatian and Roman Christians. In both letters the basic problem was divisions, or lack of acceptance, based on ethnic or social distinctions among Christians. In the case of Galatians, Jewish ethnicity was put forward by the Judaizers as a determining criterion for acceptance with God. In the case of Romans, the question was which group, Jews or Gentiles, was the favored people of God in Christ. In both cases, though, ethnic-social distinctions were being viewed as barriers to fellowship with God or man, or both. This is not dissimilar to the problem in Phlm, where a free man was being asked to accept his slave as a full brother in the Lord. In other words, Paul was asking Philemon not to regard the social distinction between himself and

---

[123] *Cf.* Eph 4.32–5.2, where God's action is presented as the model for Christian behavior: "Be kind to one another, tender-hearted, forgiving each other, just as God in Christ also has forgiven you. Therefore be imitators of God, as beloved children; and walk in love, just as Christ also loved you and gave Himself up for us, an offering and a sacrifice to God as a fragrant aroma" (NASB).

Onesimus as in any way determinative of the fellowship they have with God or each other. Paul's exhortation in Romans could easily have been repeated to Philemon: "Therefore, accept one another, just as Christ also accepted us to the glory of God" (Rom 15.7).

To put that differently, Paul was asking Philemon to adopt the mentality described in Colossians 3.10–11: "put on the new self who is being renewed to a true knowledge according to the image of the One who created him— a renewal in which there is no distinction between Greek and Jew, circumcised and uncircumcised, barbarian, Scythian, slave and freeman, but Christ is all, and in all" (NASB). Phlm is, in a sense, about the negotiation of a way of life through the dual identities of both Philemon and Onesimus. Philemon was the master, and Onesimus was the slave, but both men were also brothers in Christ. This dual status (of both men) is a particular manifestation of the larger fact that Christians, for the moment, live in two worlds at the same time. We live in the world of men, the world of the flesh. But we also live in the kingdom of God, which is different from, and above, that world. Our citizenship is in heaven, but for the moment our bodies are still in this world. To use the familiar phrase, we are in the world but not of the world—at the same time. Living out our days in this world in such a way that respects the social realities in which we now live, but at the same time finds our true identities and fulfillment in a world that is beyond this one, and that uses our worldly roles to glorify God, is, in a sense, what Christian living is all about. And it is what lies at the core of Phlm.

This understanding, that our inclusion in Christ does not erase other markers of a person's identity, also helps us to put Paul's use of persuasion in this letter in perspective. That is, Paul used the fullness of his person to serve Christ. Paul did not argue solely on the basis of revealed, divine truth. To be sure, his argument is grounded first and ultimately in his religious convictions about Jesus. But he also argued on a human level (yet without using human reasoning, 1 Cor 1.20–2.16), as well as the personal level and the factual level.[124] As we noted above, Phlm displays an everyday kind of rhetoric by which Paul intended to persuade Philemon. We noted that this use of persuasion does not amount to coercion or manipulation, but it does mean that Paul used reason and legitimate emotional concerns

[124] See J. Zmijewski, "Der Philemonbrief: Ein Plädoyer für die christliche Brüderlichkeit," *TThZ* 114 (2005): 222–42, at 240–41.

in presenting his case to Philemon. He also argued on the basis of his personal relationship with Philemon and upon the statuses that were operative between them, using them to the advantage of the gospel. He even offered to pay Philemon for any expenses that would arise (v 18). All of this is to say that Paul used every facet of his personal being in his appeal to Philemon, because he saw all the various facets of a person as tools to be used for the accomplishment of Christ's will and for Christ's glory. This is because the whole person exists in Christ, with his/her ethnicity, social standing and status, knowledge, *etc*. It is an example of the kind of thinking Paul expressed in 2 Corinthians 10.3–5: "For though we walk in the flesh, we do not war according to the flesh, for the weapons of our warfare are not of the flesh, but divinely powerful for the destruction of fortresses. We are destroying speculations and every lofty thing raised up against the knowledge of God, and we are taking every thought captive to the obedience of Christ" (NASB). Or, as Paul also said, "From him, and through him, and to him, are all things" (Rom 11.36; *cf*. Col 1.16). Who we are, the faculties we possess, the particular situations we occupy, our stations in life, our ability to reason, our ability to empathize—all of these things have a legitimate use in accomplishing God's will. Thus Paul's relationships, his (and Philemon's) emotions, his status, his money, and the truth in Christ were all for the accomplishment of Christ's will, and to Christ's glory. All could legitimately be used to bring about the proper resolution of the problem at hand, in Christ.

To summarize our findings thus far, we have noted that the things that are most often the subject of inquiry about Phlm—whether Onesimus was a runaway or had overstayed his time with Paul, whether Paul was asking for Philemon to give Onesimus his freedom, and other such matters—are actually nowhere to be found as points of discussion within the letter itself. Instead, the text of the letter directs us to some other things that were in play: the *relationship* between Paul and Philemon, now as it touched upon the issue of Onesimus, the basis of that relationship, Paul's use of persuasion, and the interplay of the status of these three men (one of whom was a slave, and another his master) in a web of mutual giving and receiving.

However, as crucial as these elements are to understanding Phlm (they are, after all, parts of the text itself), I would suggest that they still do not get us to what is driving the discussion in this little letter. It is one thing to observe that Paul called upon Philemon to take a new view of

Onesimus that did not factor social positions into the outcome. But *why* must Philemon do this? Upon what basis could such an appeal be made? To that more crucial part of the picture we now turn.

Addendum: The Outline (Literary Structure) of Paul's Letter to Philemon. Discerning a text's organization is part of the hermeneutical process. If the text has internal divisions based on clear literary markers, this information is useful as part of the interpretive task. The fact that the markers are *literary* is important. Modern texts are printed with all kinds of *visual* markers in them—chapter headings in larger font, centered, and standing apart from the following text, paragraphs with indented first lines, section headings in different type, *etc*. We navigate our way through texts by *looking* at them. The ancients navigated texts by *hearing* them, through verbal-audible markers. The problem for us, however, is that we might not always be aware of an ancient text's verbal structural markers, and thus we may ignore them. This leads to the further problem that we may then impose our own ideas of structure upon an ancient text and "discover" a structure that simply is not there.

The most defensible approach is to assume that the outline, or literary structure, of Phlm was determined mostly by the letter-writing conventions that Paul followed. The letter has an introduction, a body, and a closing, all of which are typical of ancient Greek letters. The opening section is vv 1–7, and the closing section is made up of vv 23–25. The section between these two pieces, vv 8–22, form the body of the letter in which the main business at hand was discussed.[125]

Some scholars claim that there is a chiastic structure to Phlm.[126] However, two things make these claims doubtful. First, those who have attempted to find a chiastic arrangement in Phlm do not agree on the

---

[125] I am here following a slightly modified version of the structure proposed by John L. White, "Structural Analysis."

[126] Chiasm was a way of arranging a text in antiquity for the optimization of hearing (since, as noted above, all ancient texts were composed to be heard). That is, it is a way of arranging a text for rhetorical effect. It is basically a structure of inverted parallel lines, with the first line of a work parallel to the last line, the second parallel to the second-to-last line, and so on, with a single, unparalleled line at the center of the composition. The current thinking is that this center element was meant to be understood as the main point or climax of the text. See the excellent discussion in Ian H. Thompson, *Chiasmus in the Pauline Letters*, JSNTS 111 (Sheffield: Sheffield Academic, 1995), 15–45; also John D. Harvey, *Oral Patterning in Paul's Letters* (Grand Rapids: Baker Books, 1998). One of the most recent proposals for a chiastic structure of Philemon is in Ernst Wendland, " 'You Will Do Even More Than I Say': On the Rhetorical Function of Stylistic Form in the Letter to Philemon,"

elements of the chiasm.[127] If such a structure truly exists in Phlm, it ought to be clear. Second, the proposed chiastic structures cut across what appear to be the natural epistolary sections of the letter. A much better case, I think, can be made that the letter exhibits *inclusio*, a technique by which key terms appear at both the beginning and end of a text. The following terms appear in both vv 1–7 and vv 20–25: Christ Jesus, fellow worker, grace, Lord Jesus Christ, prayers, Christ, heart, and brother (vocative). In a similar way, others have proposed a rhetorical structure to Phlm, based on the canons of ancient rhetoric.[128] I have indicated above that, in my opinion, it is unlikely that we will legitimately find the formal structures of ancient rhetoric reflected in Paul's letters (or any ancient letters).

Part 3: The Theological Context

Where the Message of Paul's Letter to Philemon Lies. I have made the case that we cannot know the exact historical situation that produced the letter to Philemon. I have also suggested that there are other, more general parts of the situation that we can know, not only because they were woven into the culture of Paul's time, but also because these features of the situation surface in the text of Phlm itself. As useful as this reconstruction of the ancient culture is for reading Phlm, we must understand that even when we have arrived at this point, we still have not heard the message of Phlm. The matters of status, benefaction, *etc.* are simply the stage on which the actual historical situation between Paul, Philemon, and Onesimus occurred, they are the scenery, as it were, that gave meaning to the words and actions in its time, they are the bearers of the message. These were basic building blocks available to Paul by which a message could be created (via comparison and contrast). They show us the mechanics of the text's situation, as it were, and they enable us to understand how the message of the text was being communicated. However, the message of this text itself does not lie in an examination, or knowledge, of such scenery. A knowledge (even a thorough one) of the cultural metaphors, the customs, the cultural norms, the historical-

in *Philemon in Perspective: Interpreting a Pauline Letter*, ed. D. Francois Tolmie, BZNW 169 (Berlin: de Gruyter, 2010), 91.

[127] John Paul Heil, "The Chiastic Structure and Meaning of Paul's Letter to Philemon," *Biblica* 82 (2001): 178–206, who notes the previous attempts by others (in fn 1).

[128] For example, F. Forrester Church, "Rhetorical Structure and Design in Paul's Letter to Philemon," *HTR* 71 (1978): 17–33.

political situation, the rhetoric, the civil-cultural mores that framed the interaction between the various parties involved in the letter, *etc.* gives vibrant color to the message, but those things are not the message, just as a knowledge of the stage setting of a play would not give us a knowledge of the plot or message of the play. Such things are vessels to hold and present the message, as it were, but the message is something else. What is going on in Phlm is that, in a sense, Paul is trying to get beyond the scenery, beyond the immediate historical situation, beyond the culture-based metaphors, *etc.* to create a new situation.

When we speak of the message of Phlm, we are speaking about something timeless. Because we believe that the Scriptures are not just ancient literature, but that they are the living and abiding word of God, we believe that these texts can communicate something to any generation of men, in whatever cultural context they live. These texts are not limited to the social and cultural circumstances that originally framed them. They speak to the human situation at large which is not contained within any one century of history.

One of the basic assumptions that lies behind reading the Biblical texts as divine Scripture is that they are understandable. Sure, there are portions that, as the apostle Peter said, are hard to understand (2 Pet 3.16). Some individual verses are not completely clear to us (as anyone who has ever wrestled with "because of the angels" in 1 Cor 11.10 can attest). To say that the Bible is understandable does not mean we claim to have understood it perfectly. But in spite of some things in the text that challenge us, the Bible is—and always has been—an understandable book, and the individual documents that together make up the Biblical canon are each understandable as well. The message of God working to save us from the consequences of our sin is as clear as it can be. The message of God preparing the way for the coming Messiah Jesus through types and patterns in his previous words and dealings with men is clear. The fact that Jesus' teachings, life, death, and resurrection have created a new situation into which we are being invited is clear. The call to follow Jesus is clear.

It should strike even the casual reader of the Biblical documents that those documents are short on the kinds of details we would need to reconstruct their historical-cultural-social situations with precision. The Bible rarely gives us dates for events, it rarely explains to us why certain behaviors in the text were performed (such as Job scraping himself with a potsherd), what some things meant (like "a Sabbath day's journey"), or what various titles meant (like rabbi or centurion). And wouldn't we all like to know what the "present distress" in Corinth was (1 Cor 7.26)? Sometimes, to be sure, a Biblical author will give us a piece of information that he thought was crucial to understanding a story, such as the beliefs of the Sadducees (Acts 23.8), or the fact that Jesus said something at the time of a particular feast (John 7.37), but these too are rare. For the most part, the Biblical authors were concerned with something else, something that transcended those historical-cultural adornments of the stories they related, something that in the end did not even need them.

The lack of historical-cultural details in the Biblical texts themselves points us to the consideration that those things—as valuable as we might think they are to our reading of the texts—were not the focus of the texts. Our ability to understand the Biblical message, or of any one of its constituent documents, does not depend on our mastery of the details of the cultures, societies, *etc.* in which those documents were written and in which the original recipients of those documents lived.[129] Nor, we might add, is the message limited to those contexts. If it were, we could not use the Bible for our lives today. The very supposition of anyone who aims to live by the Bible's teachings is that the message of the Bible is not confined to, nor only relevant to, the times in which the Biblical documents were written. We read the Bible with the assumption, yes, the confidence, that we can be a part of what is described in the pages of the New Testament, that we can share in what they experienced as Christians, and that this is not only possible, but intended by God Himself. If the Bible was not preserved by God for later generations to join in the faith of Jesus Christ, then I would admit that I do not know what it is for.

Our confidence that we can understand and join the situation described in the New Testament is a confidence that there is a timeless message there, and that this message is sufficiently communicated to us in the Bible *as it is*. As we noted above, learning about the ancient contexts of the biblical documents can add color and further clarity to our understanding of the message, but the message exists whether we have

---

[129] This in no way means that we should ignore what we can learn about the ancient contexts in which the Biblical documents were written. Our responsibility to understand God's word accurately (2 Tim 2.15) means that we may not dispense with those things that give accuracy to our understanding.

the luxury of the colors or not. It is that message that ultimately concerns us, and getting at that message is the goal of every student of the Bible.

It would be too simplistic to jump to the conclusion that because the truths of the Bible do not lie in the historical trappings of the text we can therefore simply decontextualize a Biblical text such as Phlm in order to arrive at these timeless truths. In the case of Phlm, the letter itself was originally a situational document, written to address particular people in a particular situation, to answer a specific question or solve a problem that existed among them in their time and in their lives. And the text was communicated using the trappings of its day. We cannot simply erase the names or the references to their culture and suppose that we have therefore found the eternal truth of the text, because the text would still have its situational character, the character of calling upon someone to do something about a particular issue.[130]

Nor am I suggesting that we should boil the Biblical texts down to their most abstract forms. That would only be a more drastic version of what was described in the preceding paragraph, and it would be just as fruitless for several reasons. For one, using the Bible as if it were simply a list of theological propositions is a procedure that leads only to using Biblical statements out of context and in the process perverts and twists the Biblical message. Also, we cannot deny that there is a situational quality to some of the teaching of the New Testament, and that situational quality needs to be respected and preserved. For example, the demands laid down in Romans 14 probably do not come into play in the lives of most Christians on a daily basis. Few of us are called upon to restore an erring brother (Gal 6.1) every day or to withdraw from a member of our local church (2 Thes 3.6) every week. Part of the Biblical teaching is that some actions are required only in certain circumstances. In another sense, every document in the Bible originally had a situational character. For example, each gospel was written for people who needed to know the story of Jesus, and the authors of those gospels, who understood the needs and situations of those original readers, knew which parts of the story of Jesus would benefit them in their situations. The same is even more obvious for the epistles in the New Testament canon. Each was written to address a particular situation (and sometimes that situation was multi-faceted).

---

[130] See the discussion in Millard J. Erickson, *Christian Theology*, 3rd ed. (Grand Rapids: Baker Academic, 2013), 68–89.

Beyond the immediate situation of each Biblical document, however, lies something much larger. Every part of Scripture both partakes of and contributes to a message that is larger and higher than any specific situation or any single Biblical document. There is a big picture, and every Biblical document has something to say in dialogue with it, in both giving and receiving information about it. Since our attention here is on understanding Paul's letter to Philemon, we may concentrate on the New Testament side of the Bible as we consider this phenomenon. When the New Testament authors needed to address a situation in their writings, they did so by drawing on divine truths that transcend those historical situations. Those transcendent truths were taught and applied to correct the misunderstandings or improper behaviors of the immediate situation, but those truths themselves were not, and are not, limited to the historical contexts to which they were brought to bear and address. To put it another way, what we find in the New Testament canon is a set of documents that were originally written to apply timeless truths to the time-bound problems and issues among the earliest Christians. Even though the earliest Christians are gone, and their particular historical circumstances (along with the questions and problems they created) no longer exist, we can still discern the timeless truths that the inspired authors brought to those situations, and we can apply those timeless truths to our world today, with the questions and issues our world raises, using the New Testament documents as our guide for how to do this. It is here, in the intersection of the broader Biblical narrative, the big picture, and an individual text (written in and to a specific situation) that we will find the enduring message of any given Biblical text.

The Biblical Worldview: Apocalyptic Eschatology. Some students of Phlm have remarked that it is thin on theology (but I would disagree). Phlm is not *overtly* heavy with theology like Romans, but there certainly is much theology behind it. Paul's statements and appeal would not make sense without their theological foundations. Even a cursory reading of Phlm shows that there are some heavy theological terms in it: God, Lord, Jesus, Christ, grace, faith, love, fellowship, and saints. It does not, therefore, read like the thousands of personal letters we have recovered from the ancient world that are concerned only with business requests, family news, *etc*. Even if none of these theological terms appear in the central part of the letter (vv 8–20), this does not mean that theology disappears from the text in that section. The terms are piled up in vv 1–7 so that they paint a theological perspective from which Philemon could understand vv 8–20. The "personal" section (vv 8–20) was meant to be understood only in the context of the theology laid down before it.

As noted above, the theology that appears in Phlm is a slice of a much larger perspective upon which Paul drew when he penned this letter. When Paul wrote even a "personal" letter like Phlm, he did not set his perspective on things aside. No one does that. We all speak and act based on how we understand the world at large. That is to say, whenever a person speaks their thoughts, they must necessarily do so from the worldview they hold. A worldview is the set of beliefs, understandings, values, and assumptions that makes up a kind of internal context from which we speak and act personally, and which we use as the basis of our lives. Often this set of beliefs goes largely unexpressed in the daily course of events. We do not normally discuss our worldviews unless they are called into question specifically. Even then, many people do not even know how to discuss or explain their worldview, because worldviews tend to be a part of our sub-surface thinking. Instead, we use our worldview as the foundation for other things.

As the name suggests, our worldview is the collection of intellectual (or, if you will, philosophical) things through which we view, understand, and relate to the world around us. It is the lens, or a kind of filter, through which we look at the world, it is the way we see and understand the world. It is formed over the course of our lives from a variety of sources—parents, friends, associates, teachers, experiences, literature and media, society and culture, the political conditions under which we live, our history, *etc.* For many people, it is a fluid thing, ever changing as we acquire new knowledge, new experiences, or get to know new people in our lives, *etc.* For some it changes little over the years, for others it changes drastically.

Worldviews are one of the things that go into making up not only a person's identity, but a group's identity as well. A group of people may share not only a common ancestry, a common language, and a common land, but they may also share a common worldview, a common outlook on the world and the way it is to be perceived, understood, and negotiated. Often, the shared worldview is closely related to their shared religion.

Whether or not the Bible presents us with a worldview has been debated. Some people find it hard to imagine that authors so separated by time and culture as the Biblical authors often were could have all shared the same worldview. Perhaps the question should be framed in terms of how precisely a worldview has to be defined, and whether there can be variants within the same worldview. Not every member of a group will hold, or formulate, every element of the shared worldview in exactly the same way. Some measure of flexibility and variance is both expected and accepted. People may have minor differences between them in some of the details but may still share the same general worldview. In this way, worldviews can still unite the people who share them and create a way of defining who they are even if those people do not completely agree on every specific detail or nuance of their worldview. The Jews of New Testament times would be an example of this.

I believe that the Bible (that is, the canonical collection of what we commonly call the Old and New Testaments) provides us with a worldview, and I also believe that the various Biblical authors explored, or dealt with, various facets of it. Or, to say it differently, *the faith presented in the Bible is itself a worldview*. Different Biblical authors emphasize different aspects and components of it, but I would argue that they all shared the same basic faith (some of them more informed than others, obviously). This faith, this worldview, is the shared possession of Christians. It is, it could be argued, one of the primary things that makes us who we are, that affects how we live and speak, how we plan and decide.

Is it possible to be more precise about the worldview of the biblical authors? Was there more to it than a shared faith in God? When we examine what history has left us from the first century AD, we find that there were different worldviews in circulation. There were Eclectic Middle Platonism, Epicureanism, and Stoicism, just to name a few of the more prevalent ones. Even among the Jews themselves there were different ways of viewing different aspects of the world. Most Bible students are familiar with the fact that there were some significant differences between the beliefs of the Pharisees and the Sadducees. While they all believed they were serving the same God, and they agreed about basic things such as the necessity of circumcision for adult males, Sabbath observance, following the kosher food laws, and the centrality of the Jerusalem temple to their relationship with God, they differed greatly on how they understood things like God's operation in the world, the progress and goal of history under God's control, and the role of man in this world. The Pharisees, for example, held to a worldview that included the providence of God, but the Sadducees did not. Which of the worldviews in circulation among the ancients, and especially among the Jews, did the Biblical authors adopt—if any of them?

One of the ways some Jews in Biblical times viewed the world has come to be called *apocalyptic eschatology*.[131] I believe that a good case can be made that this perspective was a significant and critical part of the default worldview of all the Biblical authors and that it is presented not only as an important piece of their worldview, but also as something that should be a major part of how we see the world as well. I do not believe that apocalyptic eschatology, all by itself, necessarily serves as a comprehensive worldview in the sense that it alone can account for all the Bible says about God and the world. But I do believe that whatever is included in the Biblical worldview, apocalyptic eschatology is definitely part of it.

In recent years, scholars have increasingly come to recognize that the apostle Paul thought according to a paradigm of apocalyptic eschatology.[132] Statements reflecting this worldview can be found throughout his letters. There has been debate over Paul's source(s) for this way of thinking, but the details of that debate do not concern us here. It is enough to acknowledge that Paul thought in terms of an apocalyptic eschatological view of the past, the present, and the future. Of course, Paul's version of this perspective on the world was highly modified

---

[131] On the origins of the way of viewing the world, see Paul D. Hanson, *The Dawn of Apocalyptic*, rev. ed. (Philadelphia: Fortress, 1979).

[132] Most modern Pauline scholars agree that however we understand Paul's writings, apocalyptic eschatology must be a part of it, although there are the expected debates over categories, essential features, *etc.* A good "lay of the land" description of the present state of thought is Ben C. Blackwell, John K. Goodrich, and Jason Maston, "Paul and the Apocalyptic Imagination: An Introduction," in *Paul and the Apocalyptic Imagination*, ed. Ben C. Blackwell, John K. Goodrich, and Jason Maston (Minneapolis: Fortress, 2016), 3–21. On apocalypticism and Pauls' theology, see J. Christian Beker, *Paul the Apostle: The Triumph of God in Life and Thought* (Philadelphia: Fortress, 1980); *idem., Paul's Apocalyptic Gospel: The Coming Triumph of God* (Philadelphia: Fortress, 1982); Jamie Davies, *The Apocalyptic Paul: Retrospect and Prospect* (Eugene, OR: Cascade Books, 2022); Martinus C. de Boer, *Paul, Theologian of God's Apocalypse: Essays on Paul and Apocalyptic* (Eugene, OR: Cascade Books, 2020). On apocalypticism in the New Testament and the early church generally, see Wayne G. Rollins, "The New Testament and Apocalyptic," *NTS* 17 (1971): 454–76; George Eldon Ladd, "Apocalyptic and New Testament Theology," in *Reconciliation and Hope: New Testament Essays on Atonement and Eschatology*, ed. Robert Banks (Grand Rapids: Eerdmans, 1974), 285–96; and the articles in *Journal for Theology and the Church*, vol. 6 (1969).

compared to some versions of it that we know from his time, due to his experience with the resurrected Jesus. His Damascus Road experience (which had several apocalyptic qualities itself) of seeing the risen and exalted Jesus changed Paul's thinking permanently. After that experience, Paul never saw things the same way again. Therefore Paul's apocalyptic eschatology was Christ-centered (to the extreme).

Before we say one more word about this, it is important to distinguish apocalyptic theology from apocalyptic literature (or the apocalyptic genre). The latter is attested in the Bible most notably in John's Revelation, and also in the books of Ezekiel, Daniel, and a few other places. That kind of literature is recognized by its high symbolism, its portrayal of the fall of kingdoms, the presence of angels as agents of God's destructive wrath, visions or tours of the heavenly realm, *etc.* Paul did not write in the apocalyptic genre. But Paul *thought* that way. That is, Paul thought in terms of cosmic forces at war with each other, of an ultimate triumph of God over them all, and a time of restoration, renewal, or re-creation—all important elements of what we today call apocalyptic theology. Paul thought in terms of the kinds of story that we see in Daniel, Ezekiel, and Revelation, and his letters are saturated with it, even if he does not express it the way those prophetic books did.

The Elements of Apocalyptic Eschatology. So what is apocalyptic eschatology? We will begin with the concept of "apocalyptic." The word itself means an uncovering, a revealing. Something that is apocalyptic has the quality of being disclosed, being exposed so that we can now see it. In particular, what is exposed or revealed in an apocalyptic event is the working of God and the new situation that his work creates. The association of "apocalyptic" with "event" is important. Events, actions of God in history, become the vehicles by which God reveals what he is doing and what his will is. Of course, events by God are usually accompanied by words from God. God does not simply act and not speak. But God's revelation is much more than his words. God is revealed in his deeds, and his words explain the proper significance of those deeds.

An apocalyptic event is one in which God intervenes with his great power into a situation which has become wicked, corrupt, and hostile to him, in order to destroy what opposes him and to re-establish righteousness. When such an event comes, the intervention by God is (relatively) sudden[133] (even though God had warned of its coming; *i.e.*, "sudden" does not mean "unannounced"), radical, drastic, catastrophic, and violent. An apocalyptic event is an event of judgment. It is also destructive and (re-)creative at the same time. The apocalyptic action of God destroys evil and its consequences and establishes a new order (or, restores the original order) of righteousness. Apocalyptic events are about God's power, they are about conquest, they are about God's victory over forces that oppose him and that have been set up to ruin his creation.

Apocalyptic events are therefore, in a sense, acts of warfare. Think of it this way: imagine there is a king and his kingdom, but an enemy recruits an army, invades this kingdom, takes the king's people as prisoners and enslaves them to himself, and sets himself up as the new king. In his power and in his anger against his enemy, and in his love for his own people, the king goes to war against the invader. He destroys the rival king and his army, and he sets the prisoners free so they may again be his own subjects. Such is the picture behind God's apocalyptic actions. That is, apocalyptic actions are those in which God fights back and destroys a rival kingdom that has sprung up to challenge and oppose his reign over his people (either universally or locally), and wherein God reestablishes his reign, or kingdom, over the people he has created for himself.

The easiest way to understand an apocalyptic event is to think of what is probably the most well known example for most readers of the Bible: the flood of Noah's time. Since the time of Adam's sin, the world became increasingly corrupt and sinful. It eventually reached the point where "every thought of man's heart was only evil continually" (Gen 6.5). Or, to put it another way, the world had become the kingdom of Satan (recall Gen 3.1ff and 6.1–3). This was completely contrary to God's purpose for the world. Then, suddenly, God intervened. He "pushed the reset button," as it were. Although God warned man about it in plenty of time, the flood itself came suddenly when the appointed time arrived. In just a few days the world was de-created, as it were. Whereas God had

---

[133] If we do not get caught up too much into modern notions of time, we can understand the conquest of Canaan to be an apocalyptic event, although it took about seven years. Previously, the peoples of that place had lived there for hundreds of years. By comparison, a seven-year period is "sudden," and the conquest certainly would have seemed sudden to the ancients who lived through it. One day they were living in their land, and before their children had even grown up the Israelites had conquered it.

separated the waters above from the waters below as part of his creative work, now they came together again. Whereas God had separated the water from the land as part of his creative activity, now in the flood they were brought together again. The world returned, in a sense, to the jumbled mess it had been before God ordered it during the creation week, formless and void, with water and land and sky mixed together. It is clear from how the story is told that God was bringing the world back to its primeval condition, where water covered everything.[134] Also, the world was washed clean. The evil humanity was destroyed, the rival kingdom was eliminated (at least for a while). After it was over, all that was left was righteous Noah, who stood as a new Adam,[135] a man from whom the world would be (re)populated. After the flood the waters returned to their place, and the dry land appeared again. A cleansed, new, or restored, world was revealed, again under the reign of God.

The flood was not the only apocalyptic event in Biblical history. Think about the destruction of Sodom, the exodus from Egypt (especially the plagues), the death of king Saul, the conquest of Canaan, the destruction of Samaria and especially the destruction of Jerusalem (more than once), just to list a few examples. Although these events were not as universal in their scope as the flood of Noah's time, all of them share an apocalyptic quality. In every one of these instances the situation had become corrupt, defiled, and hostile to God. Evil (evil people, and especially evil kings, encouraged by evil spiritual forces) had overtaken what God had originally established as good. The situation was not what God wanted it to be. In fact, the situation was the opposite of what God had originally made. Into these situations God came with his great power (having warned them first), he judged and destroyed the evil people and forces that had perverted the situation, and he restored the situation to that of his original design. Even the creation of the world can be understood as an apocalyptic event: God, in only six short days, conquered the disarray and chaos of the original world that was "formless and void," using his power to bring order that was "good."

---

[134] Gordon J. Wenham, *Genesis 1–15, Vol. 1*, WBC 1 (Dallas: Word, 1998), 206–07. *Cf.* also the discussion in G. K. Beale, *A New Testament Biblical Theology: The Unfolding of the Old Testament in the New* (Grand Rapids: Baker Academic, 2011), 58–63.

[135] For example, note the similarity in the command given to Adam (Gen 1.28) and the command given to Noah (Gen 9.1). Paul J. Kissling, *Genesis*, College Press NIV Commentary (Joplin: College Press, 2004–), 32, 321–22.

We may define an apocalyptic event, then, tentatively as: An event of intervention by God ("from above") into a situation ("below") that has become corrupt. The intervention is warned and announced beforehand, but those warnings are typically ignored or reinterpreted so that when the time comes, God's intervention has an unexpected quality to it. When it comes, it is "sudden" and "quick," violent and catastrophic, resulting in the destruction of what was corrupt and defiled and the creation of a new beginning of things, just as God said he would do. Or we may define it in more practical terms as an event in which God displays (reveals) his great power, which results in change and even reversal, and a change (for the better) in the human situation. The change that results is also accompanied by new revelation, so that the new situation can be understood more fully. In fact, the new revelation is part of the newness of the event. The new revelation corrects misunderstandings of God's promises and shows how the new "event" by God is indeed the fulfillment of what he promised. The apocalyptic way of doing things also involves "dualistic" elements, things that are in opposition to each other, and this way of looking at God's actions further posits an ultimate resolution, restitution, and restoration by God. That is, the apocalyptic mentality tends to see that there is a struggle for control of the world by two great, opposing forces, and in the end God wins.

It is important to see that apocalyptic events follow a recognizable pattern. This is part of God's way of revealing things in general. As Christians we have learned (from the New Testament itself) to read the Old Testament as the groundwork for understanding what was to come later. Solomon was not just a king, but an example of another coming king. Moses was not just God's appointed leader, but was a special kind of prophet to God's people who himself was the model for another who was to come. We can multiply examples easily. Things that were previously done by God established patterns by which he would act again. We call this typology. The typological nature of prior Biblical events includes the several apocalyptic events in the Bible as well. All events that we can identify as "apocalyptic" in the past record of Biblical history were themselves types or examples of a much greater apocalyptic event, or as the Bible writers might prefer to think of it, *the* apocalyptic event, that was coming.

Apocalyptic Eschatology and the New Testament. The greatest apocalyptic event of all was the coming of Jesus into the world. This event "fulfills" all the others; all previous apocalyptic events foreshadowed this one. The world had become, once again, corrupt and hostile to God. It had become the domain of the enemy, a place of sin and death. Or, as John reminds us, it had become a place of darkness, just as "in the beginning" (John 1.1). Then, suddenly, God changed it by an exertion of his power. Just as God dispersed (or conquered) the darkness when he said "Let there be light" (Gen 1.3), so again, in an even greater way, God sent his Light, his Son, into the world that had become dark with sin and death, to overcome it (John 1.9; 2 Cor 4.6). During the course of his earthly ministry Jesus introduced the kingdom of God to men. He came to re-conquer the world and to release those who had been taken captive by Satan (*cf.* Luke 13.16). His miracles of casting out demons were a particularly clear sign of his mission to drive the enemy out and to reclaim this world as God's domain. Also, through his teachings Jesus taught a new way of living (often presented in contrast to the Pharisaism of his time, as in the Sermon on the Mount, Matthew 5–7). In short, he came to liberate us from Satan's grip, to show us the way back to God, to remake us for the kingdom, and to restore us to our rightful selves and our proper relationship with God. All that Jesus said and did was with the purpose of changing the human situation, of destroying the enemy's hold on mankind (whom God had created for himself), and of setting us right with God again.

While the entire earthly ministry of Jesus could be rightly called an apocalyptic event, there is a particular double-event in his life that is especially so: his death and resurrection. With that particular event God destroyed the power of sin (by Jesus' death) and of death (by Jesus' resurrection from the dead), which were the powers by which Satan kept us enslaved to himself (*cf.* 2 Tim 2.26). That double-event was the final and climactic piece of his work on earth. From that moment onwards the world is not a place where people are held in the prison of sin and death with no hope of escape. From that moment onwards the world is a place where people can come out of sin and can come out of death. A "new world" has now opened up,[136] a new situation has been created and revealed because of the appearing and work of Jesus, and specifically because of his death and resurrection.

We can hear this scenario being described in Romans 5.12–21:

[136] *Cf.* the new heavens and earth predicted in Isa 65.17 and 66.22.

> Therefore, just as through one man sin entered into the world, and death through sin, and so death spread to all men, because all sinned— for until the Law sin was in the world, but sin is not imputed when there is no law. Nevertheless death reigned from Adam until Moses, even over those who had not sinned in the likeness of the offense of Adam, who is a type of Him who was to come. But the free gift is not like the transgression. For if by the transgression of the one the many died, much more did the grace of God and the gift by the grace of the one Man, Jesus Christ, abound to the many. The gift is not like that which came through the one who sinned; for on the one hand the judgment arose from one transgression resulting in condemnation, but on the other hand the free gift arose from many transgressions resulting in justification. For if by the transgression of the one, death reigned through the one, much more those who receive the abundance of grace and of the gift of righteousness will reign in life through the One, Jesus Christ. So then as through one transgression there resulted condemnation to all men, even so through one act of righteousness there resulted justification of life to all men. For as through the one man's disobedience the many were made sinners, even so through the obedience of the One the many will be made righteous. The Law came in so that the transgression would increase; but where sin increased, grace abounded all the more, so that, as sin reigned in death, even so grace would reign through righteousness to eternal life through Jesus Christ our Lord. (NASB)

God's work in Jesus is here described as God's making of a new world with a new Adam. This new world is not characterized by sin and death (like the old world was), but by righteousness and life. Through Jesus God has performed the ultimate apocalyptic event.

Woven into this apocalyptic way of thinking about things is another element, the eschatological. The Greek word *eschatos* means "last," but not merely in the sense of the end of a chronological sequence (although that idea is present). It can also mean last in the sense of consummation, of reaching a goal; it is an end in the sense of something being finished (perfected, in the Biblical sense) and having arrived at the situation that was planned.[137] The end is the accomplishment of a plan, the fulfillment of a goal or promise, the finishing of a process to bring something to a

---

[137] Franco Montanari, *The Brill Dictionary of Ancient Greek* (Leiden: Brill, 2015), 831.

desired state or condition (so it what is "last" is therefore not followed by anything else of its kind). A thing is "last," therefore, when it belongs to this finished, completed state of things.

It can be argued that all the Bible shares in an eschatological view of history.[138] All of history is headed toward a goal, all of it is moving to an end in which things will be restored (this is the apocalyptic element) as God had originally planned them to be. By his providence God is working his plan, a plan that will one day be finished.[139] When we understand that God is working to restore all things to their original good condition, this naturally leads us to see that all that God is doing therefore has an end, or goal, to it. Restoration naturally includes a goal. Or, to say it differently, apocalyptic activity naturally implies eschatology.

God's Apocalyptic Power and Transformation. The ultimate goal of God's apocalyptic action in Jesus is the reclaiming and reconciliation of his people who had become estranged from him. He has been working this plan from the moment that Adam sinned. In fact, the plan was in place even before that, because God knew it would be needed (Eph 1.4, "before the foundation of the world"). God's goal is to bring his people to himself (*cf.* Heb 2.10, "bringing many sons to glory"), and everything God has done has been with this purpose in view. God's people being with God is the "end," the goal to which God is working. The plan came to an apocalyptic expression when Jesus came to this earth.

The problem that God's apocalyptic activity is especially designed to solve is the problem of sin, and its corresponding problem of death.[140] Fixing the effects of sin is the goal, or end, of God's work. All humanity (and part of the population of the heavenly realm) had joined the side of the enemy. We all (from Adam onwards) have rebelled and sinned against God, rejecting his reign over us and making ourselves his enemies (Rom 5.8, 10), making ourselves allies of the enemy, Satan. This does not mean that no one wants to be with God. It means instead that all of us

---

[138] It begins in the first story of the Bible, the creation. God worked for six days and then rested on the seventh day, by which God made the seventh day a day of rest for man. From the very beginning God built into the fabric of the world the idea of looking forward to the end (of the week), of looking forward to the time of rest.

[139] On the importance of providence in the apocalyptic worldview, see N. T. Wright, "Apocalyptic and the Sudden Fulfillment of Divine Promise," in *Paul and the Apocalyptic Imagination*, ed. Ben C. Blackwell, John K. Goodrich, and Jason Maston (Minneapolis: Fortress, 2016), 111–34, esp. 116.

[140] Paul refers to death as "the last enemy" in 1 Cor 15.26.

have failed to maintain our dedication to that end. We have sinned, we have rebelled, and we have defiled ourselves with spiritual and moral uncleanness, we have joined the side of the enemy. But God will not have a sinful, rebellious people for himself. He is a holy God, and those who would be his must be holy as well (2 Cor 7.1; *cf.* 1 Pet 1.15–16). The problem is worse than this, however. We are powerless to free ourselves from the predicament into which our sin brought us. We cannot forgive ourselves, we cannot free ourselves from our captivity and enslavement to Satan. Even if we paid for our sin with our own lives, the result would be a people who were "legally" right with God but dead. But our sin consumes our lives anyway. As punishment for our sin our bodies are subject to death (Gen 3.14). Because of our sin we will one day die and, as our bodies decay, they will "disappear" back into the dust from which they were made. The Biblical picture is that our sin produced a complete estrangement from God. Whereas we were once righteous and alive in the presence of God, our sin has made us guilty and dead (spiritually and physically) and, in the end, a small pile of lifeless dust, de-created as it were. We have become, in a sense, the very opposite of what God originally made us to be.

Therefore, in order for those who want to be with God to actually come into God's possession as his people, they must be changed, they must be *transformed*. They must be changed from enemies into friends, they must be changed from dead to alive, from sinners into saints. We lack in ourselves anything that could come even close to achieving this change. No, it requires a drastic intervention of God's power to change the dead back into the living, to change the guilty into those who are justified. That is to say, it requires an apocalyptic event. It is only by an exertion of God's power in a radical, situation-changing way that we can be changed, or transformed, back into what we are supposed to be. Thus the accomplishment of God's desired end or goal (the eschatological part of the picture) is accomplished by a drastic, overwhelming exertion of God's power (the apocalyptic part of the picture) that transforms things into the state and condition that God wants for them.

The problem of sin and death corresponds precisely with what we are as human beings, as people. We, as human beings, are dual creatures, as it were. We are spirit and body joined together. Sin has affected the totality of our being. It has caused us to be dead spiritually (Eph 2.1), and it also causes the death of our bodies. The end result of sin is that it makes us completely dead. It is because we are dual creatures, made of spirit plus body, that it took a dual event to fix our problem. The death of Jesus provides the forgiveness of our sins so that we may be alive again spiritually, and the resurrection of Jesus opened up the door of escape from the death of our bodies. By his death and resurrection, therefore, Jesus fixed our dual problem of sin and death (respectively).

The apocalyptic reversal of our individual, personal condition does not happen all at once. Just as God took six days to create the original world, so he does not re-create the world, nor does he remake us, in an instant. It is not that God lacks the power to do so, but it is probably because we would not understand it if God did not "slow down" the event and turn it into a process that developed at a pace by which we could see how God is doing things and how he works. It is for our sakes, that we might see and appreciate what God is doing, that our transformation and re-creation does not happen instantly. Just as Moses recorded that "by the seventh day God completed His work which He had done" (Gen 2.2), so Paul said that "He who began a good work in you will perfect (complete) it until the day of Christ Jesus" (Phil 1.6). The rejuvenation of our spirits is a down payment of a more complete transformation still to come (2 Cor 1.22; 5.5; Eph 1.14). The resurrection of Jesus to eternal life and glory is the first fruits of a greater, coming harvest (1 Cor 15.20–23). Transformation is a process, a process that has now begun with the work of Jesus, but will reach its "finishing" at the last day.

Our estrangement from God was a two-part event, corresponding to the two parts of which we are made. Man is spirit and body. As a sinner, man is dead spiritually, and his body dies as a result. Likewise, our restoration to God, our re-creation, is a process in two parts. We must be made alive again in both spirit and in body, and the process happens in this order. We are made alive again on the inside first, with the rejuvenation of the outward part of us (our bodies) coming afterwards.

The rejuvenation of our spirits begins when we hear and obey the gospel of Jesus Christ. This was the appeal of Peter on Pentecost as well as the appeal not only of the apostolic preaching, but also of the New Testament as a whole. The word of God is a form, or perhaps better to say *the* form *par excellence,* of God's apocalyptic power, his life-changing, life-making, restorative power (recall Rom 1.16). God can destroy evil and establish a new order of righteousness with his word (*cf.* Isa 55; Ezek 37). We become alive again spiritually when we join ourselves to Christ through the gospel (Rom 6.11; 8.10; Eph 2.5). Or, to put it in the language of the apostle Paul, when we join ourselves to Christ through the gospel, we receive his Spirit, the Spirit that makes life, we become one spirit with him (1 Cor 6.17). As we take Jesus into ourselves, as he comes to live in us and we live in him, we take on his Spirit that makes us alive unto God.[141] God's word about Jesus creates within us a new heart and spirit and mind. Through God's holy truth (*i.e.,* his word) we are made again in the image of God (Eph 4.24). If we will hear the voice of God's Son, we come alive again in spirit (John 5.25).

However, the complete renewal or rejuvenation of ourselves is not yet finished, and this is where eschatology comes into the picture. Our re-creation will be finished on the day when God raises, and transforms, our bodies, so that we have new bodies to go with our new spirits. We can hear the eschatological element clearly in Philippians 3.21, where Paul speaks of "the Lord Jesus Christ who will transform the body of our humble state into conformity with the body of his glory, by the exertion of the power that he has even to subject all things to himself." We also detect it when Jesus says that those who are in the tombs will, one day, hear the call of the Lord and will rise (John 5.28). The sudden nature of this grandest of all apocalyptic events comes through clearly as Paul says our transformation will happen "in a moment" (1 Cor 15.52).

Apocalyptic Eschatology and New Testament Ethics. When we combine the apocalyptic and the eschatological, we have arrived at a key part of the perspective of the Biblical authors.[142] For them, God

---

[141] For a discussion of how our taking on this Spirit happens, see the author's essay "Paul's View of the Holy Spirit," in *From the Pen of Paul,* 2nd ed., ed. Nathan Ward (Temple Terrace: Florida College Press, 2022), 88–120.

[142] We should avoid the idea that some Jews, or some Biblical authors, were apocalyptists and others were not. Apocalypticism (which is a term of our invention) is not a separable "school of thought" among the Biblical writers, but is a pervasive perspective. This explains why individual features of apocalypticism regularly appear in basically all the Biblical texts, although only a few of those texts are specifically written in the apocalyptic genre. As Koch put it, "Generally speaking, apocalyptic is understood to mean a complex of writings and ideas which were widespread about the turn of the era in Palestine, in the Israelite diaspora and in early Christian circles; but which can also appear in similar form in other religious situations and mental climates" (Klaus Koch, *The Rediscovery of Apocalyptic,* trans. Margaret Kohl, Studies in Biblical Theology, Second Series, 22 (SCM, 1972), 13). See his list of eight characteristics of apocalyptic on pp. 28–33.

has intervened into the world of sin and death in the person of Jesus in order to conquer it and set it right. The death of Christ provides for our forgiveness, and His resurrection has begun the abolition of death so that God can accomplish his desired goal of bringing us to himself. Through the gospel God is inviting us to step out of the old world and into the new one. He is inviting us to leave the present world behind, with its sin and death, and to enter into the new world of righteousness and life in Christ. This is what basically accounts for the ethical instruction of the New Testament. Apocalyptic eschatology brings with it a moral demand. It is highly ethical. People must turn from the old way that is being destroyed, and willfully and deliberately step into the new situation that God brings. To stay in the old world of sin and death is to chose destruction.[143]

The ethical demands placed upon Christians in the New Testament are various ways of describing the turn from sin to righteousness, from death to life, from the worldly plane to the heavenly plane. God is calling us to become transformed in every way—in our minds (Rom 12.2), in our spirits, in our behaviors, in our thoughts, in our speech, *etc.* We are to become new people, born again into a new world, rising above and out of the old world and into the heavenly places in Christ. In other words, all of the moral teaching of the New Testament is grounded in, and is an expression of, the apocalyptic eschatology that controls the larger situation. The apocalyptic theology becomes morality. A theology of change brings with it an ethics of change. Or, as others have put, it, the indicative (the apocalyptic eschatological reality) becomes imperative (a way of life that must reflect this reality).[144]

It is precisely here, at the moral dimension of our transformation, that we must notice two other important elements in this whole process. The first is love. If we think again about what an apocalyptic event is, and if we think of the dimensions of the fall of man, it leads us to understand the role of love in God's plan for us. The world became the domain of Satan, a kingdom of sinners, because all people have followed in the footsteps of Adam (as we noted above, Rom 5.12ff). Adam acted in his

[143] The preceding paragraphs are meant to serve as a sketch of the basic ideas of "apocalyptic." Scholars debate the finer points and nuances of the picture, and there is debate over what the "core" idea of apocalypticism is, specifically whether it represents a continuity with Judaism or a break.

[144] For two examples of this approach, see Beale, *A New Testament Biblical Theology*, 835ff; and Victor Paul Furnish, *Theology and Ethics in Paul*, New Testament Library (Louisville: Westminster John Knox, 2009), 224ff.

own selfish interests. Adam decided that he did not want God to be his king, but that he wanted to be his own king. He decided to listen to himself rather than to God. All sin has this basic character. Sin is not simply disobedience, it is disobedience in rejection of God's reign over us. Until Jesus came, the world was a place where selfishness, selfish ambition, pride, arrogance, and rebellion ruled the thoughts and lives of everyone. Or, to use Pauline phraseology, all lived in the lusts of the flesh, doing the desires of the flesh, living "in the flesh," that is, in the mode of the flesh, dominated by the desires of the flesh (which are self-centered). The results of such a way of life are necessarily the various indulgences of the flesh, or obedience to the flesh, such as adultery, coveting, *etc.*, but also hatred of others, jealousy, deception (to get one's own way over others) and lying, and even murder. In a world dominated by hatred born of selfishness, the appearance of love is an apocalyptic event. Jesus' conquest over the world's situation was not just a conquest over sin and death, it was not just a conquest over Satan. By conquering Satan and the kingdom based on the lust of the flesh, Jesus made it possible for us to learn a new way—the right way—of living, the way of living in selfless love. He made it possible for us to enter into a life characterized by truth, integrity, honesty, kindness, patience, and forgiveness. Living according to love is part of the apocalyptic reversal Jesus has accomplished.

What does it mean to become a new person? What does it mean to have a transformed mind, or spirit, or character? What does such a thing actually look like? The answer is that it looks like the love of God in Christ. Immediately after Paul exhorted the Roman Christians to be transformed by the renewing of their minds in Romans 12.2, he launched into a discussion of Christian love that extended to chapter 15. The old self who was characterized by sin and death was a self of fleshly passion, envy, jealousy, strife, dissension, faction—a self characterized by various forms of hatred. But the more we grow into likeness to Christ, the more we become people of love: "…that Christ may dwell in your hearts through faith, and that you, being rooted and grounded in love …" (Eph 3.17). Love is the goal (the "end") of instruction in the gospel (1 Tim 1.5). Spiritual transformation looks like love. In short, the spiritually transformed person becomes a person who embodies the love of Jesus Christ in himself, not just as a recipient of that love, but as one who is filled with it and in turn dispenses that same kind of love to others, one who, like Christ, speaks and acts out of love always. "We know that we have passed out of death into life [*i.e.*, that we are being transformed], because we love the brethren" (1 John 3.14).

This brings us to the second element, the church.[145] It is only natural, when one thinks about it, that those who are being transformed to become unlike the world should be considered as a group. Accordingly, the identity of this group is not defined by anything worldly, because it is by definition a group that is coming out of the world. Therefore the world's categories will not suffice to describe or define it. The church is the group of people that have been called out of the darkness of the world and into God's marvelous light (*cf.* 1 Peter 2.9), out of the realm of death and into the world of life in Christ. That is, the church is, to use the Greek term, a *koinōnia*, a fellowship, a collection of people who have something in common, namely that they have appropriated the grace of God by faith in Christ, and by that grace they are being transformed more and more into the image of Jesus (Col 3.10; Rom 8.29; Eph 4.15) that truly defines sonship to God. Through the Son, people come into a familial relationship with God the Father and thus become brethren to each other. While Christians exercise love toward all people, it is especially (and only) in the church that the love that marks transformation and newness can be endlessly reciprocated (*cf.* Gal 6.10). The church thus becomes the showcase not only for God's love, but also for what the new humanity looks like: a humanity characterized first by Christ-like love. Above all, then, the church *must* be the place where divine love is reflected among its members as brotherly love. "By this all men will know that you are my disciples, if you have love for one another" (John 13.25). Furthermore, it is by this love that Christians (the church) encourage each other. "Love edifies" (1 Cor 8.1). The church builds itself up in love (Eph 4.16).

To exist in this group—that is, to be a Christian in a loving fellowship with other Christians—means that we take our newness, or transformation, seriously. All other identities or self-definitions are secondary to this one. As we noted above, this does not mean that we lose all other identities, that they are somehow erased. The church exists in the world. Christians, for all of their otherworldly character, are still fathers, wives, masters, *etc.*

---

[145] As Rollins notes ("New Testament and Apocalyptic," 463), the ethics that come with an apocalyptic-eschatological worldview necessarily create a group of people who share that outlook and its values. With an apocalyptic worldview comes also a peculiar lifestyle and the formation of a community.

in this world, but they are expected to transform those roles into vehicles for proclaiming their newness and for serving God. Those earthly roles do not constitute our primary identity. As Christians, we are first and foremost now the children of God. This means not only relating to God truly as our Father, but also relating to each other truly as brethren. In short, it means that we accept one another as brethren first, and all other (worldly) roles become subservient to that. To put that negatively, it means that we do not allow worldly distinctions, which are coupled with equally worldly judgments of value, to determine the relationship we have with each other as Christians.[146]

God's intervention to conquer the world of sin and death has begun, but it has not ended. The transformation of ourselves on the inside by becoming people of love must be completed by the transformation of our bodies. One day, God will transform our bodies, at the resurrection, so that we will be new in every way, inside and out, in spirit and in body. Then we will be fully fit to be God's possession, then God will bring his people to glory. Once we see this big picture, we understand that we are now living in an in-between time, we are living in the middle of the final or "master" apocalyptic event. It is half over, as it were. The first part has happened (with the resurrection of our spirits by the gospel, by virtue of our relationship with Christ), and soon the second part will happen (with the resurrection of our bodies at "the last day," again by the power of God in Christ). We now live in between the accomplishment of these two parts of the final apocalyptic event.[147] Just as Adam existed for a brief while and "then the Lord God took the man and put him into the garden of Eden" (Gen 2.15), so we too are living for a short while here until God will put us into the eternal home he has prepared for his people. "We ourselves, having the first fruits of the Spirit, even we ourselves groan within ourselves, waiting eagerly for our adoption as sons, the redemption of our body" (Rom 8.23 NASB). The goal of the lives we are now living is to become transformed on the inside to conform to the image of Jesus Christ himself. We are to take on his Spirit, his mind, and let him live in us as we live in him. Like Israel in the wilderness, our time on earth is meant

[146] *Cf.* James 2.1ff, where James urges his readers (hearers) not to allow their treatment of each other to be determined by outward and worldly markers such as wealth, but to treat each other as brethren, in love.

[147] See Stanley E. Porter, *The Apostle Paul: His Life, Thought, and Letters* (Grand Rapids: Eerdmans, 2016), 125–26.

to be a time of testing for the purpose of refinement and purification. We are to use our lives and the circumstances God delivers to us to become the people God wants us to be, in anticipation of the day when God will finish his work of re-creating us by giving us new, transformed bodies and bringing us to live with him as people who properly belong in the new heavens and new earth.

Once we know what to listen for, we can hear several of the dimensions of the Biblical apocalyptic eschatology in passages such as Romans 13.11–14: "Do this, knowing the time, that it is already the hour for you to awaken from sleep; for now salvation is nearer to us than when we believed. The night is almost gone, and the day is near. Therefore let us lay aside the deeds of darkness and put on the armor of light. Let us behave properly as in the day, not in carousing and drunkenness, not in sexual promiscuity and sensuality, not in strife and jealousy. But put on the Lord Jesus Christ, and make no provision for the flesh in regard to its lusts" (NASB). Change, transformation, an event of God's doing—they are all reflected not only in this passage, but throughout the Bible (in various ways, of course).[148]

I would further suggest that this change-oriented apocalyptic view of the world and of the Christian life is part of what is packed into Paul's favorite phrase, "in Christ." It would be hard to argue that this phrase is itself an apocalyptic term. Paul did not find it in Old Testament (or other Jewish) apocalyptic texts. The phrase encompasses all kinds of blessings and realities that are part of the results of the work and reign of Jesus. It denotes closeness, union, commitment, fellowship, and many other things. But I would suggest that a part of its significance is also that it summarizes the crucial apocalyptic event of the death and resurrection of Jesus, and all that comes from it. "In Christ" is the sphere, the mode, of the new situation that has come about because of the work of Jesus. Since Christ is the agent of the apocalyptic newness, to be in Christ is to participate in that apocalyptic reality. To be in Christ is to be in that new situation, to have stepped out of the old and into the new, to begin to partake of the new and transformed reality brought about by God in Christ. To be in Christ is to be a new creature (2 Cor 5.17), it is to have

[148] For apocalyptic notes in Galatians, for example, see Michael J. Gorman, "The Apocalyptic New Covenant and the Shape of Life in the Spirit according to Galatians," in *Paul and the Apocalyptic Imagination*, ed. Ben C. Blackwell, John K. Goodrich, and Jason Maston (Minneapolis: Fortress, 2016), 317–37.

begun the transformation by God's powerful word that will end in the final transformation of our bodies in glory.

What does all of this have to do with Paul's letter to Philemon? It may seem by this point that we have strayed far from a consideration of Paul's little letter to Philemon, but we have not. The worldview of apocalyptic eschatology with its message of transformation through Christ is, I would argue, the Biblical worldview, and it is certainly the worldview of the apostle Paul. We noted near the beginning of this chapter that whenever a person speaks, they do so from the standpoint of their worldview, and Paul was no different. Paul's letter to Philemon must be understood as sitting squarely within the worldview we have outlined briefly above. That is, the message of Phlm does not lie in whether Onesimus had run away from Philemon or whether he had simply stayed too long away from home (and was now asking for Paul's help to smooth this over). It does not lie simply in the idea that Paul needed, or wanted, someone to help him in his ministry. The message of Phlm does not lie in Paul's rhetorical appeal nor in the status of Paul, Philemon, or Onesimus (although understanding these things helps us to understand more accurately what Paul was saying). *The message of Phlm consists of a particular expression of the apocalyptic eschatological worldview held by Paul and taught to the early Christians.*

As we noted in a previous chapter, Paul's shortest letter does not itself tell us the specifics of Onesimus' situation. Despite thousands of pages of scholarly debate on the subject, the bottom line remains that we do not know exactly what Onesimus had done, or why he had done it. We do not know exactly what the problem was between Philemon and Onesimus, and my point is that it does not matter what it was, because the message of this short letter does not lie there, but it lies in the fact that Paul is asking Philemon to transform his thinking about Onesimus as part of the total Christian call to be transformed completely. The heart of the letter is Paul's appeal to think of Onesimus "no longer as a slave, but more than a slave, as a beloved brother" (v 16). Paul's appeal makes perfect sense in an apocalyptic scenario. Paul understood that we are now living in the time of the great apocalypse, the time of God's drastic intervention into the world in Jesus Christ in order to change it and set us right once again. The apostle's call for Philemon to change his view of Onesimus is simply the application of the apocalyptic transformation in that situation. It is the apocalyptic change put into practice in its proper context, the church, the fellowship of love. In other words, Paul is asking Philemon to allow the apocalyptic change brought about by Jesus to become operative in his relationship with Onesimus. He is asking Philemon to allow the gospel to transform his relationship with his slave into one that properly reflects the renewed reign of God in his life. He is asking Philemon to step more completely out of the old world in which a person's value was determined by their social status, and more completely into the new world in Christ, in which being in Christ is the sole determiner of a person's value.

How would this solve the problem between Philemon and Onesimus? If Philemon could transform his thinking about Onesimus, he would come to see Onesimus in such a way that the problem between them—whatever it was, it does not matter—would be resolved in love. Although our curiosity would like to know what "the right thing" (v 8) actually turned out to be (giving Onesimus his freedom? forgiving his wrong?), my contention is that such details would naturally work themselves out in the application of brotherly, Christian love coming from a transformed way of thinking about Onesimus. Once such new thinking was in control of the situation between Philemon and Onesimus, and once love became the spiritual power injected into the situation, a satisfactory resolution would be relatively easy to find.

This, I suggest, explains why the letter reads as it does, lacking a specific action demanded by Paul to be taken on the part of Philemon. It is because one specific, singular action was not necessarily in view or even necessary. Love could find any number of solutions to the problem between Onesimus and Philemon. What was most important was the adoption, on Philemon's part, of a transformed point of view that brought brotherly love to bear on the problem at hand. Philemon needed to become a transformed person, a person whose spirit was characterized by the newness of love. He needed to break free from the world around him with its fleshly, worldly ways of looking at others, and see Onesimus in a completely new way, as a fellow citizen of God's kingdom, as a brother in Christ, as another one of God's new people. It is not as if none of this was already true of Philemon, for it was. But Paul was urging Philemon to grow, or expand, his transformation to now include Onesimus. Once Philemon did that, the situation was practically resolved, and it did not matter to Paul what the particular manifestation of love actually turned out to be, because Paul was not in the business of micromanaging the faith of other people (2 Cor 1.24). What Paul wanted was something greater than any specific action, namely the maturing of a loving mind and heart on Philemon's part. If Philemon could come to that, the problem would, as we say, then solve itself.

Are there any particular indicators that Phlm was written from the point of view of apocalyptic eschatology? I believe there are. First, there are repeated references to Jesus as Lord. While this is not exclusively apocalyptic language, it is not possible to speak of the Lordship of Jesus in a Biblical way and not include his current conquest of sin and death by virtue of the apocalyptic dual event of his death and resurrection. Second, there is the perspective Paul presents in vv 4–7, of a man (Philemon) who has proven that he truly is a person of faith in Christ and whose faith has been demonstrated by acts of love towards the saints. Philemon was one of God's apocalyptically new people, and his love was the proof. Moreover, the terminology of love, which is the characteristic mode of God's apocalyptically new people, permeates the letter as well. Forms of the word "love" appear five times in the letter (vv 1, 5, 7, 9, and 16). But third, the greatest indication comes in the part of the letter that many people suppose lacks theology, the appeal section of vv 8–20. The language of change, which is a chief characteristic of apocalyptic eschatological thinking, occupies that section powerfully. The apocalyptic way of thinking appears in three of the most crucial statements of the letter. In v 11, Paul called on Philemon to change his thinking toward Onesimus because Onesimus himself had changed through the gospel of Jesus Christ. In v 15, Paul pointed out the change in Onesimus' condition that corresponded to a then-vs-now perspective. And in v 16, Paul said that Onesimus was "no longer" what he used to be, but was now different. This emphasis on a changed situation because of the gospel is apocalyptic. This repeated emphasis on the change in Onesimus and the corresponding need for change in Philemon bears the stamps of an apocalyptic perspective, and stands at the heart of the letter.

So how does apocalyptic eschatology relate to the status, slavery, and rhetoric that so thoroughly characterize the letter? These latter things are the "situation" of the text, they are the fabric of the problem Paul was addressing, they are the realities by which the historical context was defined, both in the culture and in the letter. But the solution to the problem lay in applying an apocalyptic, eschatological perspective to them and thereby subjecting them to transformation in Christ. The rhetoric now served to communicate and, if possible, achieve, an apocalyptic decision on Philemon's part to change his view of Onesimus. Likewise, the status of all three men was carefully recast in the letter to reveal the difference between the former relationships of the three men and their present relationships. An apocalyptic event had happened, namely the conversion of Onesimus. Before that event, Paul related to Philemon as a fellow Christian, and Philemon related to Onesimus as a master, but no relationship existed between Paul and Onesimus. Now, everything was different. Onesimus now shared in the brotherhood that once only the two other men had shared, and Onesimus now belonged to both Philemon and Paul in that he was now the brother and the servant of both men. What was formerly two overlapping relationships (with Philemon as the point of overlap) was now a fully triangular relationship. The conversion of Onesimus now powerfully reconfigured the status of each man. The apostle now presented himself as a prisoner, the slave was now a brother, the master who had the highest social position of the three was now the debtor to Paul. And yet none of this erased the fact that Philemon was still a master, Onesimus was still a slave, and Paul was still an apostle. All of these roles or statues took on a completely new character in light of the apocalyptically new identity of Onesimus. The transformation of Onesimus triggered the high to become low and the low to become high for the sake of fellowship. The spiritual realities involved now overpowered the social realities and made them different from what they used to be.

Therefore, even though Paul did not expound upon the apocalyptic Christ-event in this letter, the epistle's subject matter, its appeal, stands on this foundation. Reading the letter from this perspective helps us to understand why the letter says what it does (and what it does not include), and how it works.

COMMENTARY

v 1 Paul, a prisoner of Christ Jesus, and brother Timothy, to Philemon, our beloved and our fellow worker,

The letter follows a standard format for letter-writing in Paul's day, with the name of the letter's author / sender coming first. However, Paul usually expanded upon this by adding descriptions of himself that were appropriate to the occasion of the letter. What is interesting here is that Paul did not describe himself as an apostle. This does not mean that this office, or status within the Christian community, was unimportant to Paul, nor that it was irrelevant to the situation in this letter. He hints at it in vv 8, 14, and 21.[1] In fact, Paul's apostleship can fairly be assumed to be understood by Philemon, who was no stranger to Paul. Instead, the lack of citation of Paul's apostolic credential is related to the strategy of the letter, in which Paul did not wish to demand, command, or coerce his request from Philemon (v 8), especially "up front."

Instead of citing his apostleship. Paul described himself as a **prisoner of Christ Jesus**. This involves something of a play on the idea of "prisoner," because technically Paul was (as we surmise) a prisoner of (*i.e.*, imprisoned by) Roman authority. But his imprisonment was due to his obedience to, and his preaching the gospel of, Christ, and this spiritual reading of his situation is what is expressed here. We should undoubtedly take Paul's reference to being a prisoner literally here and throughout the letter. The appeal made in the letter would lose its force if Paul were not actually in prison, or if his bonds (vv 10, 13) were only figurative.

Imprisonment was, in Paul's day, a shameful thing. The ancient view of self was such that control over one's own being was the mark of an honorable, free person. To have that control taken away and to have one's body put under the power of another, especially involuntarily, was

[1] See Jeffrey A. D. Weima, "Paul's Persuasive Prose: An Epistolary Analysis of the Letter to Philemon," in *Philemon in Perspective: Interpreting a Pauline Letter*, ed. D. Francois Tolmie, BZNW 169 (Berlin: De Gruyter, 2010) 29–60, at 33.

considered shameful.[2] Lowliness is what is communicated here. Yet Paul, in characteristic fashion, found his present condition, although shameful in the eyes of the world,[3] to be a point about which he could boast in Christ. Paul often asserted the same thing that Jesus himself taught, that in the kingdom of God, greatness looks like lowliness (*cf.* Matt 18.1–4; Phil 2.5–8). The approach here is probably similar to 2 Corinthians 11.21–33, where Paul's point was that his sufferings are the proof of the genuineness of his apostleship. So here, Paul's lowly, imprisoned condition was a kind of proof of the apostleship, with its accompanying authority, that lay behind the sending of the letter. Thus in Paul's understanding of things in Christ, his title of "prisoner" actually gave him a (paradoxically) increased status[4] and thus a kind of boldness. For Paul, the designation "prisoner of Christ Jesus" expressed his complete surrender to Christ, as one who had been taken captive to serve an overlord.[5] This self-identification with lowliness begins Paul's strategy in this letter, because he will later ask Philemon to adopt this same attitude of lowliness in a new attitude toward Onesimus. But this is also the first out of five times that Paul's then-present imprisonment is mentioned (vv 1, 9, 10, 13, and 23).[6] The force of the repetition further enhances the example Paul is setting for Philemon, and is meant to persuade Philemon to have such a sacrificial spirit himself in the matter at hand.[7] It may also be meant to underscore Paul's need for Onesimus.[8]

---

[2] See Rapske, *Book of Acts and Paul in Roman Custody*, 283ff. "The first century Mediterranean culture was dominated by honour and shame; it is thus easy to underestimate the stigma attached to incarceration and bonds. Ancient literary sources link prison with dishonour. … Public exposure, irrespective of innocence or guilt, resulted in a shame that could be life-long." (283)

[3] "Whether convicted or not, those who became prisoners no longer possessed their former dignity in the public view and hence merited a negative perception." *Ibid.*, 291.

[4] Wright, *Paul and the Faithfulness of God*, 6.

[5] *Cf.* 2 Cor 2.14, where Paul describes himself as a prisoner in Christ's triumphal procession. The idea of Christ having come and defeated his enemies (including Saul of Tarsus) fits with the apocalyptic worldview I am suggesting as the lens by which to read Phlm.

[6] Other significant repetitions in the letter (which reveal its emphases) are: love (5x), Christ-Jesus-Lord (9x), "heart" (3x), "brother" (5x), partnership (2x), and compound words with the preposition *sun* ("fellow-"; 4x). Roy R. Jeal, *Exploring Philemon: Freedom, Brotherhood, and Partnership in the New Society* (Atlanta: SBL Press, 2015), 60–62.

[7] Wiema, "Paul's Persuasive Prose," 34; David W. Pao, *Colossians and Philemon*. ZECNT (Grand Rapids: Zondervan, 2012), 63.

[8] Wiema, "Paul's Persuasive Prose," 35.

Timothy was with Paul at the time of writing. We know from Hebrews 13.23 that Timothy was imprisoned at some point, but whether he was in prison with Paul when Paul wrote Phlm, we cannot say. Paul did not describe him here as a fellow prisoner. Although Timothy was with Paul, from the letter itself it becomes clear that Timothy was not meant to be understood strictly as a co-author of the letter. The letter's appeal comes from a singular person, Paul (as the singular verbs in vv 4–22 attest).

Why mention Timothy here, and not with the others in v 23? While part of the answer is that Timothy was apparently known to Philemon, the fact that Timothy's name comes here in the letter's opening seems to suggest that something more significant than simple acquaintance is in view. It is not impossible that Paul wished to imply to Philemon that the issue that is the subject of this letter was something that was known to other Christians (Timothy in particular) and that Timothy agreed with Paul's judgment about what needed to be done.[9] In this sense, then, the letter's appeal was shared by Timothy even if the dominant voice of the letter was only Paul's. Therefore, Philemon's handling of the matter was not just a matter between himself and Paul. Philemon needed to act in such a way to show his Christ-likeness to his brethren, to encourage them and set a good example in the process. This will become even more apparent in v 2 (see below). The idea that Philemon was being called upon to act in the sight of other Christians (including, in v 2, the whole church) may account for why Timothy is here called "the **brother**."[10]

This little letter is primarily addressed to "**Philemon**[11] our beloved and our fellow worker." Other than what we can glean from this letter,

[9] Fitzmyer, *Philemon*, 85; Dunn, *Colossians and Philemon*, 311.

[10] The phrase in Greek literally says "the brother," but could mean (according to regular Greek usage) "my brother" or "our brother."

[11] Knox famously proposed that "you" (singular) in v 4 refers to the last-mentioned person on the list, Archippus, thus making him the main recipient of the letter and thus the owner of Onesimus (John Knox, *Philemon Among the Letters of Paul: A New View of Its Place and Importance* (Chicago: University of Chicago Press, 1935)). His view is neatly summarized in Donald Guthrie, *New Testament Introduction*, 4th ed. (Downers Grove: InterVarsity Press, 1996), 661. The majority of scholars have rejected Knox's approach. "You" in v 4 undoubtedly refers to the first person in the list of addressees, Philemon. From an interpretational standpoint, it actually matters little if the letter's main recipient (the repeated singular "you" in the letter) is Philemon or Archippus, because we do not know enough about either man for this to make a difference in our understanding of the letter, and it does not change what Paul is asking the "you" to do. But there is a long tradition of understanding Philemon as the letter's main recipient, and it rests on solid grounds. Guthrie answers Knox's points on pp. 662–63; see also Lohse, *Colossians and Philemon*, 186–

nothing else is known about this Christian man. His name is a form of the Greek word for friendship and means something like "affectionate one."[12] Paul's description of him as "**beloved**"[13] may be a subtle play on the meaning of his name. However, there is surely more to it than this. This is the first of five references to love in the letter (vv 1, 5, 7, 9, and 16). Love, which is the essential mode of relationship of those who live in the new situation brought about by Christ, would be the key to the successful resolution of the problem at hand.[14] Furthermore, Paul was framing his request (which does not come until much later in the letter) as one that came in a context of Christians who love each other in the Lord.

The fact that Paul identified Philemon as a **fellow worker** is significant. We do not know exactly how Philemon shared work in the gospel with Paul, but the details are not important to understanding what is going on here. By describing Philemon as his fellow worker (with Timothy included, "our"), Paul hereby laid another piece of the groundwork upon which the main issue of the letter rested (see also on v 5 below). With this simple phrase, "our fellow worker," Paul established a common goal between Philemon and others who labored in the gospel, with the assumption that this goal remained a high priority to Philemon. The purpose of our fellowship is to encourage and support each other in the Lord, to work toward the well-being of God's people. If Philemon was committed to this (as his past actions would suggest, vv 5 and 7), then

---

87, 191–92. An argument for Knox's view is presented by Lamar Cope, "On Rethinking the Colossians-Philemon Connection," *BR* 30 (1985): 45–50. He points out that Philemon's name never appears again, but Archippus is named in Col 4.17, where he is told to "fulfill his ministry," which he takes to be the matter of Onesimus. He also suggests that it would have been more likely that Archippus owned the house in which this church met than Philemon, who is presented as one of Paul's fellow workers. None of this, however, is conclusive. Greek pronouns need not always refer to the most recently mentioned noun in the context, Colossians 4.17 does not imply that our letter must have been written to Archippus, and the matter of Archippus owning the house is conjecture (although not impossible). Sara Winter also defended Knox's position ("Paul's Letter to Philemon," 2).

[12] BDAG 1057. The name was not uncommon. See MM 670; *NewDocs* 3:91 (reporting 60 examples of this name known from Rome).

[13] Some Greek manuscripts, and English translations, supply the word "brother" here so that the adjective ("beloved") has a pronoun to modify, and because this fuller phrase appears in v 16 (ancient scribes often liked to make expressions match). However, the text makes perfectly good sense with Philemon as the noun: "beloved Philemon."

[14] On the topic, see Pieter G. R. de Villiers, "Love in the Letter to Philemon," in *Philemon in Perspective: Interpreting a Pauline Letter*, ed. D. Francois Tolmie, BZNW 169 (Berlin: De Gruyter, 2010), 181–203.

he was implicitly committed to doing what he could to achieve this. The problem in the context is that this commitment may cut across another of Philemon's interests, namely the behavior of his slave, Onesimus. Recognition of what is most important, therefore, comes "up front" in the letter. Without this shared commitment to the well-being of God's people, the rest of the letter might well have been an exercise in futility.

v 2 and to Apphia our sister, and to Archippus our fellow soldier, and to the church that is in your house;

The letter has three secondary addressees, Apphia, Archippus, and the church there. Appia was a fairly common name among Roman women, but the name **Apphia** is attested in inscriptions from ancient Phrygia in Asia Minor, and it is therefore usually assumed that Apphia was a Phrygian name.[15] However, just because Apphia is a Phrygian name does not necessarily mean that Phlm was sent to Christians in Phrygia. Who was the Apphia mentioned in this letter and what role does she play in the situation with Onesimus?[16] Four basic scenarios emerge:

1. Apphia was the wife of Philemon and the church met in Philemon's house (and thus similar to Aquila and Priscilla in Rom 16.3),
2. Or Apphia was the wife of Archippus and the church met in the house of Archippus,
3. Or Apphia could have been a wife to one of the men and a sister to the other one, and Archippus could have been either a son or a brother to the others,
4. Or Apphia belonged to neither man, and perhaps she was mentioned because she was like Phoebe (Rom 16.1; *cf.* also vv 6, 12, and 15) or Nympha (Col 4.14), Christian women who had rendered some special service to Paul and who were worthy of special mention.

Whatever her relationship to the others mentioned here, Apphia was a Christian, as Paul included her within the family of God by calling her "**our sister**." The most we can say with certainty is that Paul knew

---

[15] Joseph Barber Lightfoot, *Saint Paul's Epistles to the Colossians and to Philemon*, 3rd ed. (London: Macmillan and Co., 1886), 306–08.

[16] See F. Gillman, "Apphia" *ABD* 1:317–18. For a history of views on her relationship to the others here, see Batanayi I. Manyika and Cornelia van Deventer, "The Curious Case of Apphia, Our Sister" *Conspectus* 29 (2020): 134–50.

Apphia and thought she was worthy of a special greeting in this letter. She is never mentioned in any other New Testament document.

Archippus could be simply another Christian to whom Paul wanted to give special greeting (why?), or he could have been related to Philemon and/or Apphia in some way. On the assumption that entire families became Christians when the father of the household did (*cf.* Acts 16.15, 34), it would be easy to imagine Apphia to have been Philemon's wife, and Archippus their son. This approach would fit well with the fact that Onesimus was the slave of Philemon and thus technically the property of the family. In this approach, all of them had a concern in the reconciliation that was the subject of this letter, they all presumably shared Philemon's view of the situation, and all of them needed to take Paul's appeal to heart. As the *paterfamilias* (the legal head of the household), however, Philemon would have been chiefly responsible. Archippus was in Colossae when Paul wrote his letter to the church there (Col 4.17), but this does not necessarily mean that Colossae was his home, or that Philemon was in Colossae when Paul wrote Phlm.[17] Since Paul told the Colossians to remind Archippus to fulfill his ministry, Archippus was most likely a teacher and minister of the gospel. He may have been the minister with the church that met in Philemon's house[18] (see below), and this (instead of a familial relationship with Philemon or Apphia) may explain his inclusion in the letter's address.[19]

Paul called Archippus his **fellow soldier**. This designation appears elsewhere only in Philippians 2.25 (of Epaphroditus, along with "brother" and "fellow worker"), so its precise sense is uncertain. The image is obviously one of warfare (which echoes apocalyptic themes) wherein the preaching of the gospel is thought of as aimed at the destruction of Satan's kingdom (*cf.* 2 Cor 10.3). It may that this is how Paul sometimes spoke of evangelists. The term is perhaps latent in Paul's admonition to Timothy (another evangelist) to "fight the good fight of faith" (1 Tim 1.18; 6.12), and is possibly confirmed by the inclusion of Timothy in the

---

[17] See Balabanski, "Where is Philemon?"

[18] Lightfoot thought that he might have been the minister with the church in Laodicea. *Colossians and Philemon*, 307.

[19] Dunn, *Colossians and Philemon*, 312. The singular "your" in the phrase "the church in your house" could suggest that Archippus and Apphia were *not* related to Philemon. If they were family, we might have expected the plural pronoun instead. Pao, *Colossians and Philemon*, 365, citing an example from a 2nd cent. BC letter. *Cf.* also 1 Cor 16.19 and Rom 16.5, "Aquila and Priscilla and the church in *their* house."

address of Phlm, so that Archippus is a fellow soldier with both Paul and Timothy ("our fellow soldier"), the common thread among them being that all were evangelists.

The letter's address also includes **the church in your** (Philemon's) **house**. Since designated or dedicated "church buildings" are unknown until the third century,[20] we are probably correct to assume that many local churches in the first century met in the homes of wealthier members who had houses large enough to accommodate the group gatherings.[21] In the ancient Hellenistic world, Philemon would then have been the host of the church gatherings, and thereby he would have attained a status as a kind of benefactor for the group. When Paul included the church in the address to this letter, then, he was partially acknowledging Philemon's beneficence to the church there.[22] But the inclusion of the church in the address of the letter also made the matter between Philemon and Onesimus the business of the whole group. Remember that Paul's letters would have been read out loud to the churches. Because Onesimus was now a brother in the Lord (vv 10, 16), the recognition of Onesimus as such naturally involved the brethren (plural), and not just Philemon alone.[23] This did not mean that the final decision of how to receive Onesimus would lie with the church. The letter switches to singular address starting in v 4. It does mean, however, that the church was being called upon to listen to the problem.

There are at least two likely reasons for inviting the church into this discussion, and they are not exclusive of each other. First, the church

---

[20] The building at Dura-Europos, which was used as a Christian church building beginning in 240 AD (destroyed in 256 AD), "remains both the earliest and most completely known pre-Constantinian church building." L. Michael White, *The Social Origins of Christian Architecture, Vol. 1.* Harvard Theological Studies 42 (Valley Forge: Trinity Press International, 1990), 7. The Christian prayer hall discovered near Megiddo in Israel is possibly contemporary with the Dura-Europos building. Edward Adams, "The Ancient Church at Megiddo: The Discovery and an Assessment of Its Significance," *ExpTim* 120.2 (2008): 62–69.

[21] See Acts 12.12; 16.40; Rom 16.5, 14, 15; 1 Cor 16.19; Col 4.15. However, some early Christian churches probably also met in shops, warehouses, gardens, and other places. Edward Adams, *The Earliest Christian Meeting Places: Almost Exclusively Houses?*, rev. ed., Library of New Testament Studies 450 (London: Bloomsbury, T&T Clark, 2016).

[22] The idea that Philemon's position as host to the local church was understood to put him in a position above Paul, and that Paul was, in this letter, subtly re-establishing his position over Philemon (as argued by Elliot, " 'Thanks But No Thanks' ") seems more than the text can bear. See the Introduction to this commentary.

[23] Ernest Bursey, "The Puzzling Plurals in Philemon," *Journal of Applied Christian Leadership* 9 (2015): 10–13.

would be able to encourage Philemon to make the right decision and accept Paul's appeal.[24] We see the same kind of thing in Colossians 4.17 or Philippians 4.2, where Paul gave instructions for individuals in the hearing of the whole church. It is the duty of Christians to encourage each other in love, with the goal of each one becoming like Christ (Eph 4.15–16). Phlm is a concrete example of this as Paul called upon the church there to get involved in this situation and help Philemon do the right thing. Second—and this is speculation—it is possible that any resentment Philemon had toward Onesimus was shared by his family, and perhaps also by the church. Or, less drastically, the church was waiting to see what Philemon's attitude would be, and would feel obliged to support the sentiments of their benefactor. Either way, the spirit of acceptance and reconciliation Paul wanted as the outcome needed to be adopted by everyone who shared Philemon's attitude.[25]

From our perspective today, some might think that including the church in a personal matter was inappropriate on Paul's part. Did this not put pressure on Philemon? Did it violate Philemon's privacy to make this issue between himself and his slave a matter known by the whole group? Such perspectives probably did not dominate the thinking of people in the world in which Paul wrote this letter. In fact, almost the opposite perspective, in some ways, was operative. As noted in the Introduction, Paul and the early Christians lived in an honor culture, and honor was reinforced by the group that defined it. Rather than violating Philemon's privacy, Paul was putting the matter exactly where it belonged in their culture. The issue between Philemon and Onesimus was one that involved honorable conduct as Christians, and thus it was within the purview of the group, the church, to know about it and encourage Philemon accordingly. In our churches today, under the influence of our culture, we are often careful to draw lines between private matters and church matters, but we ought to ask if this is always helpful for each other. How many disastrous decisions on the part of Christians could have been avoided if the church had been called in to encourage someone for good? And how often could the honor of the church be saved if the group were called upon to help individuals make good decisions?

[24] Hock, ("Paul's Plea," 77) notes that involving an assembly in a personal decision that affected the group was not uncommon in the Greek world.

[25] *Cf.* Petersen, *Rediscovering Paul*, 100.

The name that is conspicuous by its absence here is "Onesimus," Philemon's slave, who gets no voice in the letter. This is our first clue to an important aspect of this letter. The focus is on the relationship between Paul and Philemon. Onesimus comes into it, but as an element of the Paul-Philemon relationship. Whatever Paul would ask for, the opening of the letter framed it as coming in the context of a conversation between Paul and his friend Philemon (with the church listening in), not as a conversation between Paul, Onesimus, and Philemon. Part of the reason for this is undoubtedly the delicate nature of the matter Paul would address in this letter. He will not mention Onesimus until v 10, after he has laid the proper groundwork to hear the main business of the letter, the appeal in v 17. Even then, however, the letter maintains its character as an appeal from Paul, not an appeal from Onesimus.

v 3 grace to you and peace from God our Father and from the Lord Jesus Christ.

Grace to you (Greek *charis humin*) is a normal Pauline greeting, replacing the usual "greetings" (*chairein*) in a Hellenistic letter. The two phrases would have sounded similar, but their meanings were quite different. Although this form of greeting became Paul's ordinary way of beginning his letters, it was not simply a formality for Paul. "Grace" was a kind of "umbrella term" that, for Paul, summarized all that God has done for us. This is clear in passages such as Ephesians 2.5, 8 ("by grace you have been saved"), and Romans 5.2 ("this grace in which we stand"). We must remember that what God has done for us is that he has begun the destruction of the old world of sin and death, and begun the new creation in the work of Christ. Ultimately, the grace of God consists of his apocalyptic shattering of the world of sin and death and his call for us to join him, through Jesus, in the new world of life and righteousness.[26]

---

[26] In some contexts, "grace" can have an apocalyptic character. *Cf.* Titus 2.11 "the grace of God has appeared, bringing salvation to all men and instructing us to deny ungodliness and worldly desires." Also 3.24 and Rom 5.17–21, where God's grace is said to be the cause of the believer's new life in a context of new-creation language (Jesus as the new Adam): "... those who receive the abundance of grace and of the gift of righteousness will reign in life through the One, Jesus Christ" (v 17). So also in v 21, grace is the key term that describes the apocalyptic new situation: "so that, as sin reigned in death, even so grace would reign through righteousness to eternal life through Jesus Christ our Lord." *Cf.* also Zech 4.7, where the fall of the "great mountain" and the establishment of God's temple are proclaimed "with shouts of 'Grace, grace to it.' " Beale summarizes the Biblical

Whatever Paul wanted Philemon to do, it was to be done within the sphere of people who stood in, and lived their lives in and because of, God's grace that creates a new world for his people.

"Grace" had a different sense in Paul's world than it does in ours. Through the Christian theological tradition, largely mediated through Martin Luther, the term "grace" in modern theological parlance has come to mean "unmerited favor" and, perhaps even more significantly, a gift from God "pure and simple." We certainly did not earn it, but we do not repay it either. However, this is not the sense that "grace" had in Paul's time. "Grace" was the usual word for "a favor," understood in the Hellenistic context of benefaction (see the Introduction). That is, when someone did you a favor, that favor was called a "grace." More importantly, grace was not unmerited favor that was absolutely free. Instead, grace was a favor that created a relationship in which the recipient was always honor-bound to reciprocate the favor with service and by publicly honoring the giver.[27] This relationship, created by grace, also served to define the recipient. The recipient of grace thereafter knows him/herself to be a person whose blessed existence is bound up with the giver of the gift. For Paul, this experience of God's grace is one of the things that defines not only the individual Christian, but also the group, the church. The "**you**" in this verse is plural. The church is the group of those who, in common, have experienced the grace of God (in the gospel about Christ's death and resurrection) and thus who are now defined as the recipients, the beneficiaries, of God's grace and who now collectively reciprocate this grace with praise and service. But grace not only recalibrates the identity of its recipients, it also resets the worth of each member because God's gift is given across the human spectrum and does not respect human judgments of value or worth. In this way, members of the Lord's church attain a new worth in Christ which is the same for each of them (thus they are brethren).[28] People who were

picture as "Jesus's life, trials, death for sinners, and especially resurrection by the Spirit have launched the fulfillment of the eschatological already-not yet new-creational reign, bestowed by grace through faith" (*New Testament Biblical Theology*, 16 (but the statement appears repeatedly throughout the book).

[27] See deSilva, *Honor, Patronage, Kinship & Purity*, 22–42; Barclay, *Paul and the Gift*, 24–51 and 183–88; and Thomas R. Blanton, *A Spiritual Economy: Gift Exchange in the Letters of Paul of Tarsus* (New Haven: Yale University Press, 2017).

[28] See Barclay, *Paul and the Gift*, 350. Recall also, from the Introduction to this volume, that equality of worth does not erase social positions or roles.

formerly defined only by worldly hierarchies and roles (such as slave, master, *etc.*) are now redefined primarily as people who have benefited from the death and resurrection of God's gift, Christ.

This new worth must be respected in the way Christians accept each other, which is part of the practice of Christian love. Additionally, when the members of the church practice genuine Christian love towards each other, this mutual love counts as reciprocating God's love. In Philippians 4.15–18, Paul thanked the Philippians for their material (financial) support of his ministry, but also said "Not that I seek the gift itself, but I seek for the profit which increases to your account. But I have received everything in full and have an abundance; I am amply supplied, having received from Epaphroditus what you have sent, a fragrant aroma, an acceptable sacrifice, well-pleasing to God" (vv 17–18 NASB). Note that their demonstrated love for Paul is characterized as a gift to God.[29] Their gift ultimately expressed their gratitude not just to Paul, but to God, whose gift of grace in Christ first provided their fellowship and salvation.

"Up front," therefore, in this letter Paul frames his appeal as one that will take place within, and that will fulfill, the obligations of a person (Philemon) who is the recipient of divine grace, and who lives in a community in which the practice of love reciprocates God's love. Grace is mentioned again in v 25, so that through the literary device of inclusio the entire letter is framed in this way. Also in the case of Philemon, Paul had a part in that grace coming to him, and so Paul was a participant in the circle in which grace could be reciprocated.

The inclusion of **peace** was not part of the Hellenistic letter form. In Paul's letters, it was his own modification, taking the place of the more usual expression of concern for the recipient's health. We should best understand its presence in the greeting section of Paul's letters as due to Paul's Jewish background, where "shalom" was a usual way of greeting other members of God's people, or due to Numbers 6.24–26.[30] We cannot rule out, however, that Paul also had in mind a Hellenistic, that is, Roman, sense of peace as the destruction of enmity (*cf.* Rom 16.20).[31] In the Roman

---

[29] *Cf.* Blanton, *Spiritual Economy*, 22. *Cf.* also Hebrews 13.16, where doing good and sharing with each other is described as a sacrifice to God.

[30] Fitzmyer, *Philemon*, 90.

[31] Thus Eph 2.15: "by abolishing in His flesh the enmity ... thus establishing peace." See Klaus Wengst, *Pax Romana and the Peace of Jesus Christ*, trans. John Bowden (Philadelphia: Fortress, 1987); also Werner Foerster, *"eirēnē," TDNT* 2:400–402.

view, peace was a function of power.[32] To the extent that peace from God means the destruction of the old way of hatred, arrogance, jealousy, *etc.*, through the power of the gospel, peace thus has an "apocalyptic," new quality to it. Peace is part of the new world ushered in by the work of Christ (*cf.* Rom 5.1; Eph 2.14–18), and the new people who live in Christ are characterized by it (recall Gal 5.22). Such a sense would fit the context of Phlm well, as Paul will ask for a reconciliation based on the destruction of Philemon's old attitude toward Onesimus.

The terms grace and peace, while not usually understood as strictly apocalyptic vocabulary, nevertheless point to the apocalyptic-eschatological new reality that has dawned from the work of Christ.[33] Therefore this grace and peace are **from God our Father and the Lord Jesus Christ**. As is usual with Paul's letters, the terms in the opening lines of the letter are significant for the discussion that will follow in the body of the letter.[34] The **Father**hood of God will lie behind Paul's appeal in v 16 that Philemon accept Onesimus as a brother in Christ, as well as bind Paul and Philemon together (vv 1, 7, 20). The fact that Jesus the Messiah[35] is called **Lord**, especially here

[32] Wengst, *Pax Romana*, 10.

[33] *Cf.* Barclay, *Paul and the Gift*, 354, where he says that God's call in the grace of Christ (Gal 1.6) refers to "to a 'singular universal,' a particular historical event that has redefined and re-divided the whole of reality." While Barclay does not explicitly call this "apocalyptic," the idea is there. Similarly, he says "the Christ-gift" is "the definitive act of divine beneficence" (350).

[34] *Cf.* Pao: "Though part of Paul's typical opening formula, the concepts of "grace" and "peace" form the foundation of his argument in this letter where human forgiveness and reconciliation form the proper responses to divine acts of grace." *Colossians and Philemon*, 366.

[35] "Christ Jesus" means "Messiah Jesus." It is often said that "Christ" had become basically a proper name in Christian usage (similar to the double names Herod Antipas, John Mark, *etc.*; *e.g.*, Fitzmyer, *Philemon*, 84), but this is more a matter of English readers reading Western naming conventions into the text than it is a matter of historical fact. Although the combination of "Jesus Christ" or "Christ Jesus" probably sounded like two proper names to Roman hearers who were unacquainted with the gospel (as Acts 11.26 suggests), it is hard to imagine that these two words had that same ring to first-century Jewish listeners, much less to the apostle Paul. It would be better to acknowledge that for Paul, Christ is not a second name for Jesus (or sometimes a first name, "Christ Jesus"). The Greek word Christ, which translates the Hebrew "Messiah," always retains its significance for Paul as the title of the prophesied king of Israel. See Wright, *Paul and the Faithfulness of God*, 817–24; Aquila H. I. Lee, "Messianism and Messiah in Paul: Christ as Jesus?," in *God and the Faithfulness of Paul: A Critical Examination of the Pauline Theology of N. T. Wright*, ed. Christoph J. Heilig, J. Thomas Hewitt, and Michael F. Bird (Minneapolis: Fortress, 2017), 375–92; *cf.* Walter Grundmann, *"christos," TDNT* 9:541, esp. fn 317; David B. Capes, *Old Testament Yahweh Texts in Paul's Christology* (Waco: Baylor University Press, 2017), 52; Joshua W. Jipp, *The*

in conjunction with God, should be taken as an affirmation of the deity of Jesus. The Lord of the Old Testament is often interpreted to be Jesus in the quotations of the Old Testament in the New Testament.[36] But the designation "Lord" is not a gratuitous reminder of the deity of Jesus. The title also reminds Philemon that it is the Messianic king (**Christ**) Jesus who reigns over the new world God is creating,[37] the same world in which both Philemon and Onesimus now existed as brethren. Paul often called Jesus "Lord" in contexts where obedience was an issue.[38] By the simple language of this verse, then, Paul has set forth the initial conceptual groundwork by which his appeal to Philemon was to be interpreted.[39]

v 4 I give thanks to my God, always remembering you in my prayers,[40]

"**You**" here is singular. At this point, the plural address of vv 1–3 gives way to the singular, as the conversation becomes one between Paul and Philemon, and remains so until v 25.[41]

Messianic Theology of the New Testament (Grand Rapids: Eerdmans, 2020), 148–53. To pagan ears, "Christ" would have sounded more like an honorific than a name (like Augustus; Matthew V. Novenson, *Christ Among the Messiahs* (Oxford: Oxford University Press, 2012), 93–97). It would be good to get oneself into the habit of mentally reading "Christ Jesus" as "(the) Messiah Jesus," and mentally reading "Jesus Christ" as "Jesus the Messiah," *etc.*

[36] See Capes, *Old Testament Yahweh Texts.*

[37] Jesus, as the new Adam (Rom 5.12–21) fulfills the original mandate to man to subdue and rule over all the earth. *Cf.* Psa 2. This is undoubtedly part of what it means to say that Jesus is Lord.

[38] "While *kyrios* serves as a christological title in nearly every part of Paul's Letters, it appears most prominent in the hortatory sections. In dealing with matters relating to conduct and practices within his churches, the apostle tends to refer to Jesus as *kyrios.*" David B. Capes, *The Divine Christ: Paul, the Lord Jesus, and the Scriptures of Israel* (Grand Rapids: Baker Academic, 2018), 57.

[39] See Weima, "Paul's Persuasive Prose," 29–60. "rather than being insignificant, the letter opening serves an important function in the overall argument of the letter. … Paul skillfully uses these opening sections to place himself and his readers in such a relationship to one another that his purposes in the letter are furthered." (32)

[40] Post-verbal participial phrases, such as we have here ("always remembering …") can define, specify, or clarify the action represented by the main verb. Steven E. Runge, *Discourse Grammar of the Greek New Testament: A Practical Introduction for Teaching and Exegesis.* (Bellingham, WA: Lexham Press, 2010), 262. Paul's thankfulness for Philemon was not just something that existed as a sentiment within him, but was expressed in his prayers. This may explain the choice of the periphrastic construction here. Markus Barth and Helmut Blanke, *The Letter to Philemon: A New Translation with Notes and Commentary,* ECC (Grand Rapids: Eerdmans, 2000), 270.

[41] All the first-person verbs in the letter have Paul as subject, and most of them have Philemon as direct or indirect object; the second-person verbs in the letter have Philemon

Thanksgivings were a regular feature in Hellenistic letters, and Paul modified this convention in a particularly Christian way. These sections of Paul's letters, when they are present, were not gratuitous, however, but were intended to be both a recognition of Christian fruitfulness and an encouragement to continue in the matters for which Paul expressed his thanks. Their tone is "I am so thankful for what you have done, and keep doing it."[42] That is, they functioned as both righteous praise and rhetorical encouragement. Since the thanksgiving section had this forward-looking component to it, it encapsulated important ideas that were developed in the body of the letter.[43]

Having said that, we should also note that the rhetorical function of these sections was not simply utilitarian. Paul was typically thankful for *spiritual* things among his readers, and prayed for the increase of these same spiritual things among them. Christianity is not mere performance. It is the living of a life out of a renewed spirit that partakes of, and is filled with, spiritual blessings and power from God. It is continued and increased fulfillment in these spiritual blessings that is the primary focus of the thanksgiving sections of Paul's letters. When Christians are filled with the spiritual blessings and power that comes from God, their lives will naturally demonstrate it in their actions and words. Without that spiritual aspect, Christianity would be reduced simply to good-deed-doing.

Paul gave **thanks to God** for something Philemon had done (vv 4, 7). This may seem strange to some, but it is the normal practice in the New Testament. Paul understood that Philemon's Christian character and behavior would not have existed were it not for the fact that God had intervened in the person and work of Jesus (*cf.* 2 Cor 5.19), making us new and bringing to us the knowledge of a new way of life (*cf.* Titus 2.11–14).[44] The brotherly love of Philemon therefore owed its existence to God. The apocalyptic, new-creational work of God in Jesus is the conceptual foundation upon which the conversation of this letter was possible.

---

as the subject; all occurrences of the singular forms of "you" (including "your") refer to Philemon. Jeal, *Exploring Philemon*, 59–60.

[42] White, "New Testament Epistolary Literature," 1741.

[43] P. Schubert, *Form and Function of the Pauline Thanksgivings*, BZNW 20 (Berlin, 1939), 77; Peter O'Brien, *Introductory Thanksgivings in the Letters of Paul*, NTS 49 (Leiden: Brill, 1977), 15.

[44] Lohse, *Colossians and Philemon*, 192.

v 5 as I hear about your love and faith, which you have toward the Lord Jesus and for all the saints,

The fact that Paul heard of Philemon's love and faith does not necessarily mean that Paul had *only* heard about it, and had never met Philemon personally. Verse 10 most likely means that Paul taught the gospel to Philemon. Presumably Paul had met, and taught, Philemon somewhere in Asia Minor.[45] If this was the case (and it is not certain), then it is possible that Paul had not personally seen Philemon for as much as four or five years.[46] However, we simply do not know the history between these two men. Whatever it was, "**as I hear**"[47] conveyed that Paul had kept up with news about his friend.[48] The relationship, as far as Paul was concerned, was fully intact. This relationship between Paul and Philemon lies at the core of this letter, and Paul's appeal occurs within its sphere. This is how Christian exhortation works. It is not strangers exhorting or rebuking strangers, but is meant to be done in a context of personal relationships that are characterized primarily by love.

The Greek grammar of this verse has generated much discussion. There are two basic ways to understand it. The first would be to apply both faith and love to the Lord and to the saints, but this seems to create an unusual statement about faith in the saints. One solution to this problem would be to understand that faith works through love (Gal 5.6), so the faith-love combination can have both Christ and Christ's people,

---

[45] But probably not at Colossae, because Paul had not yet been to Colossae when he wrote his letter to the church there, and Phlm seems to have been written around the same time. See Introduction.

[46] After Paul left Ephesus he got arrested in Jerusalem, detained in Caesarea for two years, transferred to Rome, and then spent two years under house arrest there. Acts 20–28.

[47] The Greek text has a present participle, and this further elaborates on the character of Paul's prayers (v 4). By the Greek present participle an author portrayed the action imperfectively, "from the inside," portraying the event as unfolding before the viewer's eyes. The present participle also usually "expresses action that is contemporaneous with its leading verb" (which in this case is also present tense, v 4 "I thank"). Constantine R. Campbell, *Basics of Verbal Aspect in Biblical Greek* (Grand Rapids: Zondervan, 2008), 60 and 72. Verses 4–6 are punctuated as a single sentence in the Nestle Greek text. Lightfoot noted that the jumbled grammar of the sentence seemed to reflect Paul's eagerness to express what was in his heart at this time (*Colossians and Philemon*, 332).

[48] As Dunn noted, this news could have come from Onesimus or from the "network of communication among the Pauline churches," undoubtedly also involving Paul's fellow workers who tended to the churches while Paul was confined. *Colossians and Philemon*, 317.

the saints, as its object.[49] Faith in Christ becomes love for the saints, as vv 6–7 below make clear. But another way to resolve the difficulty with this reading is to understand the Greek word *pistis* to mean faithfulness or loyal commitment.[50] The second way to understand the verse is to see it as written in inverted parallelism,[51] so that "love" goes with "saints," and "faith" goes with "the Lord Jesus":

> I hear of your love
>   and faith
>   which you have
>   toward the Lord Jesus
> and for all the saints.

This would make the verse speak similarly to Colossians 1.4 ("since we heard of your faith in Christ Jesus and the love which you have for all the saints" NASB) and Ephesians 1.15 ("… having heard of the faith in the Lord Jesus which exists among you and your love for all the saints" NASB). While I prefer this second approach, we must acknowledge that the particular expression Paul penned here is unusual. The more important point, I think, is the close connection between faith and love.

The two things Paul had heard are, in a sense, the defining qualities of Christians, their love and their faith. Christian **love** can be defined as a commitment to what is good or best for others first. It is a "rights-renouncing and others-oriented cruciform love."[52] The word **faith**, like grace (v 3), is an "umbrella" term that summarizes the Christian's stance toward God (*cf.* Eph 2.5, where grace and faith summarize all of salvation).

---

[49] So Dunn, *Colossians and Philemon*, 317; also Marvin Richardson Vincent, *A Critical and Exegetical Commentary on the Epistles to the Philippians and to Philemon*, ICC (New York: C. Scribner's Sons, 1897), 178–79.

[50] So Seth M. Ehorn, *Philemon*, Evangelical Exegetical Commentary (Bellingham, WA: Lexham Press, 2011); also G. K. Beale, *Colossians and Philemon*, BECNT (Grand Rapids: Baker Academic, 2019), 386–87.

[51] So Barclay, "*Koinonia* and the Social Dynamics," most commentators, as well as A. T. Robertson (*A Grammar of the Greek New Testament in the Light of Historical Research*, 4th ed. (New York: Hodder and Stoughton, 1923), 1200). Inverted parallelism also appears in 2 Cor 2.15–16 (saved—perishing—death—life). Concerning the combination of love and faith here, Paul elsewhere has these two terms in the order of "faith and love." The reversed order here perhaps previews the letter's emphasis on love (as suggested by Lohse, *Colossians and Philemon* 193; Barth and Blanke, *Philemon*, 272).

[52] Michael J. Gorman, *Cruciformity: Paul's Narrative Spirituality of the Cross* (Grand Rapids: Eerdmans, 2001), 197.

It obviously begins with the idea of believing that God exists and believing what he says, but it goes much further. "Faith" describes an orientation, one's commitment and dedication to God, a putting of one's life in God's hands (*cf.* Gal 2.20).

The fact that Paul had been hearing about Philemon's **faith** means that it must have been more than the belief and trust that he held in his heart (*i.e.*, subjectively), otherwise how could Paul have heard about it? Real faith is known by its manifestations in words and deeds (*cf.* Jam 2.14–26; Acts 14.9), manifestations that are expressions of submission and obedience to Jesus because he is the **Lord**. Thus Paul had heard about the conduct and behavior of Philemon, which he attributed to Philemon's faith. But not to be missed is the fact that faith and love are always intimately connected.[53] It was Philemon's demonstrations of Christian *love* of which Paul had heard, that prompted him to say he had heard of Philemon's *faith*. Verses 5–7 together present a picture in which faith and love go together. The person who genuinely has the former will have the latter because faith works through love.[54] When faith works, or manifests itself, it does so in the form of deeds and words of love. Love is, in this sense, the application of our common faith to each other[55] because the gospel is, at its core, a story of divine love that becomes not only experienced, but appropriated so that it characterizes God's new people in Christ.[56] Love becomes the way of life for people of faith.

Rhetorically, Philemon's record of love for the saints now becomes a basis upon which Paul will ask him to act in love for another saint (Onesimus). Paul was acknowledging that it was perfectly characteristic of Philemon to act out of love for other Christians. Therefore Paul's request (when it finally arrives in v 17), will not come as something

---

[53] Grammatically, the relative pronoun here ("which") is singular. It is possible, in Greek, to use a singular relative pronoun to refer to more than one antecedent in the context. See William W. Goodwin, *Greek Grammar* (Boston: Ginn and Company, 1892, repr., Eugene, OR: Wipf and Stock, 2003), 218 (section 1021a); Herbert Weir Smyth, *Greek Grammar* (Cambridge: Harvard University Press, 1956), 563 (section 2502c); Barth and Blanke, *Philemon*, 272. See the discussion of the grammatical options in Beale, *Colossians and Philemon*, 386–87.

[54] Gal 5.6, 13; *cf.* 1 Cor 13.2; Eph 1.15; 3.17; 4.2; 6.23; Col 1.4; 1 Thes 1.3; 3.6; 2 Thes 1.3; 1 Tim 1.5, 14; 2 Tim 1.13; Titus 3.15.

[55] *Cf.* Rom 14; Jam 2.1, 8–9; 1 John 3.17.

[56] *Cf.* Eph 4.32–5.2; 1 Thes 4.9; 1 Pet 1.22; John 13.34–35; 1 John 3.11, 23; 4.7, 11.

unusual for Philemon. It will, instead, become a matter (although a challenging one) of Philemon acting consistently with the record of loving service he has already established in his life.[57]

v 6 that the fellowship of your faith might be effective in the knowledge of every good thing that is among us in(to) Christ.

Some English translations supply the words "I pray" at the very beginning of this verse to make the grammar smoother. The idea is that Paul's prayers (from v 4) include the request that Philemon's love and faith will be for the purpose of something else, which Paul will specify.[58] However, the meaning of this verse is difficult to attain. The questions are:

1. What does the phrase "the fellowship of your faith" mean?
2. What does the word "fellowship" mean here?
3. How does the phrase "in the knowledge ..." modify what goes before it?
4. What is "every good thing"?
5. Is the best reading "among you" or "among us"?
6. What does "into Christ" mean here?

1. We begin with the phrase "**the fellowship of your faith**," which is the grammatical subject of the clause. "**Your**" is singular, referring to the faith of Philemon. Since v 4, the language of the letter has been directed specifically towards Philemon. The phrase could mean "the fellowship that consists of your faith," or "the sharing of your faith" (ESV, RSV), or "your participation in (the) faith" (HCSB), or "your sharing a common faith." "**Your**" could go with either "fellowship" or "faith." Clearly, the interpretation of this phrase is bound up with the second question.

2. The meaning of the word "**fellowship**" (Greek *koinōnia*) is important not only in this context but for v 17 as well.[59] Scholars debate whether the

---

[57] A similar text is Heb 10.32–35, where the author urged his audience to persevere in their trials based on their proven perseverance in the past.

[58] "That" translates the Greek word *hopōs,* which, when used with the subjunctive mood (as here) indicates the purpose for an event or state of things. BDAG 718. Pearson notes that "The *hopōs* subjunctive clause in v 6 is, however, somewhat obscure. Whether it depends on v. 4, or is to be seen as a parenthetical comment, is difficult to tell, but the likelihood is that vv. 5 and 6 are to be seen as individually dependent on v. 4." "Assumptions," 271–72.

[59] Several have noted that fellowship (*koinōnia*) lies at the core of this letter. "The whole letter is actually a concrete expression of what Paul understands by *koinōnia*." J. Hainz,

basic or primary sense of the word is "association" or "participation," but there is little practical difference between the two.[60] Either way, the word denotes a relationship that exists because people have something in common, because they share something. The phrase "fellowship of faith" would denote an association or sharing in faith, or sharing by faith.[61] Also, in this context, "faith" can only mean what the Bible sometimes calls "the faith," the faith in Christ Jesus that was the primary marker of Christian identity. The idea that is being communicated is that Philemon was in a relationship with other Christians because they all shared a common faith in Christ.

In an extended sense, sharing can denote "generosity" in the sense of sharing material goods with fellow Christians (Phil 1.5, often translated "participation"; *cf.* Phil 4.15 "giving and receiving"; Rom 15.26 "contribution"), which would be akin to sacrificing for others. If we apply this extended sense of the word here, it would create the idea of the generous and sacrificial sharing (or giving) that came from Philemon's faith. But that may be reading more into this verse than is warranted by the context.[62]

3. Does the phrase **"in the knowledge of** ..." refer to Paul's knowledge (since Paul is describing the content of his prayer), or Philemon's (that is, does this indicate what Paul prays Philemon will understand)? And is this knowledge produced by the effectiveness of Philemon's faith (so that its effectiveness brings him to a greater knowledge), or is this knowledge the basis of it (so that the effectiveness of his faith springs from this knowledge)? Greek grammar does not answer these questions.

Koinōnia: "Kirche" als Gemeinschaft bei Paulus (Regensburg: Pustet, 1982), 110; quoted in Barclay, "*Koinōnia* and the Social Dynamics," 151; Wright, *Paul and the Faithfulness of God*, 10: "The whole letter is both an expression of, and an exhortation to, the central Pauline theme of *koinōnia*, 'fellowship' or 'partnership.' "

[60] Julien Ogereau ("A Survey of *Koinōnia* and Its Cognates in Documentary Sources," *NovT* 57 (2015): 275–94) has shown that both senses were operative in the word. He describes the attempt to isolate either "association" or "sharing" as the primary meaning of the word as "hairsplitting" (292). Also, the word was not a religious term in Paul's day, although it has become a religious term for us because of Paul's usage of it.

[61] *Ibid.*, 278. With the noun (which we have here), the genitive is usually a partitive genitive, subjective genitive, or genitive of person (286). The subjective use ("the fellowship that your faith creates") would make sense here.

[62] Although this is how Lightfoot understood it (*Colossians and Philemon*, 333).

We start with the second set of questions. It is certainly true that experience and practice makes us understand things better. The more a person practices Christian love, the more he/she will understand its character. But it seems better to take the phrase as referring to the reason for, or basis upon which, Philemon will make his fellowship active or effective. That is, Paul's prayer is that Philemon will make his faith active because knowledge will lead him to this conclusion.

If "the knowledge" Paul speaks of here is his own knowledge, then the sense is "I pray that your generosity might become effective, because (or based on the fact that) I know every good thing that is among us." But it seems more natural to understand the phrase as referring to Philemon's knowledge, because the thrust of the context is about Philemon, his attitude, his character, and his action. Therefore the sense is "as (or because) you know every good thing that is among us." Paul is calling upon Philemon to combine his knowledge and his faith, resulting in an "action" in this case. This would make the verse here similar to Philippians 1.9: "I pray that your love may abound still more and more in real knowledge and all discernment." That is, the more they know and discern what it is to be in Christ, the more they will become people of love (*cf.* Eph 3.17). Philemon had a relationship with other Christians by virtue of the faith they all had in common, and he knew what goodness was possible, but Paul wanted to see that faith and knowledge now come to a concrete expression ("become effective"). Paul did not want Philemon to have a static faith, but an active one. Of course, Philemon's faith had been active in the past (v 7), but Paul wanted it to be active in the present situation as well.

4. "**Every good thing**" can be a generic reference to all the good that Christians learn and know as they come to develop spiritually. Some have argued that the phrase should be understood in a narrower vein as referring to the good things that accompany, or make up, our salvation. That is, the good things mentioned here are things done by God and Christ.[63] With this approach, Paul's reasoning would be that Philemon's knowledge of all the good things God has provided to us should prompt Philemon to reciprocate by providing something good himself (which will be specified later in the letter). Alternately, "every good thing" can be understood as things that Christians do as expressions of their faith,

[63] *cf.* Rom 8.28; 10.15; Phil 1.6; Jam 1.17. So Barclay, "*Koinōnia* and the Social Dynamics," 156; Wright, *Paul and the Faithfulness of God*, 18; Lohse, *Colossians and Philemon*, 194.

the good things that characterize the Christian way of life.[64] In the end, Paul simply did not specify which kind of goodness was primarily in view here, which can be taken as Paul's own clue that the phrase was meant to be interpreted broadly. The good things that God provides to us in his saving grace are to be used for his service and glory (Heb 13.21), so perhaps in the end the two become one, as it were.

The only thing that is not unclear is that Paul hoped that something would be done ("**become effective**"), that a practical good would come out of Philemon's faith. Paul approached the subject of the letter, which he has yet to reveal at this point, delicately. He has not yet said what that "something" will be. He only says that he prays that Philemon's faith, which has a record of expressing itself in love, will produce such an expression now in the present case.

5. On top of the exegetical difficulties in this verse, there is a textual difficulty as well. Are these good things among "**us**," or among "you"?[65] It makes little difference to the sense of this verse. It is a matter of whether Paul included himself in the discussion ("us") or not. At this point, the letter has become a conversation between Paul and Philemon, so "us" fits perfectly. In either case, the "us" and "you" are Christians, and that is the focus. The good things are things known and appreciated by Christians because they partake of the mind and spirit of Christ.

6. The final phrase of this difficult verse is sometimes translated "**in Christ**" (RSV, NKJV), and that is a perfectly legitimate translation. However, it is verbally different (in Greek) from the phrase "in Christ" that so often colors Paul's letters. The phrase here is not the usual *en Christō*, but *eis Christon*. That is, the preposition is different in Greek, with the primary

---

[64] *cf.* Eph 6.8; 2 Tim 2.21; Titus 3.8; 1 Pet 2.12.

[65] "Us" is the choice that appears in the printed Nestle-Aland[28] text, although "you" (pl.) is well-attested. "Us" would pick up the Paul-Philemon relationship, but "you" would presumably include the church from v 2 and would be more characteristic of the thanksgiving sections in Paul's other letters. Metzger argued that "us" was more likely original on the premise that scribes would have been prone to change the pronoun to "you." (Bruce Manning Metzger, *A Textual Commentary on the Greek New Testament, Second Edition, A Companion Volume to the United Bible Societies' Greek New Testament*, 4th rev. ed. (London; New York: United Bible Societies, 1994), 588. Solomon argued that "us" was the better reading based on internal and external considerations ("The Textual History of Philemon," 585). Fortunately, "nothing fundamental rests on this textual decision" (Barclay, "*Koinōnia* and the Social Dynamic," 155).

meaning of *eis* being "into."[66] There is considerable semantic overlap between *en* and *eis*,[67] and it is possible that Paul chose *eis* here for stylistic reasons, without any significant change in meaning, because he had just used *en* twice before: "in all knowledge" and "in (among) you." In that case, *eis* might simply mean "in." But it is also possible, if not likely, that the choice of *eis* in this final phrase is deliberate, and that it is not simply synonymous with *en* ("in") here.

If we respect *eis* as a conscious choice, we still need to narrow down the sense here, because *eis* has a wide semantic range. A few different interpretations are possible. First, it can mean "into or unto Christ" in the sense of "for him, for his sake, for his glory" (NASB, ESV, HCSB, NIV, NRSV), that is, with Christ viewed as a goal. This would mean "every good thing" is for the sake of, or for the glory of, Christ.[68] Second, it could mean that "every good thing" is designed to make us into the image of Christ, so that we grow "into" him, that is, we become more and more like him.[69] This would mean "every good work" transforms us into the image of Christ. Third, it could mean "with respect to, with reference to, with relation to."[70] This interpretation would sharpen the understanding of either the knowledge or of "every good thing" Paul has mentioned, making it a knowledge or goodness with reference to Christ (*i.e.*, a specific kind of knowledge or goodness). Any of these interpretations could work here, since this context lacks anything that would sharpen the focus of the phrase. Since Paul thought that all things are summed up in Christ (Eph 1.10) and everything is through him and for him (Col 1.16; *cf.* Heb 2.10), the phrase "into Christ" here possibly reflects that same perspective. Everything leads to Christ.

To summarize our findings, then, v 6 means that Paul prayed that Philemon's sharing in faith in Christ with other Christians would produce an action, an action based on Philemon's knowledge of the

---

[66] BDAG 288. The primary definition is "extension involving a goal or place" and the glosses provided are "into, in, toward, to."

[67] BDAG 289, 1aδ.

[68] Lohse, *Colossians and Philemon*, 195; and others.

[69] N. T. *Wright, Paul and the Faithfulness of God*, 18, citing Eph 4.12f as a similar thought. *Cf.* also Col 1.9–10.

[70] Murray J. Harris, *Prepositions and Theology in the Greek New Testament: An Essential Reference Resource for Exegesis* (Grand Rapids: Zondervan, 2012), 85. So also Barclay, "*Koinōnia* and the Social Dynamic," 156–57.

goodness that is wrapped up in Christ.[71] The specific action Paul had in mind will be revealed in v 17.

The overall purpose, or effect, of vv 5–7 is to begin to shift the paradigm in Philemon's thinking concerning the issue of Onesimus. What is absent from these verses is any talk of Philemon's status or authority as a slave owner, or any word about Onesimus or slaves. Those are social-temporal categories that, while they do not disappear from the present situation, do not define that situation as a Christian would view it. Instead, the present problem needed to be addressed and decided as dominated by the context of a mutual faith and love among Christians, and v 6 provided such a focus.

v 7 For I have had much joy and encouragement in your love, because the hearts of the saints have been refreshed through you, brother.

The connective "**for**" connects the next statement with what had just been said, but without the idea of developing a new aspect of the discussion. Instead, it introduces a statement that should be understood as strengthening or supporting what was just said.[72] Here, the support is the historical fact of Philemon's past services to the saints.

Paul rejoiced when Christians demonstrated their faith and their love for each other.[73] It was proof that the gospel was doing its work of changing the hearts and lives of God's people and producing its fruit. As in v 6, so here also the spiritual dimension of faith and love is emphasized, even though it expressed itself in concrete acts. That is, Paul did not say "I'm thankful, Philemon, that you provided brother ___ with some money, or that you provided a meal for sister ___." Instead, Paul was thankful for the love that prompted such actions (which remain unspecified). The **love**, the spiritual component, was the important thing. This gave Paul not only **joy**, but also **encouragement** that God's people were taking their transformation seriously. This verse, then, acts as an expression of Paul's confidence in Philemon's spirituality, a confidence Paul will express again in v 21.

---

[71] The latter part of the verse has the definite article acting like a relative pronoun, connecting "every good work" with "into Christ." A textual variant changes the gender of the article so that the sense is "the knowledge … that is into Christ," but its attestation is poorer.

[72] Runge, *Discourse Grammar*, 51. The material introduced by "for" (Greek *gar*) is therefore "offline," not a piece of the main point.

[73] 2 Cor 7.9, 13; Phil 1,18; 2.18; 4.10; 1 Thes 3.9.

The love in Philemon's heart had refreshed the hearts of other Christians. The word "**refreshed**" means to give rest, and thus to cause someone to be refreshed.[74] It is a Christ-like thing to do (Matt 11.28–30). The picture is one of providing a restful refuge from hardships or toil, but Paul qualified it in such a way that he meant spiritual refreshing here. It may well be that Philemon had opened his home to other Christians in hospitality (*cf.* v 22 below), and thus refreshed their bodies, but what gave Paul joy and encouragement was that the hearts of the saints had been refreshed by Philemon's love toward them. The word "**hearts**" here (and also in vv 12 and 20) is the Greek word *splanchna,* a plural word that literally means "inward (bodily) parts."[75] The ancients believed that emotions came from one's "guts," so the word acquired a figurative meaning. English translations render it "heart" in order to communicate the sense as we would say it. It is often suggested that this word was more emotionally charged than the regular Greek word for "heart" (*kardia*).[76] There may be some truth to this, but it is the kind of thing that can easily be overstated. Paul apparently used the two terms synonymously in 2 Cor 6.11–12 and in 2 Cor 7.13, 15. Nevertheless, *splanchna* probably focuses more on the emotions whereas *kardia* can include intelligence, will, *etc.*

Love, when put into action among people of faith in Christ, results not only in the meeting of physical needs through shared material resources, but it also strengthens the hearts of those who receive it. The sharing of goods carries with it a message of love, care, and concern, much more strongly than words alone would communicate. It makes people feel accepted, it makes them feel that they are truly part of the group. Ancient culture was largely group-oriented (in contrast to the largely individualistic culture of today—with some exceptions[77]), and therefore such an effect was important. Sharing of goods reinforced group identity, it reinforced the sense of "us," the sense of belonging. This would have been especially important among the early Christians, who often had to choose between being part of their families, or their local culture, and

---

[74] The verb here is a compound form of *pauesthai*: *anapauesthai*. The compounded form with *ana* meant to give temporary relief, and the uncompounded form expressed final cessation. Lightfoot, *Colossians and Philemon*, 334–35, citing the usage in Plutarch.

[75] It is the word for "intestines" in Acts 1.18.

[76] "It thus remains a very strong and forceful term which occurs only when Paul is speaking directly and personally." Helmut Köster, "*splanchna*," *TDNT* 7:555.

[77] I am thinking here of the modern "cancel culture," by which groups clearly express who may be considered "in" and who is considered "out" among them.

being part of God's people. For them, it was not always possible to have both. Christians quickly developed the unfair, shameful reputation of being troublemakers (Acts 16.20; 17.6; 24.5) who cared for no one else. In cases where people had been rejected from their native cultures or their families because they had become Christians, strong signals of being accepted by their new family in Christ were important. By acts of love among each other, Christians gave and received the message that "you may not be acceptable to the world, but you are acceptable to God, to me, and to your fellow Christians." When Paul told Philemon that his acts of love had refreshed the hearts of the saints, these kinds of things were included. Philemon had done things to make sure that fellow Christians knew they were welcomed and accepted. This becomes a foundation for the request later in the letter for Philemon to receive (accept) Onesimus in the same way he received Paul (v 17).

We noted in the comments on v 1 that since the church there met in Philemon's house, Philemon would have been viewed as the group's benefactor. In the Hellenistic world of status and honor, this would have been important. It implies that Philemon was a man who was relatively more wealthy than other Christians there, if he had a house large enough to accommodate the group's gatherings.[78] This would have given him a higher status than others within the group, a status that Paul consistently respected in this letter. Benefactors were expected to provide for others, partly because it increased their own honor and status. Here in v 7 Paul continued to lay the groundwork for the appeal that is coming in v 17. He was establishing Philemon's record of Christian love, which was a legitimate credit to him, because he will call upon Philemon to show that love to Onesimus in the present situation. The gist of vv 4–7 is to establish Philemon's public honor among all the saints.

We should again emphasize that Paul was not manipulating Philemon with flattery that appealed to selfishness.[79] It is perfectly reasonable to ask

---

[78] On average group size and ancient associations: Philip H. Harland, *Associations, Synagogues, and Congregations: Claiming a Place in Ancient Mediterranean Society*, 2nd ed. (Waco, TX: Baylor University Press, 2013), 13; Richard S. Ascough, "Paul and Associations," in *Paul in the Greco-Roman World: A Handbook*, ed. J. Paul Sampley, rev. ed. (London; Oxford; New York; New Delhi; Sydney: Bloomsbury; Bloomsbury T&T Clark, 2016), 1:68–89, at 72; and John S. Kloppenborg, *Christ's Associations: Connecting and Belonging in the Ancient City* (New Haven: Yale University Press, 2019), 116.

[79] For an example of what manipulative flattery looks like, see Acts 24.2–4. Weima notes that the charge of manipulation fails because, among other things, Paul nowhere

someone to act in a way that is consistent with their past good actions, especially if they are known to be one who genuinely loves others. Sometimes we need other Christians to help us see how we can apply our proven faith in situations where it has been deficient or lacking. The situation with Onesimus opened an opportunity for Philemon to show the same kind of love that he had shown to others in the past. The problem, of course, was that the relationship between Philemon and Onesimus was that of master and slave (and possibly a strained one at that), and this represented a considerable boundary in their culture. Paul will show Philemon how to overcome this obstacle in v 16. But if Philemon could refresh the hearts of other Christians through acts of love that communicated fellowship and acceptance, then he had every reason to consider showing this same attitude toward Onesimus.

The verse ends with Paul once again addressing Philemon as "**brother**," solidifying the reference to brethren (saints) earlier in the sentence.[80] Philemon truly had been a brother to other Christians. The repetition of the address also serves to indicate a break in the discourse.[81] The spiritual foundation that frames the upcoming request in v 17 has been laid. At this point the letter moves to the personal context between Paul and Philemon.

v 8 Therefore, even though I have much boldness in Christ to order you to do what is fitting,

vv 4–7 established Philemon's honor, as well as the perspective through which Paul wanted Philemon to think about the problem at hand. These are summarized with "**therefore**." If what Paul had said in vv 4–7 was true and correct, then a particular kind of solution to the matter with Onesimus would come from it, one consistent with Philemon's recognized honor and his loving commitment to God's people. Grammatically and rhetorically, however, Paul had some other things that he wanted to include in the matrix of factors that would inform Philemon's decision, and these occupy vv 8–9.

---

resorted to false praise or feigned emotions in this letter, and to read Phlm in terms of modern individualistic sensitivities is to read the letter out of its historical-cultural context. "Paul's Persuasive Prose," 58–59.

[80] Lohse, *Colossians and Philemon*, 195.

[81] Runge, *Discourse Grammar*, 122. This discourse function of the term here undoubtedly accounts for its unusual placement in the sentence. BDF §474, 6.

We must remember that, at this point in the letter, Paul has yet to tell Philemon what he wanted from him. This verse communicates that the yet-unmentioned request was very important to Paul, so important, in fact, that he had every right to use his apostolic authority to command Philemon to do it. But it also communicated Paul's respect for Philemon's position in the problem. For Paul to command Philemon, especially in front of the church (v 2), would have been a public challenge to Philemon's status within the group and especially with Onesimus. An apostolic command in this situation might have had the effect of belittling, humiliating, and embarrassing Philemon and destroying his credibility. It might have publicly communicated that Paul thought Philemon was so incompetent as a Christian leader that Paul had to intervene to make something right. This is the last thing Paul wanted, because it would have effectively ruined the future relationship between Philemon and Onesimus, as well as the relationship between Paul and Philemon. So Paul therefore openly communicated that he would not take an approach with Philemon that damaged his standing with others.

The effect of this verse is that Paul issued a strong request that, pragmatically, approached the force of a command without issuing a command. But we should not simply think of this as a way of disguising a command. The personal and spiritual nature of Paul's intervention is what is important.[82] The love and gentleness of Paul is on display here.[83] He prefaced his appeal by dismissing one of the approaches he could have taken. "**Even though**" communicates the concessive use of the participial phrase that comprises this verse. It is true, that Paul knew how to be **bold** and direct, as Galatians and the Corinthian letters show us at points.[84] His status as an apostle gave him the prerogative to do so, but interestingly that is not the protocol he cited here. He kept the discussion on the level of "**in Christ,**" the common participation of all believers in

---

[82] As Barth and Blanke note, Paul did not "plead, as it were, from a safe distance. He does not pretend to be in the position of an objective judge over Philemon and Onesimus. In every verse (except 15 and perhaps 20) he speaks pointedly of himself, out of a total involvement with the person and the history of the master and the slave; both are his close friends." *Philemon*, 306.

[83] On the features of politeness in the letter, see Scot McKnight, *The Letter to Philemon*, NICNT (Grand Rapids: Eerdmans, 2017), 63, drawing on Andrew Wilson, "The Pragmatics of Politeness and Pauline Epistolography: A Case Study of the Letter of Philemon," *JSNT* 48 (1992): 107–19.

[84] Gal 1.6–9; 1 Cor 5.1–2; 2 Cor 10.2.

the new situation brought about by Christ.[85] Not every situation called for boldness. In fact, if we note how rarely Paul asserted his apostolic boldness, it would seem that in Paul's judgment few situations actually called for such levels of directness. According to 2 Corinthians 10.1, instead Paul's policy was to urge Christians, by the meekness and gentleness of Christ, to do the right thing. In that same context Paul revealed why: because to adopt a general policy of ordering people around would be to use fleshly weapons in the warfare against sin (2 Cor 10.3–6). Warfare against Satan and his kingdom is part of the reality that now exists because of the apocalyptic appearing of Jesus, whose work aims to conquer sin and death, and ultimately destroy them both. The new situation that Christ has brought about creates warfare with the old one. But the warfare is not fought according to the enemy's (fleshly, worldly) methods. It is fought with spiritual weapons, chief of which is love. So here, Paul wanted Philemon to demonstrate his Christian love (v 6), and love cannot be coerced and still be love. Acts of love, by their nature, must come freely from a loving heart. So Paul, out of love and respect for Philemon, signaled that he needed Philemon to act out of uncoerced love in this situation as well.

But what Paul wants in this act of love has yet to be revealed. Instead, it is described here as "**what is fitting**," and that is about as close as the letter gets to a specific request (see also vv 16 and 17). It is roughly equivalent to our expression "do the right thing." For centuries, commentators have guessed, and argued over, exactly what Paul was asking for. Specifically, the main argument has been over whether Paul wanted Philemon to set Onesimus free. While it is certain that most slaves would have greatly preferred freedom over slavery,[86] Paul comes short of asking for Onesimus' freedom in this letter. This lack of specificity has engendered a sometimes-fierce debate over Paul's attitude toward slavery and whether the church is tasked with social reform. It has often been noted that even though Paul never specifically condemned human slavery in his letters, he certainly sowed the seeds that would produce its

---

[85] See McKnight, *Philemon*, 76, who notes the "inaugurated eschatological reality" communicated by the phrase. Dunn suggested that "boldness" here might signal that Paul was subtly acknowledging his social inferiority to Philemon, since "boldness" could describe speech that was unexpected because the speaker was of lesser status than the one addressed. *Colossians and Philemon*, 325.

[86] Peter M. Head, "Onesimus the Letter Carrier," 649–56.

demise among men. Some have even interpreted the vagueness of Paul's language here to indicate uncertainty on Paul's part, that he himself did not know what the correct solution was.[87] But such debates, as useful as they might be, miss the point here.[88] What Paul wanted was for Philemon to act out of love, as a new man in Christ Jesus. That is, "the right thing" here is the *Christian* thing to do.[89] He wanted Philemon to act according to the new situation that Jesus has established, a situation in which our actions deny the flesh and, by that denial, destroy it and its works. As noted above, Christian love can be defined as a commitment to what is good or best for others first. In any given situation, love might find several different expressions that are suitable for the moment. Acting out of love is not something that can be spelled out with an endless set of commands that cover every possible scenario of human interaction. It is a spiritual quality that is manifested by spiritual people who, like Philemon, are endowed with a knowledge of what is good (v 6) and who approach life's issues with spiritual wisdom and discernment. Love adapts to the current situation without ever diverting from its commitment to the good of others. "What was fitting" in the situation now before Philemon could equally have been several things. There was more than one solution to this problem.[90] Setting Onesimus free *might* have been one of the options, but we do not know enough about the actual problem to say that with certainty. But Philemon *did* know the situation, and his Christian love would be able to discern the best solution, and Paul would be happy with that.

v 9 instead, because of love, I appeal—such a one as Paul the aged and now also a prisoner of Christ Jesus—

---

[87] So Barclay, "Paul, Philemon and the Dilemma," 175.

[88] Not to mention that those who want to read Phlm as calling for Onesimus' freedom sometimes seem to be reading modern ideas of freedom into the context here. In the Hellenistic world, the lives of ex-slaves were often not significantly different from when they were slaves. "The act of manumission did not significantly change the circumstances of most slaves, or how they were perceived or treated." Setting Onesimus free would have changed very little about the situation, and might, in fact, have made Onesimus' life even harder. Craig S. de Vos, "Once a Slave, Always a Slave? Slavery, Manumission, and Relational Patterns in Paul's Letter to Philemon," *JSNT* 82 (2001): 89–105, at 100.

[89] Lohse, *Colossians and Philemon*, 198; Fitzmyer, *Philemon*, 104; Dunn, *Colossians and Philemon*, 325.

[90] *Cf.* Lohse, *Colossians and Philemon*, 202: "Rather he is encouraged to let love do its work, for love is resourceful enough to find the right way in accomplishing the good."

Instead of using his rightful authority as an apostle to issue a command, Paul chose instead to make an **appeal,**[91] leaving the decision in Philemon's hands. Demand comes from authority as compulsion, but appeal comes from friendship as encouragement. The key difference: the appeal comes **because of love**. It is not just a love for Onesimus or a love for Philemon that prompted Paul's method here. Rather, Christian love itself demanded that Paul take the course that was most beneficial for both men, and in this case it meant refraining from giving Philemon a direct apostolic command while at the same time voicing what was necessary for Onesimus. From the legal point of view, the right of what to do lay with Philemon, but Paul was not writing from the legal point of view. He was writing from a higher perspective, that of "in Christ." Additionally, Paul was modelling the very approach he wanted Philemon to take: Paul was dealing with Philemon out of love just as Philemon needed to deal with Onesimus out of love. In so doing, Paul was demonstrating what power in the kingdom looks like among brethren. *Cf.* Matt 20.24–28. "Paul has—ironically—exercised his apostolic authority by *not* exercising it, but rather by imitating the cruciform love of Christ."[92] The appeal here also stands on the basis established in vv 4–7, of Philemon's established record of demonstrating his faith in love towards saints.

---

[91] This verse contains a well-known grammatical difficulty, namely, the verb often translated "I appeal" (Greek *parakalō*) lacks an object (which is not usual). Normally, an author will say "I ask you to ___" (using an infinitive) or "I am asking so that …" (using a *hina* clause), but here we simply have "I ask you," leaving the content of the request unknown (in 1 Cor 4.13 Paul also uses the verb without an object, but there the sense of the verb is "we conciliate," which does not need an object). A similar construction appears in 2 Cor 10.1 "I Paul myself am urging you by the meekness and gentleness of Christ," but the content of the request is eventually picked up in v 2 with "I am asking you that, when I am present, …." A similar thing may be going on here, since the verb is repeated in v 10. The result is that we can understand the words in between to be parenthetical: "I appeal to you—such a one as Paul the aged, and now also a prisoner of Christ Jesus—I ask you concerning …" (Pearson, "Assumptions," 258). But this grammatical solution may not cover all that is going on here. Since v 4, Paul has been laying a careful foundation, brick by brick as it were, to set the proper frame for understanding the request that in coming in v 17. The use of "I appeal" here without an object could also be Paul's methodical care at work. He had just said in v 8 that he would not command Philemon. Instead, he says here, "I am making an appeal," which he further characterizes as coming from one who is now an old man and a prisoner. That is, the verb without an object simply serves to highlight, emphatically, the contrast between demand (v 8) and appeal in Paul's approach to Philemon.

[92] Gorman, *Cruciformity*, 198.

This is the only place in Paul's writings where he explicitly refers to himself as **aged,**[93] or an old(er) man. The term certainly meant something different in Paul's culture than it does in ours. First, the numbers involved seem to have been different.[94] Generally speaking, in Paul's day there probably existed at any given point mostly two generations of people.[95] "Young" men were those under the age of 30, and "old" men were those between the ages of 30–59 years. We do not know the dates for Paul's birth or death, so we do not know Paul's age when he wrote Phlm. It is not unlikely that Paul was in his mid-to-late 50's during his confinement in Rome (Acts 28.30–31).[96] Second, in 21st-century America, the phrase "old man" is nearly a synonym for senility and carries with it much negative stereotyping. In our culture, an old man is often known for what he is not: he is not strong, and his senses of sight and hearing are not sharp, as well as his memory. An old man is past his prime, and to act as if he were not is comical. These negative perceptions existed in Paul's day as well, but there was also a set of positive perceptions attached to age that are, in my opinion, so not readily associated with an "old man" in 21st century America. Old age (remember, ages 30–59) could represent superior

---

[93] The Greek word translated "aged" is *presbutēs,* but some scholars have suggested that the original text of Phlm read *presbeutēs,* which means "ambassador," on the argument that the meaning "ambassador" fits the context better (since Paul was appealing on behalf of another person like an ambassador would do), and some have questioned how "old man" could make sense in this context. The matter cannot be decided on orthography (spelling) alone, since variations in the spellings of Greek words are well known from ancient manuscripts (including the spelling of *presbutēs;* see Henry St. John Thackeray, *A Grammar of the Old Testament in Greek: According to the Septuagint* (Cambridge: Cambridge University Press, 1909), 97). The ancient translations consistently rendered the word as meaning "old man," and Hock has shown that this meaning makes perfect sense when the rhetoric of Phlm is recognized ("Paul's Plea." See also Metzger, *Textual Commentary,* 588). See also J. N. Birdsall, "*Presbutēs* in Philemon 9: A Study in Conjectural Emendation," *NTS* 39 (1993): 625–30.

[94] It is proper to note that determining lifespans in the Greco-Roman world is extremely difficult. See Tim G. Parkin, *Demography and Roman Society* (Baltimore: Johns Hopkins University Press, 1992); Walter Scheidel, ed., *Debating Roman Demography* (Leiden: Brill, 2001); Keith Hopkins, "On the Probable Age Structure of the Roman Population," *Population Studies* 20 (1966): 245–64. A good overview of the problems and complexities of the topic is Walter Scheidel, "Roman Age Structure: Evidence and Models," *JRS* 91 (2001): 1–26.

[95] Barclay, "There is Neither Old nor Young?," 228.

[96] The chronology of Paul's life is not much help, since we do not know precise dates for many of the events mentioned in Acts or his letters. It would not be unreasonable to assume that Paul was 30 years old (or almost so) when we first meet him in Acts 7, since he is there called a "young man" and 30 was the age in which a man was considered eligible to participate in public life. If Paul's confinement in Rome was from 60–61 AD, then Paul could have been around 55 years old then.

wisdom, maturity in decision-making, and fuller life experience, and by virtue of these things it was assumed the older generation generally had acquired more sense.[97] In this way, then, there was a kind of moral power associated with old age. We can also safely assume that Paul thought in terms of the Law, where respect for the aged was demanded (Lev 19.32; *cf.* Prov 16.31; 20.29), akin to children respecting their parents.

What, exactly, did Paul infer by calling himself "aged" in this context? Why does he bring this up? The fact that Paul otherwise avoided this self-characterization might suggest that it was a factor that, in his estimation, did not automatically act as a "trump card" in discussions. Paul never argued for a position based on his age or the age of his opponents.[98] The truth found in Christ was what mattered. Instead, it is probably better to understand Paul's self-characterization here as part of his overall rhetorical appeal. "Aged" was meant as a request for Philemon to recognize and give due respect to Paul and to the spiritual wisdom behind his appeal (*cf.* Lev 19.32), and to evoke a sense of compassion (pathos) for Paul as an aged "father" who deserved the support of Philemon by granting his request.[99]

The repetition from v 1 of the fact that Paul was now a **prisoner** because of his service to the Messiah (**Christ**) of Israel, **Jesus**, reminded Philemon that Paul needed his help. This complements an aspect of "aged," of someone who needs support. But it also evokes a sense of commitment, as the reason for Paul's restricted condition was that he was faithfully serving the Messiah regardless of the personal consequences to himself. By adding these descriptions of himself here, Paul was not merely trying to play on Philemon's sympathies (although his sympathies were a legitimate part of his consideration), but was also showing Philemon how his help in the present case was a "reasonable" thing to do. Here was an older, wiser man in a situation where his ability to act was limited, who

---

[97] *Cf.* Plutarch, "Whether An old Man Should Engage in Public Affairs," *Moralia* 783b-797f ("An old man active in word and deed and held in honor is a sight to arouse reverence" (788a-b), "the hoary hair and the wrinkles that people make fun of appear as witnesses to a man's experience and strengthen him by the aid of persuasiveness and the reputation for character" (789d) (Fowler, LCL), and Cicero, *De Senectute,* 17–26 ("For just as wise men, when they are old, take delight in the society of youths endowed with sprightly wit, and the burdens of age are rendered lighter to those who are courted and highly esteemed by the young, so young men find pleasure in their elders, by whose precepts they are led into virtue's paths" (26)) (Falconer, LCL).

[98] As rightly noted by Lampe, "Affects and Emotions," 65 fn 11.

[99] So Hock, "Paul's Plea," 79; Lampe, "Affects and Emotions" 65; Fitzmyer, *Philemon,* 106.

needed a friend's help. It would not be unreasonable for a man of love and faith, like Philemon, to act in such a situation.

v 10 I appeal to you concerning my child, whom I have begotten in my bonds, Onesimus.

"**I appeal**"[100] picks up the same verb from the unfinished sentence in v 9, but now advances the foundation of Paul's request further. Whether Paul was making this appeal at the request of Onesimus, or he was appealing because he knew something about the situation and was in a position to address it, we do not know, nor does it especially matter. While there is a line between intervening in a problematic situation because one is invited to do so on the one hand, and inserting oneself into a matter and becoming a meddler on the other hand, we should trust Paul's judgment here (either way). Paul was following his own directive to "bear one another's burdens" (Gal 6.2), and we may assume that Paul likewise did not violate his own directive to avoid being a busybody in the affairs of other people (2 Thes 3.11–12). There may be circumstances that compel a mature Christian to intervene into a situation between brethren without invitation, but there are no specific "rules" in the New Testament for when to do so. It requires above all a spiritual maturity (Gal 6.1, "you who are spiritual") to weigh the advantages against the disadvantages, and to proceed with loving discretion.

We have read the letter and we know whom Paul was talking about. But try, for a moment, to put yourself in the place of Philemon reading this letter for the very first time. Philemon did not yet know what Paul was asking for (that will not come until vv 16–17), nor whom it involved. Everything up to this point has been build-up, frame-setting, and contextualizing so that that when the appeal itself came, it would be heard in the proper way.[101]

---

[100] A well-known grammatical issue in this verse involves the verb *parakalō* with the genitive and the preposition *peri*. The question is: does this combination mean "I ask on behalf of," or does it mean "I ask for"? In the latter case, Paul would be asking for Onesimus himself, presumably for Onesimus to be "transferred" to his use on the basis that Onesimus is now considered Paul's "child" (see below). However, there is enough evidence in non-Biblical Greek to be confident that this expression means "on behalf of" or "concerning" (see the evidence cited in Fitzmyer, *Philemon*, 107. Also Arzt-Grabner, "The Case of Onesimos," 604–5, citing examples from the papyri).

[101] Petersen noted that, in this letter, Paul deferred discussion of the negative side of the situation until he had presented its positive side. *Rediscovering Paul*, 73.

Paul was appealing to Philemon on behalf of someone whom he had "**begotten**" and therefore was now, figuratively, his "**child**." Paul had taught this yet-unnamed person the gospel and led him to obey it. Paul often used the image of a father in his letters to describe the relationship he had with those whom he had taught and nurtured in the faith of Jesus Christ.[102] The imagery suggests care and concern, the provision of learning and moral guidance, as well as love. Whoever this person was, he was near and dear to Paul himself, and that should mean something to Philemon. If Philemon respected Paul (and there is no indication he did not), this description carefully communicated to Philemon that his attitude toward this person would be bound up with his relationship with Paul. He must think of, and treat, this person as someone who is special to Paul. But the imagery also carefully anticipates, in a gentle kind of way, something that Paul will spell out in v 16: if this person has been "begotten" by Paul and is now Paul's "child" in the Lord, then this same person is now a brother in the Lord, a fellow Christian.

Again, the change of situation brought about by the work of Christ can be discerned in the language of this verse. Note how Paul redefined Onesimus here. According to the secular world in which everyone lived, the correct designation for Onesimus would have been "your slave." But Paul redefined Onesimus. He is now "my child." At least two things are going on here: 1) the change from slave to child (and implied: now fellow Christian), and 2) the shift from Onesimus belonging to Philemon, to Onesimus belonging to Paul. This latter change is not meant to be literal, as if Paul were now claiming some actual legal right over Onesimus that superseded Philemon's right as slave owner. The term "child" is figurative,[103] but its force is to include Onesimus within the Christian family. Onesimus was a new person,[104] and Philemon's attitude needed to change accordingly. In Philemon's world, family was the closest bond a person knew, and family members were treated with a deference that did not extend to others.[105] The frequent use of family metaphors (such

[102] Gal 4.19; 1 Cor 4.14, 17; 2 Cor 12.14; 1 Thes 2.11; 1 Tim 1.2; Titus 1.4; *cf.* Phil 2.22; 1 Thes 2.7.

[103] Hock, "Paul's Plea," 78 fn 40 notes that "It was conventional for old people—free or slave—to regard a younger slave as a child." Paul was using conventional language here, but, in typical fashion, investing it with new meaning in a Christian context.

[104] Barclay, "*Koinōnia*," 160. Onesimus' new birth indicates the apocalyptic newness of his identity.

[105] See deSilva, *Honor, Patronage, Kinship & Purity*, 166–74.

as "household," "brethren," *etc.*) among the early Christians signals that the preferential treatment experienced in physical families was to be replicated in the family of God. "Give preference to one another in honor," Paul said (Rom 12.10). But the claim that Onesimus "belongs" to Paul as his child was a gentle assertion of Paul's apostolic status into this situation, based on the priority of the gospel and kingdom of God over all things. The issue before Philemon was no longer just a civil matter, with the primary question being Philemon's rights under the law. The issue was now a kingdom matter, with the primary question being how to treat a brother in Christ, and in the kingdom Paul had a place that Philemon needed to respect. In the kingdom, Paul had a legitimate claim on Onesimus. However, this claim was not presented in terms of rights or authority. Paul presented it instead as the interest of a father for a child. In other words, even though Paul was strongly hinting at his superior status over Philemon in the kingdom, he did so with the gentlest of terms and in a way that Philemon could sympathize with it.

Paul was **in bonds** when this person obeyed the gospel. Witherington is probably correct when he insists on understanding the term here (Greek *desmois*) to mean "chains," and not generically "imprisonment."[106] Even in chains, which was considered shameful (see the Introduction), Paul spoke the gospel to whomever he could. He told the praetorian guard (presumably in Rome) about his preaching (Phil 1.13), and he taught whomever would come to him while under house arrest in Rome (Acts 28.30–31). He told Timothy that, for the gospel, he experienced "hardship even to imprisonment as a criminal; but the word of God is not imprisoned" (2 Tim 2.9). It was under these circumstances that Onesimus had come to hear and obey the gospel from Paul.

The self-characterization of Paul as "in bonds" complements the previous metaphor of "my child." Paul presented himself as a father whose interest in his child should be respected, but also as one who was now in a situation in which he relied upon the help of others. When Paul wrote this letter, he was not free to move about as he wished. He could not tend to the people in the churches as he wished, and he needed his fellow workers (like Philemon, v 1) and fellow soldiers for these tasks. Such is the gist of Paul reminding Philemon of his restricted condition

---

[106] Ben Witherington, III, "Was Paul a Jailbird? A Response to the Response," *JETS* 61.3 (2018): 559–61. One could be in Roman chains and yet not be in a Roman prison, as Paul was in Acts 28.30.

(he had mentioned it before in v 1). Combined, the family metaphor and the mention of being in bonds communicate the sense "Philemon, I have this 'child' that I need to care for, but I'm in chains right now, and so I'm calling on you to help me in this situation." The effect is also to complement what Paul said in v 8. Instead of ordering Philemon about what to do, Paul empowered Philemon by laying before him a situation in which Philemon (and uniquely Philemon) could help, just as he had always been willing to help other Christians in the past (v 7). By presenting Philemon with a yet-unknown opportunity to do good, and based on the proven past generosity of Philemon, Paul created the context in which the action could spring from Philemon's own heart (see v 14 below). If Philemon were the man that Paul described in vv 4–7, Philemon would want to act for Paul's interests and help Paul's "child." We can imagine that, by the time Philemon had read these lines, he was thinking "Sure, Paul, I'd be happy to help someone whom you call 'your child.' " Again, Paul was not manipulating Philemon, tricking him into helping Onesimus. He was instead reminding Philemon of the new orientation his life had as a Christian, an orientation that had been proven by past deeds of faith and love, and trusting that Philemon was sincere and would further demonstrate his love and faith when the need arose.[107]

Who was this person, to whom Paul's descriptions had been building? It was none other than Philemon's slave **Onesimus**. His name comes after the descriptive phrases in a kind of apex. The name Onesimus was a typical slave name (it means "useful").[108] There are at least 185 known examples of male slaves in Rome with this name from the extant ancient papyri, plus feminine and diminutive forms of the name.[109] Many more examples are known from other ancient documents.[110] We know nothing about Onesimus' life or background, how he became a slave, his age or

---

[107] Dunn notes, "Paul's rhetoric here, as elsewhere, should not be denigrated as manipulative and contrived. It is typical of a leader with a strong personality that he should sincerely want to encourage and leave it open to his audience to respond of their own free will, while at the same time being so convinced of the rightness of his own opinion that he naturally seeks to persuade them to share it. In the end it is Paul's courtesy and restraint which leaves the greatest impression here." *Colossians and Philemon*, 323.

[108] For this reason, it is not likely that Onesimus was this man's original name. Slave owners often renamed their slaves. See Lewis, "Notes on Slave Names."

[109] H. Solin, *Die stadromischen Sklavennamen. Ein Namenbuch, part 2: Greischische Namen.* FASk Beiheft 2 (Stuttgart, 1996), 65–68; cited in Peter Arzt-Grabner, "The Case of Onesimos," 596 fn 37.

[110] Arzt-Grabner, "The Case of Onesimos," 596. See also *NewDocs* 4:179–81.

how long he had been a slave when Paul wrote to Philemon, what kind of work he did for Philemon, or how Philemon had treated him. In the first century, slaves could be workers in the house, workers in the fields, they could be used as messengers or couriers, or as household or estate managers, or as personal servants, and some were craftsmen, tutors, secretaries, and nurses.[111] We also do not know why Onesimus was away from Philemon, or how he had come to know Paul (see Introduction). These issues are part of the context that was known to all the parties of this letter and did not need to be spelled out.

We cannot help but think that Onesimus' conversion was news to Philemon, that this was a shocking new development that would (as Paul was arguing) change everything in the relationship between Philemon and his slave. The nature of the former relationship between Onesimus and Philemon is unknown to us, nor does it particularly matter. The effect of this (new?) piece of information is the point. We can almost imagine a pause on Philemon's part when he came to this name in the letter. "The 'child' that Paul wants me to help him with is—Onesimus?" Whatever Philemon had thought about Onesimus before, whatever his attitude or feelings had come to be, or whatever wrong might have been done—all of that needed to be adjusted and reconfigured to line up with the fact that these two men were now brothers in Christ. That is what was most important now, and that is what would determine the course of action (for both men) in the coming days. As noted in the Introduction, and as Paul will make clear in v 16, this new mapping of the relationship between Philemon and Onesimus did not entail the erasure of the master-slave relationship between them. That relationship would remain, but it would not remain as it had been before. Now it would be different, because it would be informed by an even higher one that cut across all social boundaries, namely, their bond as brothers in Christ.

Paul's method here is practical for us today. Paul did not begin his letter with the "cold hard facts" simply laid upon Philemon like the blow of a hammer. He could have said "Listen, Philemon, Onesimus is a Christian now, so I expect you to do some serious adjusting of your attitude." Instead, Paul built a picture of relationships in which Philemon himself had demonstrated excellence (vv 4–7), and then introduced the key fact that Onesimus was now a member in those relationships

---

[111] Arzt-Grabner, "The Case of Onesimos," 600.

(vv 8–10). Once the foundation was laid, Paul then gently brought Philemon to the problem. This is a fine example of "speaking the truth in love" (Eph 4.15) and speech "seasoned with salt" (Col 4.6).

v 11 who formerly was useless to you but now he is well-useful to both you and me,

This clause is probably a play on the meaning of Onesimus' name, "useful."[112] The adjective *chrēstos*, which Paul uses here in two modified forms, is a synonym of *onēsimos*.[113] In fact, some slaves were named "Chrestus."[114] Names were generally more significant in Paul's world than they are in ours. A name represented a person, and often the name's meaning summarized a person.[115] Previously Onesimus had not lived up to his name, but now he did.

When Paul says that Onesimus was **formerly useless** to Philemon, it could mean that Onesimus' absence from Philemon's house had resulted in a loss of labor. A slave who was not there to serve was useless. However, the background could have been something else, and our speculation will be of no benefit. *If* "useless" refers to something about Onesimus' behavior, then this would be the first clear indication in the letter that there was something wrong between Philemon and Onesimus. However, we do not know the history between these men, and frankly it does not matter because a specific wrong is not the focus of the letter. If some wrong was in view, it did not need to be re-hashed in this letter. It is possible, however, that "was useless to you" does not refer to some lack or wrong on Onesimus' part, but simply to the way that Philemon routinely viewed him.[116] The lack of mention of any misdeeds on Onesimus' part, and the

---

[112] LSJ 1231.

[113] Some scholars (Lohse, Bird, et al) note that *chrēstos* would have sounded much like *christos* in the way Greek was pronounced, and thus suggest that the word here provided an allusion Onesimus' new likeness to Christ as a disciple. I remain skeptical about this, but the wordplay was employed by later Christians (see Lohse, *Colossians and Philemon*, 200 fn 36).

[114] Lightfoot, *Colossians and Philemon*, 308 fn 4. Other Greek slave names were Karpos (Latinized: Carpus; "fruitful"), Symphoros ("profitable"), *etc.* (*Ibid.*; Fitzmyer, *Philemon*, 107). Apparently, the association of *chrēstos* with slaves was so common that in one Greek inscription slaves are simply referred to as *"chrēstoi."* Lewis, "Notes on Slave Names," 185.

[115] See the discussion in Lightfoot, *Colossians and Philemon*, 338.

[116] "this contrastive pair built on the meaning of the name Onesimus does not necessarily have to point to a reality behind both elements in the pair." Pao, *Colossians and Philemon*, 388; also Arzt-Grabner, "How to Deal with Onesimos," 121.

letter's focus on the spiritual dimensions of the problem, would point to this interpretation. In this way, the difference between "was useless" and "now he is useful" does not describe Onesimus *per se*, but serves more as a description of Philemon's attitude, the way he thought of Onesimus, which was the focus of Paul's appeal (v 17). The word "useless" appears in ancient documents where masters describe their attitudes toward their slaves.[117] However, the practical usefulness of Onesimus himself is not out of the picture, as v 13 will show.

The focus of the letter is on the change in the situation because Onesimus had entered into the fellowship in Christ Jesus. "**But now**" makes all the difference.[118] Onesimus, too, now participated in the apocalyptic newness in Christ. The perspective of the letter is forward-looking, and in this sense it is eschatological. What should be done now and forwards, in the new situation in Christ that embraced both Onesimus and Philemon, was the issue. The viewpoint needed to be one of forgetting what lay behind and pressing forward to what lies ahead (Phil 3.13). As Paul will point out in v 18, this does not necessarily mean that Philemon would be forced to lose any monetary value that might have been at stake. But it did mean that the past way of looking at Onesimus had to end, and a new way of viewing this man now had to determine every other aspect of the two men's relationship.

It is not hard to imagine how Onesimus was **now useful** to Paul. Onesimus could be another Timothy, another Epaphroditus.[119] He could help Paul spread the gospel and tend to the churches. He could deliver letters and verbal messages to Christians and to churches. As Christianity spread, Paul needed such fellow workers anyway, but he especially needed them when he was in chains. But how was Onesimus now useful to Philemon? We probably should not try to imagine specific tasks. The point instead is the new attitude that Paul was presenting to

[117] Examples in cited in *Ibid.*, 122–23.

[118] The connective *de* is not simply contrastive, but signals a new development that is about to be expressed. What follows *de* "is a new, distinct development in the story or argument." Runge, *Discourse Grammar*, 31. "But now" especially signals the change of things that has resulted from the work of Christ: Rom 3.21; 6.22; 7.6; 11.30; 16.26; 1 Cor 7.14; 15.20; Gal 3.25; 4.9; Eph 2.2, 2, 11, 13; 5.8; Col 1.21–22; 3.8; 1 Tim 1.13; 2 Tim 1.10; Heb 9.26; 12.26; 1 Pet 2.10, 25. McKnight (*Philemon*, 88) says it is an open question whether "now" in this text is a signal of new creation or simply a temporal marker of the time in the story of Onesimus. I am suggesting that in this case, it is both.

[119] The same word (*euchrēstos*) is used of John Mark in 2 Tim 4.11, where Paul said he was "useful for service."

Philemon. Rather than being dismissive of Onesimus as a useless slave who could not be counted on, Paul called on Philemon to see Onesimus now as a different person—because that is what he now was, in Christ. Conversion means change. Onesimus had now committed himself to being remade in Christ, re-created in righteousness and holiness (Eph 4.24). Philemon now needed to think of Onesimus first and foremost as a brother in Christ, as a fellow partaker of the new age, and as a fellow heir of the world to come. As a Christian, Onesimus was now another brother who could encourage and serve other Christians in the faith, including Philemon. This is the sense in which Onesimus was now **well-useful**,[120] or very useful, to Philemon. He would be useful to Philemon as every Christian is useful to every other Christian.

Beyond that, however, the letter envisions Onesimus as still being the slave of Philemon. Whether that would, could, or should change was simply not the concern of this letter. The socio-cultural relationship between the two men still existed, but as a changed man Onesimus could no longer be seen as, or behave as, a useless servant to Philemon. He would now serve Philemon as if he were serving Christ himself, and make himself useful in the true fulfillment of his role (see also v 16), and Philemon needed to consider him accordingly. There can be little doubt that with Onesimus' conversion, Paul had taught him the same thing he taught other slaves: "Slaves, in all things obey those who are your masters on earth, not with external service, as those who merely please men, but with sincerity of heart, fearing the Lord. Whatever you do, do your work heartily, as for the Lord rather than for men, knowing that from the Lord you will receive the reward of the inheritance. It is the Lord Christ whom you serve. For he who does wrong will receive the consequences of the wrong which he has done, and that without partiality" (Col 3.22–25 NASB).

v 12 whom I have sent[121] back to you, himself,[122] that is, my own heart.

---

[120] I have translated the Greek word (*euchrēstos*) this way to bring out the fact that it is a compound word composed of *eu* (well) + *chrēstos* (useful). The word is also used in 2 Tim 2.21.

[121] The verb is in the aorist tense. In this context it does not likely suggest that Paul had sent Onesimus at some vague point before he wrote the letter, but it is probably best to understand it as an "epistolary aorist" in which a writer puts himself in the time frame of the reader(s) (see BDF §334). In this case, the aorist would communicate nearly a stative temporal sense, so I have translated "I have sent." By the time Philemon read the letter, Onesimus would have already been sent (and arrived).

[122] A textual variant supplies the imperative "receive" here (see v 17), to supply a verb

Out of the utmost respect for Philemon, Paul had **sent** Onesimus **back** to Philemon (many modern scholars believe that Onesimus himself delivered this letter). He will explain his reason for doing this in the next two verses.[123] The verb "sent back" does *not* necessarily imply that Philemon had originally sent Onesimus to Paul.[124] We do not know how or why Onesimus came to be with Paul, how long he had been absent from Philemon, or how much of that absence was spent with Paul learning the gospel. What was important was that Paul was not going to keep him.

"I have sent back" clearly implies that Paul was acting with his apostolic authority in this situation, and Onesimus had agreed to submit. It almost seems to suggest that Paul was aware of some issue between Philemon and Onesimus. At the least it suggests that Paul thought there was the possibility that Onesimus' separation from Philemon might have become problematic. Whatever Paul knew, or was thinking, he judged that, in this situation, it would be best for Onesimus to return home, even if Philemon were to send him right back to Paul (v 13). Had Onesimus' time with Paul, learning the gospel, created a situation in which Paul feared that Onesimus had been away from home too long, and that this might now be a problem? Had Onesimus left Philemon improperly, and Paul now judged that it was time for this situation to end? As with so many other things in the background of this letter, we do not know. But whatever was going on, Paul thought it would be best to "reset" the situation, have Onesimus return home, and let the situation

---

for the pronoun *auton*, which stands alone. This probably represents a scribal attempt to make the syntax smoother. Metzger, *Textual Commentary*, 589.

[123] Deut 23.15–16 humanely forbade the return of runaway slaves to their owners. The question is sometimes raised why Paul did not follow it here, since he often resorted to the Law as a paradigm for Christian behavior (through his quotations of the Old Testament). The possibilities are 1) that Onesimus was not a runaway (and not a Jew) and thus Paul saw that the treatment demanded in Deut did not apply in this situation (*cf.* McKnight, *Philemon*, 89–90), but Roman law demanded his return; or 2) that Paul simply did not see himself as bound to follow the Torah, partly because Christ's demand for brotherly love superseded the Law (Witherington, *Philemon, Colossians, and Ephesians*, 75 fn 39; also his *Grace in Galatia: A Commentary on St. Paul's Letter to the Galatians* (Grand Rapids: Eerdmans, 1998), 341–56). Even when Paul quoted the Law and saw it as a paradigm for Christian behavior, it was always a specifically Jesus-oriented, Christological interpretation of the Law that resulted, not of the Law for its own sake.

[124] Even though the term was used in legal contexts in the sense of sending someone up to a higher authority for legal adjudication, no such context exists here. Paul was not suggesting that Philemon was a "higher court" for Onesimus' "case." Pearson, "Assumptions," 263–65.

from that point lie within the power of Philemon. And Onesimus' willing compliance with Paul's demand was a key part of making this work.

Paul had sent Onesimus **himself.**[125] The reason for this emphasis is given in the next verse.

Paul loaded the description of his action by characterizing the sending of Onesimus as the sending of his own heart to Philemon. The word for "**heart**" here is the same one as in vv 7 and 20. What does it mean that Paul had, in the person of Onesimus, sent his heart back to Philemon? Paul's heart was bound up with the presence of Onesimus. By sending Onesimus back, Paul was, in effect, pouring out his heart to Philemon in the appeal he was making. Onesimus' physical presence with Philemon was an expression of Paul's heart, proof of the sincerity and love in Paul's heart for Philemon. But it also suggests, as v 10 has already communicated, that Onesimus was dear to Paul.[126] Onesimus was, in a figurative sense, Paul's own heart. By sending Onesimus, Paul was sending "a piece of himself" (*cf.* HCSB "as a part of myself"). Subsequently, to receive Onesimus would be to receive Paul's own heartfelt gesture. How Philemon treated Onesimus would be the same thing as how he treated Paul's own heart.

v 13 whom I was wanting[127] to keep for myself, so that he might serve me on your behalf in the bonds of the gospel,

This verse explains the "himself" from the previous verse. Paul's personal preference was to **keep** Onesimus with himself and avoid the expense, rigor, and danger of the trip for Onesimus. Paul could have simply sent a letter to Philemon, by the hand of another one of his fellow workers,

---

[125] "Himself" is emphatic here, since Onesimus was already grammatically referenced in the relative pronoun "whom."

[126] The Greek word here, *splanchna*, can also refer to the loins of a father. In Sophocles' *Antigone* we hear of "one from your own loins" (*ek splanchnōn;* 1066; Lloyd-Jones, LCL). *Cf.* Artemidorus, *The Interpretation of Dreams*: "children are called *splanchna*" (1.44) and "it is the custom to call the child '*splanchna*' " (5.57). Therefore when Paul says "my own heart (*splanchna*)," it is parallel to "my child" in v 10, but "heart" emphasizes the emotional aspect of Paul's attitude towards Onesimus. *Cf.* Chrysostom: "He [Paul] does not give the bare name, but replaces it with a term of respect, which is warmer than 'child.' " My thanks goes to Dr. Evan Blackmore for pointing out these connections.

[127] The verb tense here is imperfect, which carries the idea of imperfective aspect and remoteness, of an action presented to the hearer as unfolding, but not as if it were directly before the hearer. Campbell, *Basics of Verbal Aspect*, 41–42. The result is that Paul presents his wish as something that occupied his thoughts for some time. Also, imperfect verbs tend to present offline (supplemental) information. *Ibid.*, 44.

explaining the new situation and why Onesimus would not be returning home for the foreseeable future. All of that would have been much easier. But Paul refused to do it. He returned Onesimus himself. The disputed element in the situation—Onesimus—would now be under the control of his master Philemon, which was proper and right.

Paul's preference in the matter was not completely selfish. It is not as if Paul wanted to keep Onesimus to bring him tea every afternoon. Paul saw that Onesimus had the qualities necessary to be a good servant of the gospel.[128] This spoke highly of Onesimus. If there was some kind of estrangement between Onesimus and Philemon, v 18 could indicate that Philemon might have felt that he had been wronged financially (perhaps in addition to other wrongs). For Paul to say that he thought Onesimus could **serve** him in the gospel could have gone a long way to allay Philemon's suspicions about Onesimus' present integrity.[129] Traveling as Paul's fellow worker could involve carrying money from churches (Phil 4.18), as well as managing expense money for the trips. It also probably involved faithfully communicating some matters orally (*cf.* Eph 6.21–22). In such matters Paul needed people who would not steal from the churches nor undermine him before others. Onesimus had apparently acted with enough integrity around Paul that the apostle saw in him a man who could be counted on to serve in the work of the gospel. If Paul thought this man was now trustworthy enough to entrust with such important work, this should therefore become a factor in Philemon's judgment and decision.

Even as Paul expressed what he would have preferred, it did not exclude Philemon. Paul understood, and wanted Philemon to know, that if Onesimus helped Paul in the gospel, it always would be **on** Philemon's **behalf**. In other words, Paul would interpret it as a service that originated with Philemon. In this way, Paul continued to express his respect for Philemon's place in the situation. He did not treat Philemon like he was an outsider or that he was "out of the loop" of decision-making now that Onesimus had come to be with Paul. Paul communicated just the

---

[128] Paul always used the verb "to serve" with a religious-theological sense. Pao, *Colossians and Philemon*, 391.

[129] deSilva, *Introduction*, 674, cites the case of the recommendation by Pliny the Younger of Voconius Romanus for an office granted by the emperor Trajan. In that request, "Trajan's favorable judgment of Pliny, not Voconius, will be the basis for Trajan's granting of this favor."

opposite. Although he had a legitimate claim to Onesimus as his "child" in the gospel, Paul was willing to hand the decision in the matter over to Philemon. It is a splendid example of Paul's own exhortation that Christians should subject themselves to one another in the fear of Christ (Eph 5.21) and "give preference to one another in honor" (Rom 12.10). Furthermore, Paul would have interpreted any use of Onesimus as a personal gift to himself—"that he might serve **me** on your behalf." By serving the gospel through Onesimus, Philemon would be serving Paul because Paul's life was joined to the gospel. The language hints at the idea that Paul would then consider himself indebted to Philemon, according to the ancient codes of gift and reciprocity. Philemon's established role as a benefactor of other Christians was intact. Of course, as the apostle in this situation, Paul would rightly have been considered the one having the superior status among the three men, but he was willing to place himself in the social debt of another (who was below him in status) if that fixed the problem.

If we take the word "bonds"[130] literally here (see on v 1), the phrase "**the bonds of the gospel**" could mean "bonds associated with the gospel" (genitive of reference), or bonds for the sake of the gospel, or bonds because of the gospel (genitive of reason), in keeping with the way Paul described his situation in v 1 as a prisoner for the sake of Christ. Paul was literally in Roman custody and wearing restraints (likely chains) as part of that custody, but he viewed them as due to his relationship with, and work for, Christ. As Acts shows, Paul's fetters were not due to illegal conduct on his part. They were, instead, the result of proclaiming the new situation that has been opened by the death and resurrection of Jesus, a situation that—to the disapproval of many—relativized the social barriers that many considered so important in their culture. Paul wore the chains "of the gospel" because he had been fighting the good fight, bringing the message of the Messiah's new kingdom to displace the kingdom of Satan. The present situation was one in which Philemon, through Onesimus, could participate in this spiritual warfare. Also, as in vv 1, 8, and 10, mention of his bonds underscored the practical need Paul had for a man like Onesimus at this time, because he could not move about as he wished.

---

[130] There is another Greek word for "chains" (*halusis*), which Paul used in Eph 6.20 and 2 Tim 1.16. "Bonds" (*desmos* in the plural) is a more generic term.

v 14 but[131] I wished[132] to do nothing apart from your consent, so that your good deed would not be, as it were,[133] according to necessity but rather according to your own free will.

Verse 13 is as close as Paul came to inserting his own preference into the decision that Philemon would make. As soon as he expressed it, however, he followed it with "**but**"—effectively deferring to Philemon. It could be argued that Paul did not express his own intentions about Philemon here in order to coach Philemon's decision, but simply for the sake of complete transparency. Adding this piece of information only made it clear that Paul refused to act in his own interests in this problem, even though Onesimus was his "child" in the Lord (v 10). Paul respected that there was another dimension of the problem that properly was the concern of Philemon, and Paul refused to rob Philemon of his rightful part in the situation. It is the same attitude as that expressed in v 8: Paul refused to use his superior status as an apostle to override Philemon's interests.

This verse further explains why Paul took the apparently contradictory course of returning Onesimus when he wanted Onesimus to stay with him (v 13). He wanted Philemon to know what was going on, and for everything to be done as his decision, with his approval. In the end, it was not about Paul, but about Philemon. Paul refused to impose his opinion upon Philemon or force an outcome upon him. The return of Onesimus was proof that Paul was acting out of love for Philemon (just as Philemon had acted out of love for other saints (v 7), and as Paul prayed he would yet do (vv 4–6)). That is, he did not say "Philemon, the best thing for you to do would be to let me keep Onesimus here for a while, so that is what I have decided to do." Even if Philemon would have been so gracious as to consent to something like that (for it would have rewarded Onesimus'

---

131 "But" translates the Greek connective *de* here, signaling a new development in the discussion. See comments on v 12 above.

132 The word here (Greek *thelō*) can sometimes have the sense of a resolution, something that one has in mind for oneself. BDAG 448. In v 13 Paul expressed what he wanted, but here he expressed what he chose. Lightfoot, *Colossians and Philemon*, 339, citing usage in Epictetus.

133 There is a word in this verse that often does not make it into English translations, the Greek word *ōs* ("as"). The NASB renders it here with "in effect." The addition of this little word softens the language ever so slightly (Lightfoot, *Colossians and Philemon*, 340), so that Paul avoided the idea that he had actually commanded Philemon to do something. Instead, he said that he did not want Philemon's response to be *like* something he did from necessity.

absence and undercut Philemon's place as master), Paul refused to put Philemon in that situation. Nor did Paul say "I'm sending Onesimus back because Roman law requires it." It needed to be handled as a situation between Christians, not just a legal matter.[134] Paul graciously gave the situation to Philemon to handle as his own decision and as an expression of his own faith and love. The power over the situation lay with Philemon. Paul urged, appealed, and encouraged, but in the end he did not force a particular outcome upon him. As Paul said to the Corinthians, "Not that we lord it over your faith, but are workers with you for your joy; for your stand firm in your own faith" (2 Cor 1.24). If Onesimus was to be of service to Paul as a show of faith and love to both men, it would need to come as a freely-chosen act on Philemon's part. That would make it an expression of Philemon's love.

Doing the right thing (a "**good deed**") when one has no other choice (*i.e.*, out of "**necessity**") in the situation is not virtuous. When it came to participating in the collection for the Jerusalem saints, Paul told the Corinthians that their participation was voluntary. "I am not speaking this as a command, but as proving through the earnestness of others the sincerity of your love also" (2 Cor 8.8), and "Each one must do just as he has purposed in his heart, not grudgingly or under compulsion, for God loves a cheerful giver" (2 Cor 9.7). He refused to command them about that effort, because that would ruin the loving character of the project. The whole point was for the Gentile churches to show their love for their Jewish brethren, but it would not be much of a show of love if they had no choice about whether to participate or not. Paul was expressing that same kind of thing to Philemon—even though Paul had yet to say in this letter what good deed he had in mind on Philemon's part. If Philemon had no choice but to go along with what Paul, from an exercise of Paul's will or authority, had already made happen, then it could not be a true act of love on Philemon's part. It would not be good enough for Paul to have decided the situation and ask for Philemon's approval after the fact, nor would it have been enough for Paul to order Philemon about what to do, and for Philemon to simply obey. For this to be an expression of love and faith on Philemon's part (v 5), it had to come from his **own free will**. So Paul sent Onesimus back to Philemon and, in a sense, "reset" the situation so that the decision about Onesimus would come from Philemon.

---

[134] Dunn, *Colossians and Philemon*, 329.

v 15 For perhaps, for this reason, he was away[135] for a short time, that you might have him back forever,

This verse is our only window into Onesimus' departure from Philemon. It tells us nothing about why Onesimus had left, only that the slave had been away from his master. The implication is that something was wrong, that the slave's absence was a problem, but we get no details. If Onesimus had acted wrongly, and if Paul knew about it, Paul kept it in the background as much as possible, because it was not the point of the letter, and bringing it up would not have accomplished any good. He suggested here that the time that Onesimus had been away could be viewed as a period of transition, a kind of "hinge," by which both Philemon and Onesimus could mark the apocalyptic power that changed the relationship between the two of them.[136] Just as in vv 10 and 16, so here in this verse there is an emphasis on the difference and newness of the situation involving these three men, now that Onesimus was a Christian. This is the force of the introductory "**perhaps**." That is, Paul was saying "Maybe you could look at it this way." It does not necessarily imply that Paul was guessing about the providential character of the events that had happened.[137] Consistent with the rest of the letter, Paul wanted Philemon to view the situation from the aspect of the spiritual character of the people involved.

In the phrase "**have him back**," Paul dropped a major hint at the "good deed" (v 14) he had in mind for Philemon. The appeal itself will come in v 17, after another important consideration in v 16.

We do not know how long Onesimus had been away from Philemon. The characterization of this period as "**a short time**" (literally "an hour") must be understood relatively. The same phrase denotes the length of

---

[135] Arzt-Grabner, "The Case of Onesimos," 607 convincingly argues that the passive form *echōristhe* does not mean "was separated" but means "went away." Danker notes that the passive form of *chōrizō* frequently has an active meaning (BDAG 1095).

[136] *Cf.* Barth and Blanke, *Philemon*, 346–50. "The experience of Onesimus is embedded in the cosmic change already effected by God" (350).

[137] Although this is a common interpretation of Paul's statement here. In my opinion, this reads providence into the word "perhaps" and into the passive voice of the verb, without any clue from the context. If Onesimus' separation from Philemon was God's plan, it is reasonable to expect that Paul would have made a significant point about this to Philemon. It would have easily settled much of Philemon's concerns for Paul to say, "Listen, there's a part of this whole thing that you do not know, and that is that God arranged all of this." I do not deny that God's providence was involved, but I question if this verse was about that.

John the Baptist's ministry, which likely spanned many months (John 5.35). The phrase does not necessarily imply that Onesimus had only left Philemon very recently. Llewelyn has argued that the fact that Paul mentions the time period and characterizes it as relatively short (in the big picture of things) might imply that a considerable period of time was involved.[138] In this context, the phrase stands as the contextual opposite of "forever." Any temporal period could be a "short time" compared to eternity (*cf*. Jam 4.14).

While Paul did not characterize it this way, it was as if Onesimus had undergone a death and resurrection in his absence from, and now reappearance to, Philemon. Onesimus was coming back as a new and different man. The contrast between "a short time" and "**forever**" highlights the change that had taken place, the nature of the new situation, and the Christian view of things.[139] Onesimus was simply a slave in his former existence, an existence that fortunately proved to be temporary. When Paul says that Philemon now had Onesimus back "forever," he jumped from the earthly to the spiritual (he did not mean Onesimus would literally be Philemon's slave throughout eternity). Philemon had now come back to live as Christian, to live in a relationship with God and with other Christians that begins here but extends throughout all eternity. It is in this sense that Philemon would now possess Onesimus, in the eternal bond of brotherhood in Christ. When Onesimus stepped out of his old life, out of his old self, and stepped into his new life, and allowed God to make him into a new man in Christ (Eph 4.24), he thereby stepped out of the realm of the temporal and earthly and into the realm of the eternal and spiritual. It is the spiritual, eschatological, apocalyptic, new perspective on the world that Paul emphasized for Philemon here, and this is how Philemon needed to look at Onesimus now. Our eschatological orientation, coupled with the newness we enjoy in Christ, behooves us to look not at the things that are temporal, but at the things that are eternal (*cf*. 2 Cor 4.18). The eternal is, by its nature, spiritual, and what is spiritual is more important and more valuable than what is temporal. Onesimus may have been useless and of little value to Philemon before (or simply viewed that way), but now he was useful and valuable because he shared in what is eternal.

---

[138] *NewDocs* 8:43.

[139] *Cf*. the contrast between temporary and eternal, corresponding to an apocalyptic re-creation and an accompanying new perspective on things, in 2 Cor 4.16–18.

The whole implication of Paul's appeal is that this change in Onesimus' spiritual condition must result in a change in how Philemon thinks of, and relates to, Onesimus in the future. Some scholars describe ancient slaves as people who were "socially dead." Slaves were a commodity. "They were mere tools. At best they were chattel."[140] Such a view toward Onesimus simply would not do in light of his conversion. The spiritual resurrection that made for the newness of Onesimus as a person now called for a correspondingly new attitude toward the relationship Philemon had with him. Of course, Paul exhorted all Christian masters to treat their slaves with a new and different kind of attitude (Eph 6.9; Col 4.1), but here there was something more in play: Onesimus himself was also a Christian.

v 16 no longer as a slave, but as more than a slave, a beloved brother, especially to me, but how much more to you, both in the flesh and in the Lord.

This verse is "the core and highlight" of the letter.[141] It contains the rationale that makes the entire letter work, and makes explicit what was implied in v 10. The fact that Onesimus was now a Christian, and especially Paul's own "child" in the gospel, means that Onesimus was not just a slave anymore. This change in the status of Onesimus is, in a real sense, the core basis for Paul's appeal. By sending this letter Paul was not trying to micromanage how Philemon related to his slaves. The letter's business was far greater than that. The situation was one in which, in a true sense, everything had now changed, and this change was essential for Philemon to reckon going forward.

What is significant here is the coexistence of two ways of looking at Onesimus.[142] He was a slave when he left Philemon, and he came back as Philemon's slave. But he was **no longer**[143] *just* **a slave**, because his

---

[140] Wessels, "The Letter to Philemon in the Context of Slavery," 167.

[141] Barth and Blanke, *Philemon*, 410.

[142] Tucker, *"Paul's Particular Problem,"* 420: "Paul still views Onesimus as a slave. He does not argue that salvation is emancipation from slavery. He does, however, see a transformation in his identity. ... Paul identifies him in the context of his existing identity as a slave *and* his transformed identity 'in Christ" as a beloved brother." (emphasis added)

[143] The Greek word *ouketi*, translated "no longer," does not technically correspond, grammatically, to the verb in v 15 ("that you might have him back"). The effect is that it presents Onesimus' new status not as dependent upon Philemon's acceptance, but as a status that is real in its own right. Lightfoot, *Colossians and Philemon*, 341; Barth and Blanke, *Philemon*, 416–17. Thus it corresponds, conceptually, with "but now" in v 11.

conversion had gifted him with a new identity, in the new order created by Christ,[144] that now determined and relativized all other identities. A new perspective was now needed.[145] He was **more than a slave** now. The strong, contrastive "**but**" (Greek *alla*) highlights the difference.[146] The old identity **as**[147] a slave *only* no longer operated. It still existed, but now redefined and transformed into something very different. The two facets of Onesimus—his social role as a slave and his spiritual identity as a brother in Christ—did not coexist equally. The latter overpowered the former and now reconfigured it. His socio-cultural identity as a slave did not cease to exist or be operative, but his entire personal identity had now been engulfed in another one that had the power to reshape everything that came within it (without erasing it).

This verse lays the essential piece of the foundation for Paul's request in the next verse. As Paul had already mentioned, Onesimus was now his "child," or to use another part of the family metaphor, he was now a **beloved brother**. The word "beloved" (Greek *agapētos*) is the same word Paul had used to describe Philemon in v 1, and Paul called Philemon "brother" in v 7. Both men were dear to Paul, both were his brothers in the family of God. But what was needed now, at this moment, was for *Philemon* to see *Onesimus* as beloved, and as a brother, as well. The use of the same terminology for both men implies that now, *in the Lord*, they were equal, and the dual identity of Onesimus (as both slave and brother) involved a subordination of his old identity (slave) to the new one (brother).[148]

---

[144] McKnight, *Philemon*, 95, notes that "no longer" expresses an "eschatological shift."

[145] The word "as" (Greek *hōs*, in the phrase "as a slave") introduces "the perspective from which a person, thing, or activity is viewed or understood as to character, function, or role." BDAG 1104.' " No longer as a slave,' therefore, points to a reception of this slave within a new framework that acknowledges the relativization of the present social and political reality without necessarily denying such a reality in the present age." Pao, *Colossians and Philemon*, 395.

[146] Runge, *Discourse Grammar*, 95 notes that "*Alla* is often used following a negated clause to introduce a positive alternative." As such it introduces an idea as a correction of another one. In this case, the correction does not involve the complete negation or elimination of Onesimus' (former) status, but an enhancement of it so that the former description is, by itself, no longer adequate.

[147] The word "as" bears much weight here. Without it, Paul would have been declaring Onesimus free—"he is no longer a slave." But the addition of "as" limits or diminishes what comes after it. In English we would say "as only a slave," or "as if he were just as slave." Barth and Blanke, *Philemon*, 418–20.

[148] "In a situation of conflicting identities he [Paul] urges Philemon to let the Christian identity of Onesimus become predominant over his legal identity." Michael Wolter, "The

"Old habits die hard," as the saying goes. Changing the perspectives that are part of our social, daily existence is difficult. In Philemon's world, attitudes about slaves and masters had been socially codified for a long time. The terminology was loaded with judgments of value, worth, and status, all of which played key roles in the way interactions worked. Especially the term "slave" represented a serious social boundary. However, Christians cannot live like Christians if they constantly think like the world, or like the culture, around them. If we think like the world, we will act like the world. So Paul here specified the precise change in thinking that was needed for this particular situation. Philemon's perspective would have to change so as to include this man—who, up to this point, he had always known first and foremost as his slave, with all the cultural baggage that went with it[149]—within a new and different circle, that of the family of God's newly-created people in Christ. This meant that the deferential treatment accorded to family now needed to be extended to Onesimus (see on v 10 above).

The challenge facing Philemon should not be interpreted as a flaw in the man. We should rather try to appreciate it for the potentially tremendous obstacle it was. What was confronting Philemon confronts every Christian throughout their lives in Christ. Repentance from the old way of life, and transformation into the new person in the image of Christ, is a process, not an event. The repentance we demonstrate at the moment of decision (such as demanded in Acts 2.38) is an initial step, but it is not the only one. Vestiges of our old ways of thinking and acting tend to survive until they are directly confronted in specific situations. It is nice when we can conceptually inventory ourselves and remove improper thoughts so that they do not surface later, but few people actually work out their salvation in this way. For most of us, it takes the inadequacy of our old ways to come to the surface in a moment of

Letter to Philemon as Ethical Counterpart to Paul's Doctrine of Justification," in *Philemon in Perspective: Interpreting A Pauline Letter*, ed. Francois Tolmie. BZNW 169 (Berlin: de Gruyter, 2010), 169–79, at 175. *Cf.* Wright (*Paul and the Faithfulness of God*, 20): "Yes, indeed: Philemon himself is part of that new creation, and so is Onesimus, so the question of their social status is radically outflanked."

[149] Bird: "Although brotherhood was known as an ideal in the Greek world, such a bond between slaves and masters would have been quite scandalous and viewed as compromising the household order. Treating slaves humanely was not unknown in the Greco-Roman world, but regarding them as brothers would have been viewed as bad for discipline and even self-deprecating for the master (was he to come down to their level?)." *Colossians and Philemon*, 140–41.

spiritual challenge before we know that further change on our part is needed. It is in that moment, the moment when our old ways prove not to fit with who we now are, that the continuing work of transformation takes place. In that moment, every Christian must re-commit to change, and change is seldom easy for us. A Christian must decide, at that moment, if the transformation he/she has begun will continue or not. In a very real sense, the issue with Onesimus now placed Philemon at a spiritual crossroad. He had to decide if he would hang on to his old view of Onesimus, or to press on and expand his spirituality now to include Onesimus as a beloved brother.[150] Sadly, some people come to a point in their spiritual development where the sacrifice, the change, is more than they are willing to commit to. They are like the rich man who had followed the demands of the Law of Moses but could not bring himself to divest himself of his love of possessions and money (Matt 19.16–22). For some people, there is a limit past which their commitment to Jesus will not go. This was the same kind of test now facing Philemon. Would he accept, as a beloved brother, the man who was socially beneath him and who had wronged him? Was the Christian faith and love that he already possessed able to grow so as to include this particular person? This is what was at stake.

In v 10 Paul had said that Onesimus was now useful "both to you and to me" (notice how he put Philemon first in that clause). The repetition of "**me**" (or "my," vv 10, 11, 12, 13, and here in v 16), however, reminded Philemon that his relationship with Onesimus now included Paul, as v 17 will make abundantly clear. But Onesimus was now "**much more**" useful to Philemon, that is, doubly so, because Philemon had an extra aspect of relationship with Onesimus that Paul did not have: Philemon was the owner and master of Onesimus. This verse therefore does two things: 1) it shows how much more benefit Philemon will gain from Onesimus in the new situation of things. Onesimus will serve Philemon better now, and that will be to Philemon's advantage; but 2) it also continues to lock the three men into a mutual relationship. The fellowship that Philemon

---

[150] *Cf.* Petersen, *Rediscovering Paul,* 269–70: "When he is confronted with Onesimus's presence on his doorstep, and after having read Paul's letter, he is confronted not only with having to decide whether or not he will receive his slave as his brother, but also whether or not *he* is and wants to be a brother, a slave of Christ, and a son of God. Paradoxically, the critical decision to be made concerns himself, not Onesimus, for Onesimus *is* a brother, a slave, or rather a freedman of Christ, and a child of God-to-be regardless of what he, Philemon, decides." (emphasis his)

has always had with Paul has now been joined by Onesimus. Philemon could not consistently reject one and receive the other.

Onesimus still needed, now more than ever, to be a good servant for Philemon (*cf.* Eph 6.5–6), but not just for civic reasons. His new identity, apocalyptically formed by the power of God, demanded that he be a person of love, a person dedicated to the service of others, and this would directly impact what he did as Philemon's slave. He was truly, therefore, still a slave, **but more than a slave**. He was a new kind of slave because he was a new kind of person. He now had a renewed relationship with Philemon, **in the flesh and in the Lord**. Note that Paul did not say that his relationship in the flesh (that is, in the social world of men) had been replaced by his relationship in the Lord. Both aspects of Philemon, his social position as a slave and his spiritual identity as a Christian, existed together, but with the latter redefining the former.[151]

Paul used the word "**flesh**" (Greek *sarx*) with a couple of different nuances in his letters. Sometimes "flesh" has a negative connotation as the seat of sinful desires (as in Rom 7.17–18 and Gal 5.17). In the present context, however, there is no suggestion that evil is part of Onesimus' new relationship with Philemon. "Flesh" here is simply a synonym for "worldly" or "earthly," and denotes the socio-cultural role Onesimus occupied as a slave.[152] That role remained, but was now transformed as a part of a new person with new motives and new goals. The coexistence of Onesimus's two statuses—relating to Philemon in the flesh and in the Lord at the same time—highlights the tension that characterizes the new time inaugurated by Christ. As a slave, Onesimus was already part of the extended household of Philemon, yet never socially equal to family members. But as a Christian, he was now a full brother in the household (family) of God.[153] To Philemon, Onesimus was now "more" in two ways,

---

[151] *Cf.* de Vos: "While he does not seek to alter the fact that legally and structurally they remained master and slave, he wants to bring about a fundamental change in the nature of their relationship as master and slave.... In effect, without changing the structures of their master-slave relationship, he expected a significant change in the quality of their relationship." "Once a Slave, Always a Slave?," 102.

[152] Cf. Schweizer, "Here, too, *sarx* denotes the circle of purely human relations irrespective of the fact that the slave and his master are also believers in the Lord's kingdom. The reference is to social relations rather than kinship. Here it is especially plain that the two spheres are not mutually exclusive. But the sphere of *sarx* is not the decisive one." (Eduard Schweizer Friedrich Baumgartel, *"Sarx, Sarkikos, Sarkinos," TDNT* 7:127).

[153] Dunn, *Colossians and Philemon*, 313.

having a new kind of relationship with him "in the flesh" (in the social world of men) but also now relating to him as a brother "in the Lord." The work of Christ in bringing the kingdom of God does not bring about the sudden destruction of the present world or its social structures. A destruction is coming, but until then the Messiah has opened up a new world and he is inviting all who would come into it. Christ's people, then, still live in this world, but in another sense they are in the process of leaving this world. Their citizenship now lies elsewhere, in heaven (Phil 3.20), even as they continue to occupy roles in this world.

v 17 If, therefore, you consider me a partner, accept him as you receive me.

Paul appealed to the existing relationship between himself and Philemon as a starting-point ("**therefore**"[154]) for the new, further relationship that now included Onesimus.[155] The way Philemon viewed Paul was to be the model for how he now viewed Onesimus. Perspective is the issue. Paul presented himself bound to Philemon in such a way (as a **partner**[156]) that Philemon ought to accept Onesimus if he accepted Paul (recall v 12).

"**Accept**" is the first imperative in the letter,[157] and fully reveals and encapsulates the content of the appeal that Paul had so far only hinted

---

[154] The connective "therefore" (Greek *oun*) links what precedes with what follows, but also with the sense that what follows is a development, or advancement, of what preceded. Runge, *Discourse Grammar*, 43.

[155] Such is the force of the first-class conditional sentence here: "If this thing is true (and let us suppose that it is), then this other thing is true or should also happen." See on v 18 below.

[156] There has been much discussion among scholars over the word "partner" here. The word (Greek *koinōnos*) could be used in secular Greek of various kinds of shared relationships: businesses, sacrifices, plans, civic associations, *etc.* (LSJ 970). It is undoubtedly going too far in this context to demand that the word here must mean "business partner" (Arzt-Grabner argues for this meaning here on the basis that this is what the term normally means in the papyri, "The Case of Onesimos," 608). Although that is a perfectly legitimate use of the word in ancient Greek, nothing in this context would impart such a nuance to it. Ogereau rightly notes that the contextual sense is more important than the lexical sense; *i.e.*, there are all kinds of partnerships, and the context (not the word) tells us what they are ("A Survey of *Koinōnia*," 292). It is much better to think that the term instead parallels the designation of "fellow worker" from v 1 (Wiema, "Paul's Persuasive Prose," 37), or that the sentiment is that of Phil 1.7, "… I have you in my heart, since both in my imprisonment and in the defense and confirmation of the gospel, you all are partakers (Greek *sumkoinōnous*) of grace with me." (NASB)

[157] A textual variant has this request (using the same word as here) coming earlier, in v 12. See the comments there.

at. Now Philemon knew what Paul wanted. It is amazing how much discussion has occupied students of Phlm over whether or not Paul wanted Philemon to give Onesimus his freedom, when the thing that Paul clearly asked for is in plain view. Acceptance was the request. The term Paul used here means to welcome, or accept, someone into their circle of acquaintances.[158] As such it is closely akin to fellowship in that it refers to an association or relationship between people, but it also implies a distinction between insiders and outsiders. Social boundaries were ingrained into the cultures and lifestyles of the ancients.[159] In the church, in the fellowship of Jesus Christ, however, these boundaries no longer operated. Fellowship in Christ cut across all social and ethnic lines (and this was a challenge for many people, both inside and outside the church) because being in Christ constituted a new "master group" for the identity of Christians. It made people of all kinds of different socio-ethnic identities brothers and sisters in the Lord. So in Rome, Jewish and Gentile Christians were divided over the issue of the status of each group before God. The Jews argued they had always been God's special, chosen people, but Gentile Christians were arguing that God had now rejected them. Paul's careful exposition in that letter showed that neither claim was correct as they were being stated, and that God now accepts both groups in Christ on the equal footing of faith in Christ. "Therefore, accept one another, just as Christ also accepted us to the glory of God" (Rom 15.7). Acceptance of people whom one's culture said were unacceptable was a difficult thing (and still is). As Wright put it, "the letter to Philemon is all about the reconciliation of people whose culture was trying to pull them apart."[160] When Paul sent Onesimus back to Philemon, it was much more than the return of a slave that was in view. That socio-cultural restoration was a symbol, as it were, of a much better kind of repair that was now possible because both men were Christians. The return of Onesimus was ultimately an appeal for Philemon to *accept* him, which ran much deeper than simply retaining him at home once again.

"**As you accept me**" provides a further basis for Philemon's acceptance of Onesimus. Unfortunately, we do not know enough about

[158] BDAG 883. See also Zachary J. Cole, "Illustrating a Pauline Imperative (Phlm. 17): *Proslambanō* in P.Mur. 2.115," *JSNT* 45 (2022): 1–16.

[159] Specifically to the point in Phlm, Aristotle, reflecting the sentiment of the time, said that there could be no real friendship between a master and a slave. *Nic. Eth.* 8.11.

[160] Wright, *Paul and the Faithfulness of God*, 68.

Philemon to know exactly how this analogy was intended. Paul was, of course, a Jew. Philemon's ethnicity is unknown to us. If Philemon was a Gentile (which seems likely), then Philemon had already learned how to cross one of the ancient social barriers in his relationship with Paul. Accepting Onesimus would be an exercise in the same kind of thing. It is possible, though, that Paul was thinking more in terms of friendship and brotherhood, since the word "brother" occupied a powerful place in the letter in the previous verse. At any rate, Paul wanted the same kind of relationship between Philemon and Onesimus as already existed between himself and Philemon.[161]

We do not know what kinds of thoughts Philemon was harboring toward Onesimus. Whatever they were, Paul encouraged Philemon to make his love "complete" in the sense of now including Onesimus within it. It is a common fault that we might excel at demonstrating our faith and love well toward some people, but we can be blind to how we are failing to demonstrate the very same faith and love toward other people. In Philemon's case, the defect came through the society of his day in which masters and slaves were never considered social equals. One of the great challenges of living the Christian life is to make sure that our treatment of others is truly being shaped by the gospel and not simply by the social norms under which we live at the moment. In Christ, Philemon could accept Onesimus in a way the world in which he lived would never have allowed.

v 18 But[162] if he has wronged you or owes you anything, charge this to me.

This verse has figured into many discussions over the nature of Onesimus' absence from his master, Philemon. It was common that runaway slaves would steal something as they fled in order to fund their escapes,[163] but we do not know if that was the case here (either of running away or stealing).

---

[161] Lohse (201 fn 45) notes an almost identical appeal (in slightly different verbiage) in a letter from the second or third century AD (*P.Osl.* 55). It reads, in part: "... Theon the Admirable, who is delivering my writings to you, stayed at my house. He regards me as his brother. Therefore, you will be well advised, brother, to receive him as you would me." Text and discussion in S. Eitrem and Leiv Amundsen, eds., *Papyri Osloenses, Fasc. 2* (Oslo: Academy of Science and Letters of Oslo, 1931), 132–35.

[162] The connective here is *de*, signaling a new development in the discussion. See on vv 12 and 14.

[163] *NewDocs* 8:13.

The first-class conditional sentence that Paul used here does not give us any certainty. The sense of the conditional is to propose something for the sake of argument. It does not mean that the thing proposed by the "if" clause actually happened or is the state of things.[164] It is possible that Onesimus may have squandered something of Philemon's resources, or damaged something, *etc*. It is possible Onesimus' absence itself was the financial loss that this verse hints at, since Philemon would have lost the value of Onesimus' labor, or it could be that the value of Onesimus as a slave had declined (if Philemon thought he had run away; slaves known to run away were worth less in resale).[165] Or it may be that Philemon had incurred expenses in trying to find Onesimus.[166] But it could, in fact, be that none of these things were the case. We just do not know. Furthermore, the conditional sentence here does not even imply that Paul knew of any wrongs Philemon had suffered in the situation with Onesimus. The language instead simply indicates that Paul was anticipating possible damages and offering to pay for them.

Paul used two words for offences here. The first is "**wronged**" (Greek *adikeō*), a verbal form of the Greek word that is often translated "unjust," but it can refer to cheating, breaking divine law, breaking human law, or causing injury.[167] In short, the word covers all kinds of violations against norms. The other word, "**owes**" (Greek *opheilō*), is less morally charged, and can include financial debt or social obligations.[168] By the combination, Paul was simply trying to cover the anticipated problem in his usual way of speaking in parallel terms.[169]

A feature of Phlm that has long puzzled scholars is its lack of any expression of remorse relayed from Onesimus himself. Not once does Paul relay "Onesimus says he is sorry, he has expressed his regret for his actions and wants me to communicate that to you," *etc*. Yet "It seems almost essential to the genre to include some overt expression of or

---

[164] Stanley E. Porter, *Idioms of the Greek New Testament* (Sheffield: JSOT, 1999), 257; Pearson, "Assumptions," 268–69.

[165] *NewDocs* 6:57.

[166] *Ibid*.

[167] BDAG 20.

[168] BDAG 743.

[169] The change in tenses signals that the "wronged" (aorist) is portrayed simply as something that happened without any special perspective intended, but the "owing" (present) is portrayed as something unfolding before the hearer. Pearson, "Assumptions," 271.

allusion to remorse."[170] The problem is based, however, on the assumption that Paul was aware of an actual offence. It may be that this letter does not contain any such expression of remorse or repentance from Onesimus simply because Paul did not know of anything that called for it.[171] His offer to repay came within the context of a hypothetical situation.

The fact that Onesimus was now a Christian and a brother to Philemon would not erase the consequences or damages (if there were any) of past actions. Nothing was being ignored as Paul continued his fully transparent handling of the problem. Furthermore, Paul did not merely offer to help. Paul instead put the offer in the form of an imperative, which communicated Paul's insistence in the matter.[172] Similar to the procedure in Acts 6, where Hellenistic Jewish Christians were put in charge of resolving complaints that they themselves had raised, so here Paul wanted the resolution of the problem with Onesimus to be to Philemon's satisfaction. He put himself in Philemon's place and imagined what could be problematic from Philemon's perspective. Paul considered that Philemon might have perceived some kind of wrong against him by Onesimus, and Paul took that seriously. His appeal on Onesimus' behalf did not mean that Paul had now "chosen sides" between the two men and that any fair concerns Philemon had were now going to be ignored. If damages had to be paid for, Paul did not object, and he would let Philemon decide what those were, and their value.

There is an unstated premise to Paul's offer: "If he has wronged you or owes you anything, charge that to me—*if that is what you think you want to do.*" The Corinthians, still steeped in their pagan ways, were at one point suing each other over alleged wrongs between them. Paul advised that they should arbitrate the matter among themselves instead of publicly exposing their disagreements with each other to the world (1 Cor 6.1–6), but he also advised them that an even better solution would be to cancel any damages they thought they were owed, because that would be the

---

[170] *NewDocs* 8:42.

[171] My thanks to Dr. Evan Blackmore for his insight on this point.

[172] The imperative here is present tense, like the one in v 22. The other two imperatives in this letter (vv 17 and 20) are aorist. Scholars have yet to resolve the semantic difference between aorist imperatives and present imperatives in Koine Greek. A good discussion may be found in Joseph D. Fantin, *The Greek Imperative Mood in the New Testament: A Cognitive and Communicative Approach*, Studies in Biblical Greek 12 (New York: Peter Lang, 2010). Perhaps the present imperative here is meant to match the verbal aspect of "owes" right before it (Pearson, "Assumptions," 271).

more Christ-like way (vv 7–8). The injured party may choose to forego compensation as a show of good will. But Paul said nothing of this to Philemon, obviously. The apostle probably did not want to place such an additional burden on Philemon, and offered to bear that burden himself if any damages came to light.

From the language Paul used we are not justified in assuming that he was anticipating some kind of resistance on Philemon's part. Instead, the conditional sentence simply suggests that he brought the matter up as an extra measure of love and generosity on his part, as a "just in case" kind of offer. Additionally, Paul was putting himself forward personally as the guarantor for any reparations Philemon might have needed or demanded. "**Me**" is emphatic here (as also in vv 10, 11, and 17).

It is not likely that Paul's years as an apostle had made him a man of means. His poverty was so obvious that it was a constant source of criticism from some of the Corinthian Christians (*cf.* 2 Cor 6.4, 10). The problem, in this case, was that it was likely that Onesimus was even poorer than Paul, because Onesimus was a slave.[173] If there had been damages, and even if Onesimus would have been willing to pay for them, he might have had almost nothing with which to pay. For Paul to offer to take on the debt related to any potential damages caused by Onesimus—debt that Paul himself might not even have known about—was a serious commitment.[174]

It is important to see the spiritual dimension here. What Paul was offering was not just to pay for a few things if that would help. Paul was acting out the gospel of Jesus Christ, putting himself in the place of the debtor for the debtor's benefit, so that the debtor could be released from any claims against him. The gospel is that God was in Christ, not counting their trespasses against them because Jesus paid for them (2 Cor 5.19). Here Paul was putting the model of Christ's sacrifice for others into action in a concrete offer to Philemon (*cf.* Rom 15.1–3). Just as Jesus' death thereby reconciled us to God, Paul's offer here would have

---

[173] Many slaves were paid (but not well), so it is conceivable that Onesimus had a savings (called his *peculium*) somewhere. Wessels, "The Letter to Philemon in the Context of Slavery," 155. Whether he had anything, or had brought it with him, we simply do not know. If Onesimus had survived apart from Philemon on the basis of something he had stolen, he had probably spent it all by now (*NewDocs* 8:40). Regardless, Paul's offer does not necessarily imply that Onesimus had nothing, but that may have been the case.

[174] See A. Deissmann, *Light from the Ancient East* (London: Hodder & Stoughton, 1910), 339.

the effect of removing a potential obstacle to Philemon's reconciliation with, and acceptance of, Onesimus.

It is possible that this intervention on Paul's part, in which he offered to stand for the debts of Philemon, further explains why Onesimus' voice is never heard in this letter. Even though the problem originated between Philemon and Onesimus, this letter makes it clear that, from Paul's perspective, the primary solution could take place within the relationship between Philemon and Paul, which now included Onesimus, who was now closely bound up with Paul.[175] He wrote to Philemon as a partner (v 17), but then urged him to "accept him [Onesimus] as you accept me" (v 17) because Onesimus represented Paul's own heart (v 12). Throughout the letter, Paul put the matter primarily as a matter between himself and Philemon, not as a matter primarily between Philemon and Onesimus (with Paul as the outsider), because Paul now stood in for him. This perspective would help Philemon, because he would be dealing with Paul (with whom he had a good relationship) rather than directly with Onesimus (with whom his relationship was damaged). Philemon would reconcile with Onesimus through his relationship with Paul.

Paul's offer of restitution should not be taken to mean that the perfect restoration of all wrongs, as if they never happened, is necessary before things can move on. That, obviously, can rarely ever be done. In some cases restoration is impossible. Instead, Paul was doing his best to be a peacemaker, to remove any potential barriers that could hinder the reconciliation of these two men, and in a Christ-like spirit he was pledging his own resources to do so.[176] If damages had been suffered, and if Onesimus could not pay for them, and if that could be an obstacle to the reconciliation of these two men, then Paul saw that offering to pay in Onesimus' place would remove the barrier and allow the reconciliation to advance in fulfillment of Paul's request (v 17).

As we have noted above, Paul was careful to handle this situation in a way that empowered Philemon. The choice to let Onesimus serve Paul while Paul was in chains, and the choice to press for any damages that might be discovered, was Philemon's to make. But these choices had to

---

[175] *Cf.* Melick, *Philippians, Colossians, Philemon*, 366: "The idea of substitution predominates in this section. There is constant interchange between Paul and Onesimus. At times Onesimus represents Paul, and at times he appears 'clothed in Paul.' "

[176] As such, vv 18-19a are, in a sense, only a secondary concern in the letter. Wolter, "Ethical Counterpart," pp. 174–75.

do with the details of the earthly situation. There was another, higher, choice that went with these, the choice to accept Onesimus, and that choice was significantly loaded with the sense of obligation that the grace of Christ, now being demonstrated by Paul, brought with it. Paul did his best to make sure that this last choice was not beset with obstacles for Philemon, so that Philemon's obligation to reciprocate the grace of Christ to Onesimus would be unmitigated.

v 19 I, Paul, have written with my own hand, I will repay (and I would not mention to you that you owe me your own self).

The repetition of **Paul**'s name here (now for the third time in the letter) underscored the personal nature of the appeal. Since Paul's letters were read out loud to the churches, the inclusion of his name within the body of his letters enhanced the sense that Paul himself was speaking to them (as in Gal 5.2; Eph 3.1; Col 1.23; 1 Thes 2.18). In several places in Paul's letters, he noted that he wrote the closing part of a letter with his own hand.[177] If Paul dictated a letter to a scribe, then the personal handwriting of Paul would have served as a mark of authenticity to the recipient for the letter's provenance. Paul's handwriting at the end of the letter—especially when punctuated by writing his own name—guaranteed that the words of the entire letter had come from Paul, as well as serving as a reminder of the authority Paul had in the letter's business.[178] However, here the point was a little different. Paul was making a solemn promise. He did not want that promise simply to be relayed by a scribe (although Paul's integrity would not have been altered). He did not want Philemon to suppose that Paul's scribe had included this promise as a mere formality. Paul wanted Philemon to know with certainty that this promise was coming from himself, and his own handwriting served as a kind of signature to the promise. "I[179] will repay" thus becomes a kind of blank IOU for Philemon.[180]

All this talk of being owed, and people making payments, and Paul's handing all the decision-making over to Philemon, would have a little different ring to it in Paul's day than it does perhaps in our world today.

---

[177] 1 Cor 16.21; Gal 6.11; Col 4.18; 2 Thes 3.17, and here.

[178] White, "New Testament Epistolary Literature," 1740.

[179] The personal pronoun "I" (twice) here is emphatic.

[180] Similar letters are known from the papyri. Deissmann, *Light from the Ancient East*, 334–35.

These things could have had the effect of putting Philemon in the place of highest status among the three men. The others, then, would have been obligated to him: Onesimus for creating a problem, and Paul because of his voluntary promise. The latter part of this verse served as a corrective to any such notions, if Philemon were tempted to entertain them. Yet in characteristic style, Paul offered the correction with gentleness. He expressed it as "I'm not going to mention this, but if I did, I would say . . . ."[181] It is not the main clause of the sentence, but it packs more power than even Paul's promise in the first part of the verse. The main part of the sentence was the promise to pay, but this clause served to clarify what this promise did, and did not, imply.

In the relationship between Paul and Philemon, the real debtor here was Philemon, and the real benefactor was Paul. The situation had to be viewed through the lens of the new reality in Christ, not through the lens of earthly social structures (where Philemon would have outranked Paul economically). Philemon was not to think that Paul's deferential treatment (*cf.* v 14) meant that he was becoming a benefactor for Paul, that is, over Paul. The fulfillment of Paul's request would instead simply count as reciprocation for Paul's prior benefaction to him. The gift Paul had given to Philemon was the new life Philemon now enjoyed through the gospel. When Paul said to Philemon "**you owe**[182] **me your own self**," it is hard to imagine that Paul meant anything other than the fact that Paul was the one through whom Philemon learned the truth and stepped out of the world of sin and death, and into the life and joy and hope found only in Christ Jesus. Paul has consistently argued in this letter on the level of the spiritual realities that made the situation what it was. Therefore, the reference to Philemon's debt to Paul for himself should be understood, in the broader context of the discussion, as having a spiritual referent. By Paul's sharing the gospel with Philemon, Philemon had been rescued from the coming wrath of God (1 Thes 1.10; *cf.* 2 Thes 1.8) and become a new man, his old self done away with by sharing in

---

[181] This was a common rhetorical technique called praeteritio, or paraleipsis. Fitzmyer, *Philemon*, 118.

[182] This is the only time this word is used in the New Testament. It is a compound verb, made up of the preposition *pros* + the verb *opheilō* ("I owe"). The proposition *pros*, when prefixed to a verb, sometimes contributes the sense of "addition." Here the idea would be that "you additionally owe," and results in the sense that Philemon owed more than Paul owed. Robert McL. Wilson, *A Critical and Exegetical Commentary on Colossians and Philemon*, ICC (London: T&T Clark International, 2005), 359.

the death of Christ with reference to sin, and putting on Christ as a new creature. As one of God's new people he now lived in the new, Messianic world of faith, righteousness, and love. Who he now was, he owed to Paul's teaching him the gospel. Thus Philemon owed his very self—who he now was—to Paul.

We might bristle at this claim. Our reaction might be to say that the credit for a person's salvation and transformation belongs wholly with Jesus. Paul would not have denied that. But the fact that our salvation lies first and foremost with God and Christ does not erase the spiritual service we provide for each other, including that of sharing the gospel, and the indebtedness created when someone serves us spiritually. Yes, the power of salvation is of God. But the favor, the gift, of sharing it with someone is significant on its own level. Paul said that elders were to be supported for their work among the flock, and if a man served well in that capacity, especially as both an elder and a minister, he was to be given "double honor" (twice the support; 1 Tim 5.17). Elders and preachers primarily work with spiritual commodities. They impart knowledge, they encourage people in the faith, and they offer loving correction. And for this spiritual work the church is indebted to repay their efforts with support. Even though it is Jesus who saves us, we are indebted to those who have taught us the gospel both initially and over the years, and it would be properly deemed an affront to think otherwise.

Some might also object to Paul even putting this into play on the assumption that Paul was being manipulative. But it would be a mistake to read Paul's words in v 19b as simply an attempt to maintain his ego. Such a reading would be inconsistent with the man we see in his letters. Paul saw himself as the servant of others. Even though he was privileged to have spiritual experiences that not even the most boastful "spiritual person" could claim (2 Cor 12.1–10), he did not have an ego problem. If anything, Paul was protecting Philemon from the temptation to think of himself more highly in this situation than he should. It was a call to humility, to avoid the arrogance of status that could have easily dominated, and ruined, the situation. Paul's words served as a gentle reminder that the disposition of Paul's appeal, although finally resting in Philemon's hands, was more a matter of obligation on Philemon's part than it was a matter of privilege. The right outcome needed to come from the right perspective.

The back-and-forth in which now Philemon, now Paul, holds the position of benefactor over the other in the letter's rhetoric illustrates the kind of relational dynamic that was also at work in the reconciliation between Philemon and Onesimus. Even though Paul had a higher status within the Christian community, he was perfectly willing to humble himself for the sake of the resolution of the problem. This did not, however, erase or invalidate Paul's status. Paul was the benefactor to Philemon when it came to spiritual things, even if Paul was willing to place the decision in Philemon's hands and put himself in the position of the one making an appeal. Paul's readiness to reshape his relationship with Philemon through humility, even though it did not reshape everything between them, paralleled Philemon's need to reshape his relationship with Onesimus in a similar way, as retaining his status as master over Onesimus yet with a willingness to sacrifice aspects of his thinking for the sake of fellowship in Christ. Furthermore, Paul brought up the matter of Philemon's debt to himself only in the context of what Philemon could now do for *Onesimus*.[183] This substitution of Paul for Onesimus, and vice versa (noted in vv 12, 17–18) continues here, and Philemon could now reciprocate the grace he experienced through Paul by accepting Onesimus.

Of course, all this talk about offering to pay for things should not veil the higher price that Philemon was being asked to pay in this situation, namely, the change in his own heart, in his attitude toward Onesimus (see on v 16). That cost Paul could not offer to bear, but he could make it easier by offering to take care of the material costs that had accumulated.

v 20 Yes, brother, give me some benefit from you in the Lord, give my heart refreshment in Christ.

The letter's gentle tone is reinforced as Paul addressed Philemon again (*cf.* v 1) as "**brother**." This is the level at which Paul wanted the discussion and its outcome to take place. While there could be hierarchies and debts among Christians, they were all mediated by the primary relationship that held them together, that they were brethren in the Lord. Furthermore, the previous talk of who-owes-whom-what now gave way to a return to the language of appeal. "**Yes**," standing by itself, has the rhetorical effect of encouraging a positive disposition toward

[183] Barclay, "*Koinōnia*," 165.

what was said and asked for. *Cf.* Phil 4.3. It was a gentle urging not too different from our modern phrase "Come on."

With the possible obstacle of payment now covered, Paul returned to his appeal, but now with a twist. Philemon's acceptance of Onesimus would also **give** Paul **some benefit**,[184] since Onesimus himself represented Paul's own heart (v 12). Just as quickly as Paul had reminded Philemon of his place as the greater debtor in this situation (v 19), he immediately softened it by putting himself[185] in the place of one who was wishing for, or asking for, a favor from Philemon. And the favor was the acceptance of Onesimus. Even if Paul had to pay for damages due to Onesimus' absence (vv 18–19), Paul communicated that he would still be "profited" by Philemon's acceptance of his slave.

"**Refreshment**" echoes the use of the same word in v 7. In his appeal concerning Onesimus, Paul was not asking for anything other than what Philemon had done for other saints in the past. In this sense it was not a new burden placed on Philemon, but the continuation of what he already did. And just as the hearts of the saints had been refreshed by their loving treatment from Philemon that gave them a sense of acceptance and belonging, so Paul wanted that same experience for himself as Philemon accepted Onesimus, who represented Paul's own heart (v 12).

---

[184] The Greek verb here, *oninēmi*, is not easy to translate into English, since we do not have a single verb that captures its sense. The verb means "to be the recipient of a favor or benefit or to have something for one's use" (BDAG 711), but it can sometimes mean "to have delight" (LSJ 1232). Lightfoot noted that the verb is often found in contexts discussing family relationships (*Colossians and Philemon*, 342–343). If this sense is operative here, it would suggest that Paul wanted the kind of satisfaction suggested by the immediately-preceding word "brother," the kind of benefit and favorable disposition given among family members. Paul here used the optative mood. Whereas the subjunctive would express what could happen from the speaker's point of view, the optative expresses what is potential "but slightly remoter, vaguer, less assured, or more contingent" (Porter, *Idioms*, 59). In the optative, this verb means "I may have profit," or in the third person, "you may (or may you) have profit" like our saying "bless you." It is not an imperative, but that is, in a very soft way, its pragmatic force here—which is confirmed as it is paralleled by an imperative ("give … refreshment"). The verb is also in the middle voice, which has the effect in this particular case of giving the verb a semi-passive sense. The active form means "I benefit, I help," and the middle form means "I have benefit" (*i.e.*, from something or someone else; LSJ 1232). The meaning of the genitive used with the optative means either "for" or "from," depending on the context. Perhaps translating the first part of this verse as a question would convey in English the sense of gentle urging here: "Might I have benefit from you in the Lord?" Some scholars have suggested that the choice of this verb by Paul was meant as a kind of play on Onesimus' name (*onaimen—Onesimus*). It is possible, but I am skeptical.

[185] The word "me" in the verse is emphatic.

As throughout the letter, Paul here kept the discussion on the spiritual plane. The benefit and refreshment Paul was hoping for was **in the Lord**, that is, **in Christ**. Paul's request, although being acted out within the social world of men, was most properly characterized as being done in that sphere or circle of relationship that bound believers to Christ and to each other.

v 21 Being confident[186] in your obedience, I have written to you, knowing that you will do beyond what I say.

Paul's respectful tone toward Philemon continued in this verse. Expressions of confidence in the context of a request are fairly usual in ancient personal letters among family members.[187] Paul did not speak to Philemon as an underling whose incompetence left him no option but to give orders. Paul had already made it clear that he was not going to order Philemon around in this matter (v 8). Instead he respected Philemon—before his family and he whole church (v 2)—and had **confidence** that he was a man of spiritual wisdom, faith, and love, and so he trusted that Philemon would comply with his request because he would see that it was, after all, what a mature Christian ought to do. This confidence was to be understood as the correct interpretation of Paul's motive in writing to Philemon.[188]

The word "**obedience**" may tend, to our ears, to shift the letter's tone to one of authoritative command, as if all the while Paul had been giving a command, just in veiled terms. However, the word here (Greek *hupakoē*) means obedience not in the sense of mindless commandment-following, but in the sense of listening. In some contexts it can mean "response," and the verb form of this word can mean to hear favorably, and thus do what

---

[186] Greek perfect participle of *peithō,* thus meaning "to be convinced" or "to be persuaded." BDAG 792. The perfect participle, like the present participle, usually expresses an action contemporary with the leading verb, but it also encodes the spatial value of proximity, the idea being that what is expressed is portrayed as directly present. Campbell, *Basics of Verbal Aspect,* 42.

[187] White, "New Testament Epistolary Literature," 1737. He cites *P.Oxy.* 745, in which the letter's author says "I know that you will do everything well." Text and discussion in *The Oxyrhynchus Papyri, Part IV,* ed. Bernard P. Grenfell and Arthur S. Hunt (London: Egypt Exploration Fund, 1904), 244–45.

[188] Pre-verbal participles (here: "being confident") "establish states of affairs" that are important background information for understanding the action of the main verb (expressed afterwards). They create a "circumstantial frame" for the information in the main sentence. Runge, *Discourse Grammar,* 243–250.

was asked.[189] I would suggest, based on Paul's approach throughout the letter, that "obedience" here should be understood in this softer way.[190] "I'm sure you'll listen to what I have said" or "I'm confident you will respond to my appeal favorably" is the sense here. It is possible that Paul had in mind Philemon's obedience to the Lord, but given Paul's apostolic status, this changes things very little, because what Paul wrote was the command of the Lord himself (1 Cor 14.37).

Paul was confident in Philemon's Christian character, a fact that in itself provides an often-needed lesson in how to deal with each other as brethren. Paul thought the best of Philemon and assumed that he would act like a Christian. His letter ("**I have written to you**") was not written in a spirit of skepticism or suspicion concerning Philemon's motives or goodness. It was written with a spirit of optimism based on the fact that Philemon was a good man whose previous actions had proven that. Just because Paul's request might be difficult for Philemon in some ways, that did not mean that Paul automatically assumed Philemon would fail to do what was right. He assumed, in fact, just the opposite. Expressed confidence in each other encourages each other. It gives others a sense that their spiritual maturity is recognized and can be depended upon, and this encourages them to continue in that same way. Paul could produce the negative tones of rebuke when they were needed, but that was not his default stance toward other Christians. "Great is my confidence in you" (2 Cor 7.4), and "I rejoice that in everything I have confidence in you" (v 16), and "We have confidence in the Lord concerning you, that you are doing and will continue to do what we command" (2 Thes 3.4). With such words Paul encouraged the best in other Christians. Here, it was his way of saying to Philemon "I know what I am saying to you might be hard, but I also know that you are the kind of person that will do what is right no matter how hard it is."

Paul was so confident of Philemon's proven Christian character that he could say that he imagined Philemon would actually do more than just accept Onesimus. This verse has often been interpreted as implying that Paul sought for Onesimus' manumission (or a similar arrangement) without saying so explicitly. Paul had expressed his preferred solution in v 13, but it is not necessary to read this verse as bringing that up again.

---

[189] BDAG 1028–29.

[190] *Cf.* Fitzmyer, who translates it "acquiescence." (*Philemon*, 121).

Given the sustained focus on spiritual qualities in the letter, we are probably better off understanding this verse in the same vein. Acceptance was what was asked for (v 17). Therefore "**beyond what I say**" could, possibly, not be a reference to manumission at all, but mean something like "you will be even more gracious toward, and more accepting of, Onesimus than I have asked," that is, more loving, more kind, more open to him. That is, it could refer to the abundance of Philemon's new attitude without implying any change in Onesimus' slave status.

There is a real sense in which we could summarize Phlm as a letter about overcoming the flesh and the world. The culture in which Philemon lived, as well as his own flesh, said to think of Onesimus one way, but the gospel said to think of him in a very different way. Only a person whose heart, mind, and spirit had changed, and been transformed into the likeness of the mind and spirit of Christ, could succeed here. Only a person who had been apocalyptically changed by the power of God to re-create us could manage it correctly. That was the challenge facing Philemon. Paul was sure he could do it, and do it very well.

v 22 At the same time also prepare a guest room for me, for I hope that through your prayers I will be granted to you.

The practice of hospitality to strangers was common in the ancient world, unlike our culture today.[191] Pagans believed that the gods sometimes took on human form and tested humans concerning their kindness (*cf.* Acts 14.8–18, where this was a factor), but hospitality was not considered only a religious gesture among them. It became especially important among Christians because of the brotherly love it demonstrated (Heb 13.1–2). Inns were available for travelers, but they were dangerous places. It was better to stay in a **guest room** in someone's home. It does not seem likely that, starting with Acts 13, Paul owned a house somewhere. For the greater part of his time as an apostle, Paul would have stayed with other Christians (*cf.* Acts 16.15; 17.7), or (when he thought the circumstances required it) in his own temporarily-rented place. However, what Paul was asking for here involved more than a place to stay. Hospitality was a kind of negotiation between strangers in which people departed as friends. It was a way of crossing a social boundary as well as expressing

[191] See Gustav Stählin, "*xenos, xenia, xenizō, xenodocheō, philoxenia, philoxenos,*" *TDNT* 5:17–19.

love, and created (or in this case, cemented) a relationship of ongoing friendship and reciprocity.[192] To practice hospitality was to display openness and acceptance of one who was otherwise considered foreign. In this context, then, Philemon's hospitality to Paul would be a clear signal of Philemon's continued openness to Paul, to which was now tied his openness to Onesimus (vv 13, 17). His acceptance of the one would entail his acceptance of the other.

By expressing his intention to visit Philemon personally in the near future, Paul was not imposing himself upon Philemon, although he used the imperative here. In Greek, as in English, imperatives could express a wide variety of nuances, depending on the context (literary or social).[193] Nor was Paul's "command" to "prepare a guest room for me," in this context, an assertion of authority over Philemon that was intended to pressure him into doing what Paul said, nor a thinly-veiled threat that Paul was going to visit to make sure Philemon complied with his demands. The context here is about trust, not mistrust. Instead, he was signaling two things: 1) the request served as a further expression of confidence in Philemon's brotherly love. Paul had just said that he could count on Philemon to act in love (v 21), even beyond Paul's request, and he was now showing that this confidence was not hypothetical. He assumed that not only would Philemon welcome Onesimus back into his home, but that he (Paul) himself would be welcome there too. "**At the same time**" has the sense of our modern phrase "And while you're at it." There was a coming, concrete situation in which that very welcome would be needed; and 2) it communicated that he continued to hold Philemon as a beloved brother. The demand for a room signaled the openness of the relationship (as far as Paul was concerned), that he planned for it to continue as the friendship it had always been, and friends were perfectly welcome to make such requests of each other. Paul probably did not want to come across as having made a demand on Philemon from afar and that would be the end of it, without any personal element to it. Letters were written to keep communication open, but Paul never thought that letters were an

---

[192] "In the first-century Mediterranean world ... hospitality was a public duty toward strangers where the honor of the community was at stake and reciprocity was more likely to be communal rather than individual." S. C Barton, "Hospitality," in *Dictionary of the Later New Testament and Its Developments,* ed. Martin, Ralph P., and Peter H. Davids (Downers Grove, IL: InterVarsity Press, 1997), 501–507, at 501. See also "Hospitality" in *Dictionary of Biblical Imagery*, ed. Leland Ryken et al (Downers Grove, IL: InterVarsity Press, 2000), 402–404.

[193] Fantin, *The Greek Imperative*, 62–63, 76–77, 87, 144–45.

adequate substitute for face-to-face fellowship. It is also likely that Paul had Philemon's well-being in mind. Philemon's response to Paul's request in v 17 might have been difficult. Even spiritually mature people struggle sometimes with obedience that is personally challenging. No doubt Paul wanted to visit with Philemon and see how he was managing his acceptance of Onesimus, and lend encouragement, as well as encourage Onesimus to continue to act appropriately in this new situation.

This verse tells us nothing about how soon Paul expected to be free, nor does it imply anything about how near the place of Paul's confinement was to Philemon's location. It does not even tell us that Paul's case had been heard when he wrote this letter. It probably means no more than what Paul meant in Philippians 1.19–26, esp. vv 18–19, where Paul said (during the same confinement?) "... I know that this will turn out for my deliverance through your prayers and the provision of the Spirit of Jesus Christ." All this verse tells us with certainty is that once Paul was released, he planned on visiting Philemon.[194]

Paul's confidence in the good condition of their friendship was further expressed in Paul's assumption that Philemon would mention Paul in his **prayers**, reciprocating Paul's frequent prayers for him (v 4). The word "**granted**" (Greek *charizomai*) means "to give as a gift." It shares the same root as the word for "grace," and is the same word Paul used in Acts 26.11 and 15 when he complained that he was about to be "gifted" to the Jews (who were planning on killing him) as a sacrificial pawn in the opening negotiations of power between the Jews and the new Roman governor Festus. But the word does not have such negative connotations here (unless Paul was being slightly sarcastic). It is also used in Acts 3.14 to describe how Barabbas was "given" to the crowd instead of Jesus, and thus in a legal setting it meant "set free."[195] In this context, who will be doing the gifting is not stated. We should probably assume Paul meant that his hoped-for visit would be a gift from God. Otherwise it would have an almost comic touch, as Paul hoped that he would become the gift of the Roman authorities to Philemon.

---

[194] Herein is another part of the difficulty of reconstructing the historical context behind this letter (see Introduction). Just before his arrest in Jerusalem, Paul indicated that he planned to go to Rome and then to Spain (Acts 19.21; Rom 1.15; 15.24, 28). If Paul wrote Phlm during his Roman detention, why does he say he would visit Philemon upon his release? *Cf.* also Phil 2.24.

[195] Hans Conzelmann, *"charizomai," TDNT* 9:393.

vv 23–24 Epaphras my fellow prisoner in Christ Jesus, and Mark, Aristarchus, Demas, and Luke, my fellow workers, greet you.

Timothy had been included in the opening of the letter (v 1), which probably meant that Timothy was with Paul as he wrote the letter. The greetings from these other coworkers may not carry such an idea. They may have been with Paul, or they may have simply been within Paul's current circle of helpers, whether they were physically present at the time of writing or not. Nothing even says that Philemon knew all of them personally, or that they knew about the problem between Philemon and Onesimus. The list of names here is nearly identical to the list in Colossians 4.10–17. The absence of Tychicus' and Justus' names here, as well as those of others of Paul's known helpers (such as Titus), the absence of the names of Philemon and Apphia from Colossians, and the different designations for Aristarchus, suggests that the circle of Paul's helpers changed, and their conditions changed, as the circumstances of Paul's wider ministerial concerns changed.[196]

The greetings here reminded Philemon that his fellowship with Paul included a larger group of people.[197] In this way, it is not completely different from the inclusion of the church in the address of the letter (v 2), as it reminded Philemon that his decision was being acted out in terms of the fellowship of God's people.

Epaphras, whose full name was Epaphroditus, helped as the gospel was taking hold in Macedonia (Phil 2.25; 4.18), relaying messages and funds for Paul. He later helped Paul in the evangelization of the western part of Asia Minor (Acts 19.10), as he was from Colossae (Col 4.12) and started the church there (Col 1.3–8). Paul here calls him "**my fellow prisoner**," but he is not described this way in Col 4.12. Epaphroditus is never mentioned in Acts, and Luke gives no indication in that narrative that another Christian was confined with Paul in Rome. We therefore lack the information we need to understand Paul's description here. It could be that Epaphras was arrested (where?) and eventually joined in Paul's confinement, or Paul could be referring to a previous experience, maybe years earlier, that is not recorded in Acts.[198]

---

[196] See Balabanski, "Where is Philemon?"

[197] *Cf.* Rom 16, where a long list of greetings helped establish Paul's connection with the Roman Christians although he had not yet been there.

[198] Paul was imprisoned more often than Acts reveals. By the time we get to the point in the narrative in Acts where Paul wrote 2 Cor, Luke has Paul spending exactly one night

Mark is probably John Mark, a Jew whose name appears in the very earliest records of Christianity. His mother's name was Mary, and they had a house in Jerusalem where Christians met (Acts 12.12). He accompanied Paul and Barnabas on Paul's "first missionary journey" (as we call it; Acts 12.25; 13.5; John Mark was Barnabas' cousin, Col 4.10), but for some reason left Paul when they got to Pamphylia (Acts 13.13). Whatever happened, Paul thought it was serious enough at the time to refuse to take him on further journeys. This resulted in Mark going with Barnabas to Cyprus (Acts 15.39), at which point he disappears from the narrative in Acts. His frequent mention in Paul's letters, however, implies that the two men reconciled, and Mark again became a helper to Paul to the end of Paul's life (2 Tim 4.11). At some point he was a helper to the apostle Peter, as Peter called him figuratively "my son" in 1 Pet 5.13.[199] The tradition going back to Papias of Hierapolis is that this same Mark wrote the second gospel in our New Testament.[200]

Aristarchus was, like Mark, one of the few helpers of Paul who was a Jew (Col 4.10–11). He is called Paul's fellow prisoner in Colossians 4.10, but not here. This, along with the absence of the name of Justus here (from Col 4.11), led Balabanski to suggest that Phlm and Colossians were not written at exactly the same time, contrary to what is usually assumed. A difference in perhaps several months between the writing of Phlm and Colossians (whichever one was written first) would explain the differences in the two lists. Unfortunately, the "prison letters" of Paul contribute little to allow us to reconstruct the movements and incarcerations of Paul's helpers. **Demas** was among Paul's helpers at this time, but is mentioned in 2 Timothy 4.10 in an unflattering way that suggests he quit working with Paul (and maybe even renounced Christianity). **Luke** is undoubtedly Luke the physician, the sometime travelling companion of Paul (the "we" sections of Acts) and the author of the gospel of Luke and the Acts of the Apostles.

---

in jail, in Philippi. Yet Paul said in 2 Cor that by that time he had been "in far more imprisonments" than his critics (11.23), as well has having been beaten as official punishments by both Jews and Romans at least eight times (11.24–25), of which Luke recorded only one (Acts 16.24–40). It is not at all impossible that Epaphras shared in one or more of those experiences.

[199] We cannot prove that the Mark mentioned in 1 Pet is the same man who is mentioned in Paul's letters. There is, however, enough overlap between the areas in which Paul and Peter worked to suppose that the same man worked with both apostles. See also *ISBE* 3:260.

[200] The tradition is recorded in Eusebius, *Ecclesiastical History*, 3.39.16.

v 25 May the grace of the Lord Jesus Christ be with your spirit.

The word "**grace**" (Greek *charis*) and the phrase "**Lord Jesus Christ**" repeats the same terms from v 3, thus reminding Philemon in closing that a larger context was operative, the context of the reign of the divine king Jesus over those who pledge their faith to him, a reign in which the love of God through Jesus to his people is to be reciprocated by love among themselves. "**Your**" here is plural, returning to the audience of vv 1–3 that includes Philemon, Apphia, Archippus, and the church there. Although the discussion has been primarily in the singular, with Paul addressing Philemon, the appeal and its attendant considerations were for all to know. The words express something like a prayer, echoing the mention of Paul's prayers earlier (v 4), and leaving his readers/hearers with the encouragement that Paul was thinking about their spiritual condition in light of their submission to the loving reign of Jesus.

Although Paul used this as somewhat of a standard closing in his letters,[201] that does not mean that it was merely a formality when he wrote these words. Here in Phlm, they are clearly appropriate to the situation. Philemon, and everyone involved secondarily in this matter of Onesimus, would need a **spirit** (or mind, or character) full of **Christ**-like **grace** to accept Onesimus as they should. True to the consistent emphasis throughout the rest of the letter, Paul focused here on the spiritual dimension of the situation. The decision Philemon had to make was not simply a practical one, but was eminently a spiritual one. It required a spiritual man, someone full of the mind, or Spirit, of Christ (Rom 8.9–11), with all his spiritual knowledge (v 6) and wisdom, to "do what is proper" (v 8). It needed to be a decision that came from a heart, or spirit, that had been formed into the likeness of the mind and spirit of Jesus himself. Although Paul did not use the language of the Spirit's indwelling here, this closing statement comes close to it. It is only by being Spirit-filled people, manifesting the mind of Christ in love, joy, peace, patience, kindness, goodness, faithfulness, gentleness, and self-control (Gal 5.22–23), that we will be able to defeat the flesh and live appropriately in this world. This was Paul's parting wish for the recipients of this letter. If they could attain to that, the problem that was the occasion of this letter would find its best solution.

---

[201] With variations; Rom 16.24; 1 Cor 16.23; 2 Cor 13.14; Gal 6.18; Eph 6.24; Phil 4.23; Col 4.18; 1 Thes 5.28; 2 Thes 3.18; 1 Tim 6.12; 2 Tim 4.22; Titus 3.15; *cf.* Heb 13.26; Rev 22.21.

BIBLIOGRAPHY

Aasgaard, Reidar. *"My Beloved Brothers and Sisters": Christian Siblingship in Paul*. London: T&T Clark, 2004.

Achtemeier, Paul J. "Omne Verbum Sonat: The New Testament and the Oral Environment of Late Western Antiquity." *JBL* 109.1 (1990): 3–27.

Adams, Edward. "The Ancient Church at Megiddo: The Discovery and an Assessment of Its Significance." *ExpTim* 120.2 (2008): 62–69.

__________. *The Earliest Christian Meeting Places: Almost Exclusively Houses?* Rev. ed. Library of New Testament Studies 450. London: Bloomsbury, T&T Clark, 2016.

Arzt-Grabner, Peter. "How to Deal with Onesimus? Paul's Solution within the Frame of Ancient Legal and Documentary Sources." Pages 113–42 in *Philemon in Perspective: Interpreting a Pauline Letter*, Edited by D. Francois Tolmie. BZNW 169. Berlin: de Gruyter, 2010.

__________. "Onesimus *erro*." *ZNW* 95 (2004): 131–43.

__________. *Philemon*. Papryologische Kommentare zum Neuen Testament 1. Göttingen: Vandenhoeck & Ruprecht, 2003.

__________. "The Case of Onesimos: An Interpretation of Paul's Letter to Philemon Based on Documentary Papyri and Ostraca." *Annali di Storia dell'Esegesi* 18.2 (2001): 589–614.

Ascough, Richard S. "Paul and Associations." Pages 1:68–89 in *Paul in the Greco-Roman World: A Handbook*. Edited by J. Paul Sampley. 2 vols. Rev. ed. London; Oxford; New York; New Delhi; Sydney: Bloomsbury; Bloomsbury T&T Clark, 2016.

Balabanski, Vicky. "Where is Philemon? The Case for a Logical Fallacy in the Correlation of the Data in Philemon and Colossians 1.1–2; 4.7–18." *JSNT* 38.2 (2015): 131–50.

Barclay, John M. G. "*Koinōnia* and the Social Dynamics of the Letter to Philemon." Pages 151–69 in *La Lettre à Philémon et L'Ecclésiologie Paulinienne / Philemon and Pauline Ecclesiology*. Edited by Daniel Marguerat. Leuven: Peters, 2016.

———. "Mirror-Reading A Polemical Letter: Galatians as a Test Case." *JSNT* 31 (1987): 73–93.

———. *Paul and the Gift*. Grand Rapids: Eerdmans, 2015.

———. "Paul, Philemon and the Dilemma of Christian Slave-Ownership." *NTS* 37 (1991): 161–86.

———. "There is Neither Old nor Young? Early Christianity and Ancient Ideologies of Age." *NTS* 53 (2007): 225–41.

Bartchy, S. Scott. "Philemon, Epistle to." *ABD* 5:305–10.

Barth, Markus, and Helmut Blanke. *The Letter to Philemon: A New Translation with Notes and Commentary*. ECC. Grand Rapids: Eerdmans, 2000.

Barth, Markus, Helmut Blanke, and Astrid B. Beck. *Colossians: A New Translation with Introduction and Commentary*. AB 34B. New Haven: Yale University Press, 2008.

Barton, S. C. "Hospitality." Pages 501–507 in *Dictionary of the Later New Testament and Its Developments*. Edited by Ralph P. Martin and Peter H. Davids. Downers Grove, IL: InterVarsity Press, 1997.

———. "Social Values and Structures." Pages 1127–34 in *Dictionary of New Testament Background: A Compendium of Contemporary Biblical Scholarship*. Edited by Stanley E. Porter and Craig A. Evans. Downers Grove, IL: InterVarsity Press, 2000.

Beale, G. K. *A New Testament Biblical Theology: The Unfolding of the Old Testament in the* New. Grand Rapids: Baker Academic, 2011.

———. *Colossians and Philemon*. BECNT. Grand Rapids: Baker Academic, 2019.

Beker, J. Christian. *Paul's Apocalyptic Gospel: The Coming Triumph of God*. Philadelphia: Fortress, 1982.

———. *Paul the Apostle: The Triumph of God in Life and Thought*. Philadelphia: Fortress, 1980.

Bird, Michael F. *Colossians and Philemon*. New Covenant Commentary Series. Eugene, OR: Cascade Books, 2009.

Birdsall, J. N. "*Presbutēs* in Philemon 9: A Study in Conjectural Emendation." *NTS* 39 (1993): 625–30.

__________. "Reassessing a Rhetorical Approach to Paul's Letters." *ExpTim* 119 (2008): 374–79.

Blackwell, Ben C., John K. Goodrich, and Jason Maston. "Paul and the Apocalyptic Imagination: An Introduction." Pages 3–21 in *Paul and the Apocalyptic Imagination*. Edited by Ben C. Blackwell, John K. Goodrich, and Jason Maston. Minneapolis: Fortress, 2016.

Blanton, Thomas R. *A Spiritual Economy: Gift Exchange in the Letters of Paul of Tarsus*. New Haven: Yale University Press, 2017.

Blass, Friedrich, Albert Debrunner, and Robert Walter Funk. *A Greek Grammar of the New Testament and Other Early Christian Literature*. Chicago: University of Chicago Press, 1961.

Boring, Eugene. "Philippians and Philemon: Date and Provenance." *CBQ* 81 (2019): 470–94.

Bradley, K. R. *Slaves and Masters in the Roman Empire: A Study in Social Control*. Oxford: Oxford University Press, 1987.

Brookins, Timothy A. "'I Rather Appeal to *Auctoritas*': Roman Conceptualizations of Power and Paul's Appeal to Philemon." *CBQ* 77 (2015): 302–21.

Bursey, Ernest. "The Puzzling Plurals in Philemon." *Journal of Applied Christian Leadership* 9 (2015): 10–13.

Byron, John. "Paul and the Background of Slavery: The *Status Quaestionis* in New Testament Scholarship." *CurBR* 3.1 (2004): 116–39.

Campbell, Constantine R. *Basics of Verbal Aspect in Biblical Greek*. Grand Rapids: Zondervan, 2008.

Campbell, William S. *Paul and the Creation of Christian Identity*. London: T&T Clark, 2008.

Capes, David B. *Old Testament Yahweh Texts in Paul's Christology*. Waco: Baylor University Press, 2017.

———. *The Divine Christ: Paul, the Lord Jesus, and the Scriptures of Israel*. Grand Rapids: Baker Academic, 2018.

Cassius Dio. *Roman History*. Translated by Ernest Cary. 9 vols. LCL. Cambridge: Harvard University Press, 1914–1927.

Cicero. *On Old Age. On Friendship. On Divination*. Translated by W. A. Falconer. LCL. Cambridge: Harvard University Press, 1923.

Church, F. Forrester "Rhetorical Structure and Design in Paul's Letter to Philemon." *HTR* 71 (1978): 17–33.

Cole, Zachary J. "Illustrating a Pauline Imperative (Phlm. 17): *Proslambanō* in P.Mur. 2.115." *JSNT* 45 (2022): 1–16.

Cope, Lamar. "On Rethinking the Colossians-Philemon Connection." *BR* 30 (1985): 45–50.

Danker, Frederick W., Walter Bauer, William F. Arndt, and F. Wilbur Gingrich. *Greek-English Lexicon of the New Testament and Other Early Christian Literature*. 3rd ed. Chicago: University of Chicago Press, 2000.

Daube, David. "Rabbinic Methods of Interpretation and Hellenistic Rhetoric." *HUCA* 22 (1949): 239–64.

Davies, Jamie. *The Apocalyptic Paul: Retrospect and Prospect*. Eugene, OR: Cascade Books, 2022.

de Boer, Martinus C. *Paul, Theologian of God's Apocalypse: Essays on Paul and Apocalyptic*. Eugene, OR: Cascade Books, 2020.

de Villiers, Pieter G. R. "Love in the Letter to Philemon." Pages 181–203 in *Philemon in Perspective: Interpreting a Pauline Letter*. Edited by D. Francois Tolmie. BZNW 169. Berlin: De Gruyter, 2010.

de Vos, Craig S. "Once a Slave, Always a Slave? Slavery, Manumission, and Relational Patterns in Paul's Letter to Philemon." *JSNT* 82 (2001): 89–105.

de Silva, David A. *An Introduction to the New Testament: Contexts, Methods, and Ministry Formation*. Downers Grove: InterVarsity Press, 2004.

———. *Honor, Patronage, Kinship & Purity: Unlocking New Testament Culture*. Westmont, IL: InterVarsity Press, 2012.

———. *The Letter to the Galatians*. NICNT. Grand Rapids: Eerdmans, 2018.

Deissmann, Adolf. *Light from the Ancient East*. London: Hodder & Stoughton, 1910.

Dunn, James D. G. *Beginning from Jerusalem*. Vol. 2 of *Christianity in the Making*. Grand Rapids: Eerdmans, 2009.

__________. *The Epistles to the Colossians and to Philemon: A Commentary on the Greek Text*. NIGTC. Grand Rapids: Eerdmans, 1996.

Ehorn, Seth M. *Philemon*. Evangelical Exegetical Commentary. Bellingham, WA: Lexham Press, 2011.

Eitrem, S., and Leiv Amundsen, eds. *Papyri Osloenses, Fasc. 2*. Oslo: Academy of Science and Letters of Oslo, 1931.

Elliot, Scott S. "'Thanks But No Thanks': Tact, Persuasion, and the Negotiation of Power in Paul's Letter to Philemon." *NTS* 57.1 (2011): 51–64.

Ellis, Earle E. *The Making of the New Testament Documents*. Leiden: Brill, 1999.

Epp, Eldon Jay. "New Testament Papyrus Manuscripts and Letter Carrying in Greco-Roman Times." Pages 35–56 in *The Future of Early Christianity*. Edited by Birger A. Pearson. Minneapolis: Fortress, 1991.

Erickson, Millard J. *Christian Theology*. 3rd ed. Grand Rapids: Baker Academic, 2013.

Fantin, Joseph D. *The Greek Imperative Mood in the New Testament: A Cognitive and Communicative Approach*. Studies in Biblical Greek 1. New York: Peter Lang, 2010.

Finegan, Jack. *Handbook of Biblical Chronology*. Rev. ed. Peabody, MA: Hendrickson, 1998.

Fitzgerald, John T. "The Stoics and the Early Christians on the Treatment of Slaves." Pages 141–75 in *Stoicism in Early Christianity*. Edited by Tuomas Rasimus et al. Grand Rapids: Baker Academic, 2010.

Fitzmyer, Joseph A. *The Letter to Philemon: A New Translation with Introduction and Commentary*. AB 34C. New Haven: Yale University Press, 2008.

Fung, Ronald Y. K. *The Epistle to the Galatians*. NICNT. Grand Rapids: Eerdmans, 1988.

Furnish, Victor Paul. *Theology and Ethics in Paul*. New Testament Library. Louisville: Westminster John Knox, 2009.

Gillman, F. "Apphia." *ABD* 1:317–18.

Goodwin, William W. *Greek Grammar*. Boston: Ginn and Company, 1892. Repr., Eugene, OR: Wipf and Stock, 2003.

Gorman, Michael J. "The Apocalyptic New Covenant and the Shape of Life in the Spirit according to Galatians." Pages 317–37 in *Paul and the Apocalyptic Imagination*. Edited by Ben C. Blackwell, John K. Goodrich, and Jason Maston. Minneapolis: Fortress, 2016.

———. *Cruciformity: Paul's Narrative Spirituality of the Cross*. Grand Rapids: Eerdmans, 2001.

Grenfell, Bernard P., and Arthur S. Hunt, eds. *The Oxyrhynchus Papyri*. 15 vols. London; New York; Boston: The Offices of the Egypt Exploration Society, 1904–1922.

Guthrie, Donald. *New Testament Introduction*. 4th ed. Downers Grove: InterVarsity Press, 1996.

Hainz, J. *Koinōnia: "Kirche" als Gemeinschaft bei Paulus*. Regensburg: Pustet, 1982.

Hanson, Paul D. *The Dawn of Apocalyptic*. Rev. ed. Philadelphia: Fortress, 1979.

Harland, Philip H. *Associations, Synagogues, and Congregations: Claiming a Place in Ancient Mediterranean Society*. 2nd ed. Waco, TX: Baylor University Press, 2013.

Harrill, Albert J. *Slaves in the New Testament: Literary, Social, and Moral Dimensions*. Minneapolis: Fortress, 2006.

———. "Using the Roman Jurists to Interpret Philemon." *ZNW* 90 (1999): 135–38.

Harris, Murray J. *Prepositions and Theology in the Greek New Testament: An Essential Reference Resource for Exegesis*. Grand Rapids: Zondervan, 2012.

Harris, W. V. "Demography, Geography and the Sources of Roman Slaves." *JRS* 89 (1999): 62–75.

Harvey, John D. *Oral Patterning in Paul's Letters*. Grand Rapids: Baker Books, 1998.

Hawthorne, Gerald F. *Philippians*. WBC 43. Dallas: Word, 2004.

Head, Peter M. "Onesimus the Letter Carrier and the Initial Reception of Paul's Letter to Philemon." *JTS* 71.2 (2020): 628–56.

Heil, John Paul. "The Chiastic Structure and Meaning of Paul's Letter to Philemon." *Biblica* 82 (2001): 178–206.

Hock, Ronald F. "A Support for His Old Age: Paul's Plea on Behalf of Onesimus." Pages 67–81 in *The Social World of the First Christians: Essays on Honor of Wayne A. Meeks*. Edited by L. Michael White and O. Larry Yarbrough. Minneapolis: Fortress, 1995.

Hoehner, Harold W. *Ephesians: An Exegetical Commentary*. Grand Rapids: Baker Academic, 2002.

Hopkins, Keith. "On the Probable Age Structure of the Roman Population." *Population Studies* 20 (1966): 245–64.

Horsley, G. H. R., S. R. Llewelyn, and J. R. Harrison, eds. *New Documents Illustrating Early Christianity*. 10 volumes. Grand Rapids: Eerdmans, 1981–2012.

"Hospitality." Pages 402–404 in *Dictionary of Biblical Imagery*. Edited by Leland Ryken et al. Downers Grove, IL: InterVarsity Press, 2000.

Isaac, Benjamin. *The Invention of Racism in Classical Antiquity*. Princeton: Princeton University Press, 2004.

Jeal, Roy R. *Exploring Philemon: Freedom, Brotherhood, and Partnership in the New Society*. Atlanta: SBL Press, 2015.

Jipp, Joshua W. *The Messianic Theology of the New Testament*. Grand Rapids: Eerdmans, 2020.

Johnson, Lewis. "The Pauline Letters from Caesarea." *ExpTim* 68 (October 1956): 24–26.

Keitzer, Larry J. *Philemon,* Readings: A New Biblical Commentary. Sheffield: Sheffield Phoenix, 2008.

Kissling, Paul J. *Genesis*. College Press NIV Commentary. Joplin: College Press, 2004.

Kittel, Gerhard, and Gerhard Friedrich, eds. *Theological Dictionary of the New Testament*. Translated by Geoffrey W. Bromiley. 10 vols. Grand Rapids: Eerdmans, 1964–1976.

Klauck, Hans-Josef. *Ancient Letters and the New Testament: A Guide to Context and Exegesis*. Edited and translated by Daniel P. Bailey. Waco, TX: Baylor University Press, 2006.

Kloppenborg, John S. *Christ's Associations: Connecting and Belonging in the Ancient City*. New Haven: Yale University Press, 2019.

Knox, John. *Philemon Among the Letters of Paul: A New View of Its Place and Importance*. Chicago: University of Chicago Press, 1935.

Koch, Klaus. *The Rediscovery of Apocalyptic*. Translated by Margaret Kohl. Studies in Biblical Theology, Second Series, 22. SCM, 1972.

Ladd, George Eldon. "Apocalyptic and New Testament Theology." Pages 285–96 in *Reconciliation and Hope: New Testament Essays on Atonement and Eschatology*. Edited by Robert Banks. Grand Rapids: Eerdmans, 1974.

Lampe, Peter. "Affects and Emotions in the Rhetoric of Paul's Letter to Philemon: A Rhetorical-Psychological Interpretation." Pages 61–77 in *Philemon in Perspective: Interpreting a Pauline Letter*. Edited by D. Francois Tolmie. BZNW 169. Berlin: de Gruyter, 2010.

Lee, Aquila H. I. "Messianism and Messiah in Paul: Christ as Jesus?" Pages 375–92 in *God and the Faithfulness of Paul: A Critical Examination of the Pauline Theology of N. T. Wright*. Edited by Christoph J. Heilig, J. Thomas Hewitt, and Michael F. Bird. Minneapolis: Fortress, 2017.

Lewis, David. "Notes on Slave Names, Ethnicity, and Identity in Classical and Hellenistic Greece." *Studia Źródłoznawcze. U Schyłku Starożytności* 16 (2017): 169–99.

Licona, Michael R. *The Resurrection of Jesus: A New Historiographical Approach*. Downers Grove, IL: IVP Academic, 2010.

Liddell, Henry George, Robert Scott, Henry Stuart Jones. *A Greek-English Lexicon*. 9th ed. with revised supplement. Oxford: Clarendon, 1996.

Lightfoot, Joseph Barber. *Saint Paul's Epistles to the Colossians and to Philemon*. 3rd ed. London: Macmillan and Co., 1886.

Lohse, Eduard. *Colossians and Philemon*. Translated by William R. Poehlmann and Robert J. Karris. Hermeneia. Philadelphia: Fortress, 1971.

MacGillivray, Erlend D. "Re-Evaluating Patronage and Reciprocity in Antiquity and New Testament Studies." *JGRChJ* 6 (2009): 37–81.

Manyika, Batanayi I., and Cornelia van Deventer. "The Curious Case of Apphia, Our Sister." *Conspectus* 29 (2020): 134–50.

Martin, R. P. *Colossians and Philemon*. NCB 48. London: Oliphants, 1974.

Martin, Troy W. "The Covenant of Circumcision (Genesis 17:9–14) and the Situational Antitheses in Galatians 3:28." *JBL* 122 (2003): 111–25.

McClister, David. "Paul's View of the Holy Spirit." Pages 88–120 in *From the Pen of Paul*. 2nd ed. Edited by Nathan Ward. Temple Terrace: Florida College Press, 2022.

McGrath, Alister and Joanna McGrath. *The Dawkins Delusion?: Atheist Fundamentalism and the Denial of the Divine*. London: SPCK, 2007.

McKnight, Scot. *The Letter to Philemon*. NICNT. Grand Rapids: Eerdmans, 2017.

Meeks, Wayne A. *The First Urban Christians: The Social World of the Apostle Paul*. 2nd ed. New Haven: Yale University Press, 2003.

Melick, Richard R. *Philippians, Colossians, Philemon*. NAC 32. Nashville: Broadman & Holman, 1991.

Metzger, Bruce Manning. *A Textual Commentary on the Greek New Testament, Second Edition, A Companion Volume to the United Bible Societies' Greek New Testament*. 4th rev. ed. London; New York: United Bible Societies, 1994.

Mitchell, Margaret M. "John Chrysostom on Philemon: A Second Look." *HTR* 88 (1995): 135–48.

Moisés, Silva. *Philippians*. 2nd ed. BECNT. Grand Rapids: Baker Academic, 2005.

Montanari, Franco. *The Brill Dictionary of Ancient Greek*. Leiden: Brill, 2015.

Moulton, James H., and George Milligan. *The Vocabulary of the Greek Testament*. London, 1930. Repr. Peabody, MA: Hendrickson, 1997.

Nordling, John G. *Philemon*. Concordia Commentary. Saint Louis: Concordia, 2004.

Novenson, Matthew V. *Christ Among the Messiahs*. Oxford: Oxford University Press, 2012.

O'Brien, Peter. *Introductory Thanksgivings in the Letters of Paul*. NTS 49. Leiden: Brill, 1977.

Ogereau, Julien. "A Survey of *Koinōnia* and Its Cognates in Documentary Sources." *NovT* 57 (2015): 275–94.

Osiek, Carolyn. "The Politics of Patronage and the Politics of Kinship: The Meeting of the Ways." *BTB* 39.3 (2009): 143–52.

Pao, David W. *Colossians and Philemon*. ZECNT. Grand Rapids: Zondervan, 2012.

Parkin, Tim G. *Demography and Roman Society*. Baltimore: Johns Hopkins University Press, 1992.

Pearson, Brook W. R. "Assumptions in the Criticism and Translation of Philemon." Pages 255, 278 in *Translating the Bible: Problems and Prospects*. Edited by Stanley E. Porter and Richard S. Hess. JSNTS 173. Sheffield: Sheffield Academic, 1999.

Petersen, Norman R. *Rediscovering Paul: Philemon and the Sociology of Paul's Narrative World*. Philadelphia: Fortress, 1985.

Plutarch. *Moralia*. Translated by Harold North Fowler et al. 15 vols. LCL. Cambridge: Harvard University Press, 1927–1969.

Porter, Stanley E. "Ancient Literate Culture and Popular Rhetorical Knowledge: Implications for Studying Pauline Rhetoric." Pages 96–115 in *Paul and Ancient Rhetoric: Theory and Practice in the Hellenistic Context*. Edited by Stanley E. Porter and Bryan R. Dyer. Cambridge: Cambridge University Press, 2016.

Porter, Stanley E. *The Apostle Paul: His Life, Thought, and Letters*. Grand Rapids: Eerdmans, 2016.

———. *Idioms of the Greek New Testament*. Sheffield: JSOT, 1999.

———. "Paul of Tarsus and His Letters." Pages 533–85 in *Handbook of Classical Rhetoric in the Hellenistic Period, 330 B.C.-A.D. 400*. Edited by Stanley E. Porter. Leiden: Brill, 1997.

Rapske, Brian. *The Book of Acts and Paul in Roman Custody*. Vol. 3 of *The Book of Acts in Its First Century Setting*. Edited by Bruce W. Winter. Grand Rapids: Eerdmans, 1994.

———. "The Prisoner Paul in the Eyes of Onesimus." *NTS* 37 (1991): 187–203.

Reed, Jeffrey T. "The Epistle." Pages 171–93 in *Handbook of Classical Rhetoric in the Hellenistic Period, 330 B.C.-A.D. 400*. Edited by Stanley E. Porter. Leiden: Brill, 1997.

Reicke, Bo. "Caesarea, Rome, and the Captivity Epistles." Pages 277–86 in *Apostolic History and the Gospel. Biblical and Historical Essays Presented to*

F. F. Bruce on His 60th Birthday. Edited by W. Ward Gasque and Ralph P. Martin. Grand Rapids: Eerdmans, 1970.

Robertson, A. T. *A Grammar of the Greek New Testament in the Light of Historical Research.* 4th ed. New York: Hodder and Stoughton, 1923.

Rollins, Wayne G. "The New Testament and Apocalyptic." *NTS* 17 (1971): 454–76.

Runge, Steven R. *Discourse Grammar of the Greek New Testament: A Practical Introduction for Teaching and Exegesis*. Bellingham, WA: Lexham Press, 2010.

Saller, Richard. "Patronage and Friendship in Early Imperial Rome: Drawing the Distinction." Pages 49–62 in *Patronage in Ancient Society*. Edited by Andrew Wallace-Hadrill. London: Routledge, 1989.

Sanders, E. P. *Paul and Palestinian Judaism: A Comparison of Patterns of Religion.* Philadelphia: Fortress, 1977.

Scheidel, Walter, ed. *Debating Roman Demography*. Leiden: Brill, 2001.

__________. "Roman Age Structure: Evidence and Models." *JRS* 91 (2001): 1–26.

Schubert, P. *Form and Function of the Pauline Thanksgivings*. BZNW 20. Berlin, 1939.

Seneca, Lucius Annaeus. *Ad Lucilium Epistulae Morales*. Translated by Richard M. Gummere. 3 vols. LCL. Cambridge: Harvard University Press, 1979.

__________. *Moral Essays*. Translated by John W. Basore. 3 vols. LCL. Cambridge: Harvard University Press, 1928–1935.

Smyth, Herbert Weir. *Greek Grammar.* Cambridge: Harvard University Press, 1956.

Soards, Marion L. "Some Neglected Theological Dimensions of Paul's Letter to Philemon." *PRSt* 17.3 (1990): 209–19.

Solin, H. *Die stadromischen Sklavennamen. Ein Namenbuch, part 2: Greischische Namen*. FASk Beiheft 2. Stuttgart, 1996.

Solomon, Matthew S. "The Textual History of Philemon." PhD diss., New Orleans Baptist Theological Seminary, 2014.

Sommers, Tamler. *Why Honor Matters*. New York: Basic Books, 2018.

Sophocles. Translated by Hugh Lloyd-Jones. 2 vols. LCL. Cambridge: Harvard University Press, 1994.

Stowers, Stanley K. *Letter Writing in Greco-Roman Antiquity*. Library of Early Christianity 5. Philadelphia: Westminster, 1986.

Temporini, Hildegard, and Wolfgang Haase, eds. *Aufstieg und Niedergang der römischen Welt: Geschichte und Kultur Roms im Spiegel der neueren Forschung*. Part 2, *Principat*. Berlin: de Gruyter, 1972–.

Thompson, Ian H. *Chiasmus in the Pauline Letters*. JSNTS 111. Sheffield: Sheffield Academic, 1995.

Tolmie, Francois D, ed. *Philemon in Perspective: Interpreting a Pauline Letter*. BZNW 169. Berlin: de Gruyter, 2010.

———. "Tendencies in the Research on the Letter to Philemon Since 1980." Pages 1–27 in *Philemon in Perspective: Interpreting a Pauline Letter*. Edited by D. Francois Tolmie. BZNW 169. Berlin: de Gruyter, 2010.

Tucker, J. Brian. "Paul's Particular Problem—The Continuation of Existing Identities in Philemon." Pages 407–24 in *T&T Clark handbook to Social Identity in the New Testament*. Edited by J. Brian Tucker and Coleman A. Baker. London: Bloomsbury T&T Clark, 2016.

Vincent, Marvin Richardson. *A Critical and Exegetical Commentary on the Epistles to the Philippians and to Philemon*. ICC. New York: Charles Scribner's Sons, 1897.

Weima, Jeffrey A. D. "Paul's Persuasive Prose: An Epistolary Analysis of the Letter to Philemon." Pages 29–60 in *Philemon in Perspective: Interpreting a Pauline Letter*. Edited by D. Francois Tolmie. BZNW 169. Berlin: De Gruyter, 2010.

Wendland, Ernst. " 'You Will Do Even More Than I Say': On the Rhetorical Function of Stylistic Form in the Letter to Philemon." Pages 79–111 in *Philemon in Perspective: Interpreting A Pauline Letter*. Edited by Francois Tolmie. BZNW 169. Berlin: de Gruyter, 2010.

Wengst, Klaus. *Pax Romana and the Peace of Jesus Christ*. Translated by John Bowden. Philadelphia: Fortress, 1987.

Wenham, Gordon J. *Genesis 1–15*. WBC 1. Dallas: Word, 1998.

Wessels, G. Francois. "The Letter to Philemon in the Context of Ancient Slavery in Early Christianity." Pages 143–68 in *Philemon in Perspective:*

Interpreting a Pauline Letter. Edited by D. Francois Tolmie. BZNW 169. Berlin: de Gruyter, 2010.

Westermann, William L. The *Slave Systems of Greek and Roman Antiquity*. Philadelphia: American Philosophical Society, 1955.

White, Joel. "The Imprisonment That Could Have Happened (and The Letters Paul Could Have Written There): A Response to Ben Witherington." *JETS* 61.3 (2018): 549–58.

White, John L. "Epistolary Formulas and Cliches in Greek Papyrus Letters." Pages 289–319 in *Society of Biblical Literature 1978 Seminar Papers, Vol. II*. SBLSPS 14. Missoula, MT: Scholars Press, 1978.

____________. "New Testament Epistolary Literature in the Framework of Ancient Epistolography." *ANRW* 25.2: 1730–56.

____________. "The Structural Analysis on Philemon: A Point of Departure in the Formal Analysis of the Pauline Letter." Page 8 in *Society of Biblical Literature 1971 Seminar Papers*. Society of Biblical Literature, 1971.

White, L. Michael. *The Social Origins of Christian Architecture, Vol. 1*. Harvard Theological Studies 42. Valley Forge: Trinity Press International, 1990.

Williams, David J. *Paul's Metaphors: Their Context and Character*. Peabody, MA: Hendrickson, 1999.

Wilson, Robert McL. *A Critical and Exegetical Commentary on Colossians and Philemon*. ICC. London: T&T Clark International, 2005.

Winter, Sara B. C. "Paul's Letter to Philemon." *NTS* 33 (1987): 1–15.

Witherington, Ben, III. " 'Almost Thou Persuadest Me…": The Importance of Greco-Roman Rhetoric for the Understanding of the Text and Context of the NT." *JETS* 58.1 (2015): 63–88.

____________. *Conflict and Community in Corinth: A Socio-Rhetorical Commentary on 1 and 2 Corinthians*. Grand Rapids: Eerdmans, 1995.

____________. *Grace in Galatia: A Commentary on St. Paul's Letter to the Galatians*. Grand Rapids: Eerdmans, 1998.

____________. *Paul's Letter to the Philippians: A Socio-Rhetorical Commentary*. Grand Rapids: Eerdmans, 2011.

____________. "The Case of the Imprisonment That Did Not Happen: Paul at Ephesus." *JETS* 60.3 (2017): 525–32.

———. *The Letters to Philemon, the Colossians, and the Ephesians: A Socio-Rhetorical Commentary on the Captivity Epistles.* Grand Rapids: Eerdmans, 2007.

———. "Was Paul a Jailbird? A Response to the Response." *JETS* 61.3 (2018): 559–61.

Wolter, Michael. "The Letter to Philemon as Ethical Counterpart to Paul's Doctrine of Justification." Pages 169–79 in *Philemon in Perspective: Interpreting A Pauline Letter*. Edited by Francois Tolmie. BZNW 169. Berlin: de Gruyter, 2010.

Wright, N. T. "Apocalyptic and the Sudden Fulfillment of Divine Promise." Pages 111–34 in *Paul and the Apocalyptic Imagination*. Edited by Ben C. Blackwell, John K. Goodrich, and Jason Maston. Minneapolis: Fortress, 2016.

———. *Paul and the Faithfulness of God*. Vol. 4 of *Christian Origins and the Question of God*. Minneapolis: Fortress, 2013.

Wuellner, Wilhelm. "Arrangement." Pages 74–75 in *Handbook of Classical Rhetoric in the Hellenistic Period, 330 B.C.-A.D. 400*. Edited by Stanley E. Porter. Leiden: Brill, 1997.

Zelnick-Abramovitz, R. *Not Wholly Free: The Concept of Manumission and the Status of Manumitted Slaves in the Ancient Greek World*. Leiden: Brill, 2005.

Zmijewski, J. "Der Philemonbrief: Ein Plädoyer für die christliche Brüderlichkeit." *TThZ* 114 (2005): 222–42.

MORE BIBLE COMMENTARIES BY DEWARD PUBLISHING

Exposition of Genesis (volumes 1 and 2), H.C. Leupold

The Growth of the Seed: Notes on the Book of Genesis, Nathan Ward

Thinking Through Job, L.A. Mott

Searching for the Meaning of Life: Studies in the Book of Ecclesiastes, Paul Earnhart

Thinking Through Jeremiah, L.A. Mott

Let Us Search Our Ways: A Commentary on Lamentations, Evan and Marie Blackmore

Christ Revealed: A Commentary on Matthew, Kenneth L. Chumbley

Invitation to a Spiritual Revolution: Studies in the Sermon on the Mount, Paul Earnhart

Original Commentary on Acts, J.W. McGarvey

Walk Worthily: A Commentary on Ephesains, Jeff Smelser

Uncommon Sense: The Wisdom of James for Dispossessed Believers, James T. South

The Lamb, The Woman, and the Dragon: Studies in the Revelation of St. John, Albertus Pieters

For a full listing of DeWard Publishing Company books, visit our website:

www.deward.com

www.ingramcontent.com/pod-product-compliance
Lightning Source LLC
Chambersburg PA
CBHW020455100426
42813CB00031B/3368/J

* 9 7 8 1 9 4 7 9 2 9 2 5 8 *